Handbook of Popular Literature

By the Same Author

- Indian Classic Literature

About the Author

Deepali Borthakur MA, MSW, MPhil working as Academic Officer and Assistant Professor in Department of Humanities and Social Sciences, Assam Down Town University.

Handbook of Popular Literature

DEEPALI BORTHAKUR
MA, MSW, MPhil, Academic Officer, Assistant Professor,
Department of Humanities and Social Sciences,
Assam Down Town University

CONCEPT PUBLISHING COMPANY PVT. LTD.
NEW DELHI-110059

ISBN-13: 978-93-88937-78-8 (H.B.)
ISBN-13: 978-93-88937-79-5 (P.B.)

First Published 2021

Published and Printed by

Concept Since 1974

Concept Publishing Company Pvt. Ltd.
A/15-16, Commercial Block, Mohan Garden,
New Delhi-110059 (INDIA)
T : 91 11 25351460, 91 11 25351794
E : publishing@conceptpub.com; *W* : www.conceptpub.com

Cataloging in Publication Data--Courtesy: D.K. Agencies (P) Ltd. <docinfo@dkagencies.com>

Borthakur, Deepali, author.
Handbook of popular literature / Deepali Borthakur.
pages cm
Includes bibliographical references
ISBN 9789388937788 (HB)
ISBN 9789388937795 (PB)

1. Popular literature—History and criticism. I. Title.

LCC PN56.P55B67 2021 | DDC 809 23

Preface

"**Handbook of Popular Literature**" will aquaint learners with popular literature, such as crime thriller, graphic fiction, children's literature and so forth, generally regarded by purists to be "low-brow" and meant for easy mass consumption. Popular Literature is literature that is enjoyed by a large mass of people. A good example would be the Harry Potter series.

In India, one might associate popular literature with the likes of Chetan Bhagat, Preeti Shenoy, Amish etc. although many serious readers would hesitate to classify their works as literature. But then, that is a subjective view, and it can't be denied that these writers enjoy large popular appeal.

Popular literature, unlike high literature, generally does not seek a high degree of formal beauty or subtlety and is not intended to endure. The growth of popular literature has paralleled the spread of literacy through education and has been facilitated by technological developments in printing. With the Industrial Revolution, works of literature, which were previously produced for consumption by small, well-educated elites, became accessible to large sections and even majorities of the members of a population.

The boundary between artistic and popular literature is murky, with much traffic between the two categories according to current public preference and later critical evaluation. While he was alive William Shakespeare could be thought of as a writer of popular literature, but he is now regarded as a creator of artistic literature. Indeed, the main, though not invariable, method of defining a work as belonging to popular literature is whether it is ephemeral, that is, losing its appeal and significance with the passage of time.

The most important genre in popular literature is and always has been the romance, extending as it does from the Middle Ages to the present. The most common type of romance describes the obstacles encountered by two people (usually young) engaged in a forbidden love. Another common genre is that of fantasy, or science fiction. Novels set in the Western frontier of the United States in the 19th century, and called westerns, are also popular. Finally, the detective story or murder mystery is a widely read form of popular literature. Popular literature has also come to include such genres as comic books and cartoon strips.

This book will give an insight into the concept of Popular Literature and the varied genres that comes under its canvas' keeping in mind the undergraduate syllabus and students. The Introduction will provide the idea of what is popular literature, its caracteristcs and how it is different from other forms of literature. It will be followed by four Chapters that deals will the various units as declared in the CBCS syllabus. The book discusses genres like Children Literature, Graphic Fiction, Crime Thriller and LGBT fiction in a descriptive pattern.

I believe "**Handbook of Popular Literature**" will be helpful for students pursuing their graduation and also to literature aspirants who have a keen interest in Popular Literature.

Acknowledgements

At the foremost, I would like to express my sincere gratitude towards Dr. Mridul Bordoloi, The Head, Department of English, Dibrugarh University for invaluable guidance and support. It would not have been possible for me to complete my book without his motivational and scholarly supervision.

I am immensely indebted to and extend my sincere gratitude to my PhD Supervisor Dr. Basil N. Darlong Diengdoh, Assistant Professor, Dibrugarh University who has been extremely kind to extend his scholarly insights that helped me accomplish the work.

The completion of this book would have been a dream without the care, concern of my family members and friends. I extend my heartiest gratitude to my loving parents for their care, patience and continuous support and for bearing with me in my difficult moments during the pursuance of this book.

At the end, I would like to thank almighty whose blessings always helped me to move forward in life.

COURSE CODE: 30200
COURSE 6: POPULAR LITERATURE
(CORE)
CREDITS ASSIGNED: 6 CREDITS

Course Objectives: Popular literature includes those writings intended for the masses and those that find favour with large audiences. It can be distinguished from artistic literature in that it is designed primarily to entertain (brittania.com). The objective of this course is to acquaint learners with popular literature, such as crime thriller, graphic fiction, children's literature and so forth, generally regarded by purists to be "low-brow" and meant for easy mass consumption. However, it would be wrong to assume such a position insofar as the lines of distinction between what is literary and what is popular tends to be blurred.

UNIT I: CHILDREN'S LITERATURE
—Lewis Carroll, *Through the Looking Glass*

UNIT II: CRIME THRILLER
—Agatha Christie, *The Murder of Roger Ackroyd*

UNIT III: LGBT FICTION
—Shyam Selvadurai, *Funny Boy*

UNIT IV: GRAPHIC NOVEL
- Durgabai Vyam and Subhash Vyam, *Bhimayana: Experiences of Untouchability.*
- Autobiographical Notes on Ambedkar (For the Visually Challenged Students)

Contents

Introduction: Popular Literature

> We are today in the presence of a discrepancy between two essential manifestations; no longer is there one single esthetic norm in our society, but two, the same measurements do not apply to "high" art and "popular" art. (Todorov 1977: 44)

The society that we live in has always been a centre of social disparities. At the base of various social norms and practices are certain ideologies which are being disseminated by those who intend to exercise their power, authority and dominance. This practice has led to the construction of hierarchical superstructures that operate in almost all domains of human endeavour. This is also visible in the world of literature where some works are considered to be more serious and hence more respectable than others. This categorization is set upon certain benchmark of standards that in turn situate some genres in the domain of literary canon, while the excluded lot gets marginalized to the periphery. The term canon stands to accord a degree of excellence to works by distinguishing between good and bad works. Works which draw considerable recognition about its excellence enjoy an advantage in terms of serious significance and are therefore inculcated into the educational program or framework of various academic institutions.

The canonical status of a literary work mainly depends on this politics of inclusion and exclusion. However, this classification is mostly based on the subjective analysis of literary critics or scholars; but the tendency to prioritize such works has been a universal phenomenon.

Popular literature is one such domain which has been trying hard to relocate itself to the center. The term 'Popular Literature' applies to those genres of fiction that has always been conveniently sidelined to the periphery of literary canon on grounds of being non-serious'. Science fiction, horror fiction, fairy tales, detective fiction etc. are some of the most widely read genres of popular literature. Their popularity rests on the large scale readership from across the globe. But such stories often find it hard to make its way to mainstream or 'high' literature, since they are considered unfit to conform to the notions of the grand canon. Popular literature is mostly looked down upon as inferior and not literary enough to deserve critical acclaim. The principal reason behind this is the labeling of the genre as 'popular' which is almost taken to be equivalent of being non-serious. Valued on the mere grounds of 'entertainment', the genre has long been facing discrimination, struggling to find its place within the grand literary canon.

Popular literature in English writing has now shown wide and continued acceptance, measured by sales, frequent imitation, adaptation to other cultural forms and general commercial success. The word "popular" is meant as a synonym for "successful," not as an antonym for "serious." Certain books are carefully tailored by authors and publishers to capture the attention of a wide range of potential readers.

There is a marked difference between true popular literature, that of folklore and folk song, and the popular literature of modern times. Popular literature today is produced either to be read by a literate audience or to be enacted on television or in the cinema; it is produced by writers who are members, however lowly, of an elite corps of professional literates. Thus, popular literature no longer springs from the people; it is handed to them. Their role is passive. At the best they are permitted a limited selectivity as consumers.

Certain theorists once believed that folk songs and even long, narrative ballads were produced collectively, as has been said in mockery "by the tribe sitting around the fire and grunting in unison." This idea is very much out of date. Folk songs and folk tales began somewhere in one human mind. They were developed and shaped into the forms in which they are now found by hundreds of other minds as they were passed down through the centuries. Only in this sense were they "collectively" produced.

During the 20th century, folklore and folk speech had a great influence on elite literature—on writers as different as Franz Kafka and Carl Sandburg, Selma Lagerlöf and Kawabata Yasunari, Martin Buber and Isaac Bashevis Singer. Folk song has always been popular with Bohemian intellectuals, especially political radicals (who certainly are elite). Since World War II the influence of folk song upon popular song has not just been great; it has been determinative. Almost all "hit" songs since the mid-20th century have been imitation folk songs; and some authentic folk singers attract immense audiences.

Popular fiction and drama, westerns and detective stories, films and television serials, all deal with the same great archetypal themes as folktales and ballads, though this is seldom due to direct influence; these are simply the limits within which the human mind works. The number of people who have elevated the formulas of popular fiction to a higher literary level is surprisingly small. Examples are H.G. Wells's early science fiction, the western stories of Gordon Young and Ernest Haycox, the detective stories of Sir Arthur Conan Doyle, Georges Simenon, and Raymond Chandler.

The latter half of the 20th century witnessed an even greater change in popular literature. Writing is a static medium: that is to say, a book is read by one person at a time; it permits recollection and anticipation; the reader can go back to check a point or move ahead to find out how the story ends. In radio, television, and the cinema the medium is fluent; the audience is a collectivity and is at the mercy of time. It cannot pause to reflect or to understand more fully without missing another part of the action, nor can it go back or forward. Marshall McLuhan in his book *Understanding Media* (1964) became famous for erecting a whole structure of aesthetic, sociological, and philosophical theory upon this fact. But it remains to be seen whether the new, fluent materials of communication are going to make so very many changes in civilization, let alone in the human mind—mankind has, after all, been influenced for thousands of years by the popular, fluent arts of music and drama. Even the most transitory television serial was written down before it was performed, and the script can be consulted in the files. Before the invention of writing, all literature was fluent because it was contained in people's memory. In a sense it was more fluent than music, because it was harder to remember.

Man in mass society becomes increasingly a creature of the moment, but the reasons for this are undoubtedly more fundamental than his forms of entertainment.

Long neglected as a topic of scholarly interest, popular culture has in recent years attracted the close and sustained attention of critics. Novels and stories of various genres, including detective fiction, mysteries, thrillers, romances, westerns, fantasies, science fiction, and the like—works rapidly consumed by a huge reading public in the United States, Europe, and around the world since the debut of the paperback in the late 1930s—have been increasingly scrutinized by academics using the tools and techniques of literary criticism. As a result, scholars have produced studies on the works of such popular authors as detective novelists Raymond Chandler and Dashiell Hammett, citing the merit of their "hard-boiled" writings as literature and as cultural documents. While many critics still denigrate works of this type as simple entertainment, "escapist" fiction, marred by formulaic narratives, superficiality, and sensationalism, some adherents of modem literary theory have challenged the accepted notions of what constitutes serious literature.

In addition, there are scholars who have opted to dismantle the barriers between elite and popular culture in order to understand both more fully. Thus, new strategies are being formulated to draw all modes of literature, from the canonical works of Shakespeare to something as seemingly ephemeral as advertising copy or paperback fiction, together in the study of cultural history, both in the past and in its most contemporary manifestations.

In Canada, whether published in paperback or cloth editions or both, trade or general books are considered to have had satisfactory sales if they have sold 1500 copies (poetry, play), 3000 (first novel) or 7000 (political commentary); at double these figures the publisher may have a BEST-SELLER. Arguably the best-selling Canadian author of all time is Arthur HAILEY, many of whose novels, such as *Hotel* (1965) and *Airport* (1968), have sold millions of copies each. The much anticipated and best-selling works of contemporary fiction writers such as Margaret ATWOOD, Ann-Marie MACDONALD, and Michael ONDAATJE might also be labeled popular literature. Popular, nonfiction authors such as Farley MOWAT, Peter C. NEWMAN, and Naomi Klein, who write serious books of particular interest to Canadians, enjoy hardcover sales of 75,000-150,000 copies per title. As substantial as such figures may seem, they pale in comparison with the sales record of Coles Notes.

The last ten years has witnessed the proliferation of popular fiction both in the number of titles and sales. For instance, Mills and Boon "publish 70 new titles each month and pulp any unsold copies after three months." (*The Independent*, 2008). And there have been changes in reading habit; a report on Market Figures from the UK National Literacy Trust cited on the website of the Romantic Novelist Association reveals that there are more people reading for pleasure than ever before (65% now read for enjoyment compared to 55% in 1979). At the international level, Mills and Boon have their books translated into 25 languages and sell in 100 international markets and a stable of 1,300 authors worldwide are working for Mills and Boom. (*The Independent*, 2008)

CHARACTERISTICS

Popular fiction is the combination of two main elements: conventions and inventions. According to Cawelti, conventions are elements which are "usually quite specific to a particular culture and period and do not mean the same outside this specific context." Stereotyped characters, accepted ideas, commonly known metaphors even favourite plot are examples of conventions. Inventions, on the other hand, are elements which are "uniquely imagined by creators". Such inventional elements could be either new kinds of character ideas, innovative plot or creative usages of language.

Both conventions and inventions play significant roles in a cultural context. While conventions represent the shared values of a society, inventions introduce new concepts to the society. Conventions maintain the traditions, customs and stability of a defined culture; inventions bring changes, new values. This explains the popularity of popular fictions since readers could find in these novels a piece of their lives, beliefs, and interests. Such findings bring them "satisfaction and emotional security". At the same time, inventions provide them with new information about the world and the feeling of escape from the ordinary life around them.

It is usually criticized that the genres of popular fiction make overuse of the literary "formula", which is "the synthesis of a number of specific cultural conventions in a period of time. Sewell (1984) stated that the value of popular fiction as literature was subsidiary because of limitations in novelty and creativity of "formula" fiction. However, such "formula" fiction fills a strong need for escape and relaxation of readers. Readers experience life, death, violence, and sex described in popular fiction in a manner that increases his sense of confidence and well-ordered existence. Furthermore, formula could be considered to be "a kind of literary art" because of its two features: (1) essential standardization and (2) its relation to the needs of escape.

The first characteristic of formula is the "essence of all literature". This is the factor creating the common background between a writer and his/her audience. Such shared experience brings basic emotional security to readers and through this readers may find it easier not only to comprehend the plot, but also to interpret between the lines. In other words, when a bridge between a writer and his/her readers is created, it enables "artistic communication".

The second feature of formula is of importance since such formulaic elements create the ideal world without limitations or uncertainties in readers' imagination. This aspect significantly distinguishes between popular fiction and serious literature. The latter describes the real world and forces its readers to face with the uncertain and unsecured reality when recognizing their involvement in characters whose fates reveal limitations and uncertainties.

THE RELATIONSHIP BETWEEN POPULAR FICTION AND POPULAR CULTURE

The term "popular culture" has been defined in numerous ways.

Mukerji and Schudson give the following definition of popular culture:

> "Popular culture refers to the beliefs and practices, and the objects through which they are organized, that are widely shared among a population. This includes folk beliefs, practices and objects rooted in local traditions, and

> mass beliefs, practices and objects generated in political and commercial centers."

Bates and Ferri mention even a broader definition of popular culture:

> "Popular culture is the television we watch, the movies we see, the fast food, or slow food, we eat, the clothes we wear, the music we sing and hear, the things we spend our money for, our attitude toward life. It is the whole society we live in, that which may or may not be distributed by the mass media. It is virtually our whole world".

From these definitions, it is evident that the "formula" mentioned above is cultural product. Culture is source for conventions, as well as is the background based on which the mutual understanding between a writer and his audiences. On the other hand, formula also has its impacts on culture since it may become conventional ways of representing and relating certain images, symbols. Flemming's James Bond, Doyle's Sherlock Homes, or recently Rowling's Harry Potter could be taken as examples illustrating influences of fictional characters on culture. For instance, Gelder observes the phenomenon of Harry Potter and ascertains that Harry Potter has spread far beyond the novels themselves. Total sales had reached around 250 million across 200 countries, with the novels translated into 60 languages, including Latin and Welsh. The first Harry Potter film adaptation by Warner Bros. became at the time the second-highest grossing film in history (beaten only by James Cameron's The Titanic). A huge amount of media spin-offs and merchandizing helped to keep Harry Potter at the centre of global cultural interest. Discovering such powerful influence of this phenomenon, Gelder concludes that "The Harry Potter phenomenon has indeed rebranded, and reglobalized, Britain, presenting to the world a country confident in its past but trying harder than usual to work out the possibilities for the future." Apparently, when a formula is widely successful, it has special appeal and becomes significant to the society. The process through which a formula develops and become a pattern of culture could be name "cultural evolution". (Cawelti, 1976, p.20).

THE RELATIONSHIP BETWEEN POPULAR FICTION AND LITERARY SYSTEM

Despite the widespread and popularity of popular fiction, in academic world, the place of popular fiction and its importance in academia are still not clear. A confession of an interest in popular fiction would be received with "doubts and uncomprehending responses." (Ashley, 1989 p.1) While genres of popular fiction-such as romance, thriller, crime fiction, or science fiction have attracted widespread attention from various perspectives, they have not been considered and investigated as "disparate categories".

To explain the overlook on popular fiction, Ashley states that such neglect is the result of the negative attitude of literary criticism, which consider popular fiction to be "the second-rate fiction", or "a kind of cultural detritus". In the sixties of the twentieth century, Tony Bennet introduced the case of popular fiction as both "symptom and cause of cultural degeneracy". And in literary scholars' views, whose focus was the language and style used in literature, popular fiction was "a meretricious cousin of real literature". (Schneider-Mayerson, 2010 p. 30). However, it is worth viewing popular fiction in the polysystem frame in order to reconsider the position of popular fiction in literature,

Even Zohar introduced his concept of polysystem with the idea that literature is an historical phenomenon that should be analyzed by systematic approaches similar to that of other sciences. He describes "The idea of structuredness and systemicity need no longer be identified with homogeneity, a semiotic system can be conceived of as a heterogeneous, open structure. It is, therefore, very rarely a unisystem but is, necessarily, a polysystem – a multiple system, a system of various systems which intersect with each other and partly overlaps, using concurrently different options, yet functioning as one structured whole, whose members are interdependent". A literary polysystem is envisaged as the interlinking chains of genres and producers which allow us to identify different types of literature and their social purposes. In the polysystem theory, all fields of literary creativity, popular literature, translated literature, children's literature, as well as semi-literary texts, may become subjects of research. The predominant factors in the polysytem concept are stratification, heterogeneity and dynamics.

The polysystem theory also assumes a series of centres and peripheries belonging to the various system within polysystem. There is always a struggle among texts created. The goal of such a battle is to move into the centre of the polysystem, but only a small number of them acquire the status of "official", "high", and become canonical. Texts which move successfully to the central position are those which are of popularity on the market, as well as among readers.

Obviously there are some certain restrictions in the polysytem theories such as the blurred boundaries between centre and periphery but the theory of Even-Zohar allows us to observe the movement and social positioning of popular fiction along with discovering the factors which influence the position of popular fiction in the national literary system. The fame of popular fiction as stated in the introduction of this section, together with the certain contribution of popular fiction to the development of current literary and cultural trend, has revealed popular fiction is an integral part of the literary system and it is worth conducting more insightful research to this field.

DIFFERENCE BETWEEN POPULAR LITERATURE AND CLASSICAL LITERATURE

Classic literature or art is above all works that survive through institutions like schools, religious traditions, or learned societies. Classical literature enjoys a long shelf-life but its popularity may be limited to literate, elite, or schooled culture. Compared to popular literature, classic literature is under-exposed except in schools.

> "A classic is something everybody wants to have read, but no one wants to read." —Mark Twain

Twain's line is funny for sympathizing with humanity's weaknesses, but "wants to have read" admits the prestige or social capital of classics.

In Literature's ongoing balancing act between entertainment and education, classic literature tilts toward education or learning and is less likely to indulge cheap thrills or escapism.

"Education" may include:

- broadening the mind,
- cultural literacy,
- vocabulary-building,
- modeling,
- ethics,
- empathy,
- critical thinking,
- cultural or historical critiques concerning social or personal justice,
- mental-emotional exercise,
- attention-span extension (deferred gratification), and discipline.

Popular literature and culture are what most people want to read, largely because they're easier and more immediately gratifying. They stick to proven formulas (as in "sequels" or "knock-offs") to capitalize on previously-proven winners. They're familiar and unchallenging, in contrast to the demands classic literature makes on a reader.

A classic text, instead of being highly predictable, self-consciously innovates, extends, reforms, or even parodies previous styles and contents from earlier texts in its tradition. Like evolution, classic literature continues what has come before but also adapts to fresh experience and challenging knowledge. (Popular literature also changes but follows rather than leads, supporting status quo).

A simple formula for classic literature is "a book that won't stay closed." A classic text keeps producing meaning for one generation after another, in different contexts, for audiences with different mind-sets and needs—even though the text still speaks with the same words!

Classics don't always stay classics, though. Competition from new texts is always crowding out some older ones, and tastes and needs change.

In sum, what counts as "classic literature" remains fairly stable but also changes according to what's being written, what gets taught, and who's sitting in the classrooms. (See representative literature below.)

Popular literature or art is the kind of literature that readers talk about excitedly and want to read as though it is news or a change in lives of people they care about—for instance, a new installment in a series like Twilight, Hunger Games, Tom Clancy's novels featuring Jack Ryan, or any other detective, spy, or action series with a glamorous, super-competent hero or team.

Instead of surviving indefinitely in schools and libraries, popular literature lives and dies by the momentary marketplace when it appears in popular culture. Successful popular literature sells well and becomes well-known to a wide audience, but compared to classic literature or art it is often over-exposed, shorter-lived, and soon forgotten or replaced with follow-ups, sequels, etc. (e.g., hit songs on the radio sound old a month or year later).

Sentimental style, sensational events, and stereotypical formulas like sensitive vampires, exploding helicopters, helpful dogs, and lost children are predictable, but they please wide audiences by reinforcing familiar tastes and attitudes, confirming what everybody already thinks and appealing to what is already known. In contrast, classic literature usually takes you beyond your comfort zone.

Unit 1
Children's Literature

Children's literature, the body of written works and accompanying illustrations produced in order to entertain or instruct young people. The genre encompasses a wide range of works, including acknowledged classics of world literature, picture books and easy-to-read stories written exclusively for children, and fairy tales, lullabies, fables, folk songs, and other primarily orally transmitted materials.

By the end of the 18th century, children's literature was a flourishing, separate and secure part of the publishing industry in Britain. Perhaps as many as 50 children's books were being printed each year, mostly in London, but also in regional centres such as Edinburgh, York and Newcastle. By today's standards, these books can seem pretty dry, and they were often very moralising and pious. But the books were clearly meant to please their readers, whether with entertaining stories and appealing characters, the pleasant tone of the writing, or attractive illustrations and eye-catching page layouts and bindings.

1.1 EARLY WRITING FOR CHILDREN

This was new. At the beginning of the century very few such enjoyable books for children had existed. Children read, certainly, but the books that they probably enjoyed reading (or hearing) most, were not designed especially for them. Fables were available, and fairy stories, lengthy chivalric romances, and short, affordable pamphlet tales and ballads called chapbooks, but these were published for children and adults alike. Take Nathaniel Crouch's

Winter-Evenings Entertainments (1687). It contains riddles, pictures, and 'pleasant and delightful relations of many rare and notable accidents and occurrences' which has suggested to some that it should be thought of as an early children's book. However, its title-page insists that it is 'excellently accommodated to the fancies of old or young'.

Meanwhile, the books that were published especially for children before the mid-18th century were almost always remorselessly instructional (spelling books, school books, conduct books) or deeply pious. Yet just because books seem dull or disciplinary to us today, this doesn't mean that children at the time didn't enjoy them. Godly books of the sort produced from the 1670s by Puritans like John Bunyan are a case in point. James Janeway's *A Token for Children* (1671-72) gives what its subtitle describes as 'an Exact Account of the Conversion, Holy and Exemplary Lives and Joyful Deaths of Several Young Children'. These children lie on their deathbeds, giving accounts of the sins too often committed by children – idleness, disobedience, inattention to lessons, boisterousness, neglecting the Sabbath – but tell those assembled round them that salvation awaits all who renounce such wickedness, and they explain how happy they are to be going to their eternal reward. Hardly fun, we might think, yet memoirs and letters, as well as continuing sales over more than a century, testify to young readers' genuine enjoyment of these descriptions of heroic and confident, if doomed, children.

1.2 THE 18TH CENTURY

In the first half of the 18th century a few books that didn't have an obviously instructional or religious agenda were published especially for children, such as *A Little Book for Little Children* (c.1712), which included riddles and rhymes; and a copiously illustrated bestiary, *A Description of Three Hundred Animals* (1730), the second part of which was published 'particularly for the entertainment of youth'. But the turning point came in the 1740s, when a cluster of London publishers began to produce new books designed to instruct and delight young readers. Thomas Boreman was one, who followed his *Description of Three Hundred Animals* with a series of illustrated histories of London landmarks jokily (because they were actually very tiny) called the *Gigantick Histories*

(1740-43). Another was Mary Cooper, whose two-volume *Tommy Thumb's Pretty Song Book* (1744) is the first known nursery rhyme collection, featuring early versions of well-known classics like 'Bah, bah, a black sheep', 'Hickory dickory dock', 'London Bridge is falling down' and 'Sing a song of sixpence'.

1.3 THE FATHER OF CHILDREN'S LITERATURE

But the most celebrated of these pioneers is John Newbery, whose first book for the entertainment of children was *A Little Pretty Pocket-Book Intended for the Instruction and Amusement of Little Master Tommy and Pretty Miss Polly* (c.1744). It was indeed a pretty book, small, neat and bound in brightly coloured paper, and Newbery advertised it as being sold with a ball (for a boy) and a pincushion (for a girl) – these toys were to be used to record the owner's good and bad deeds (by means of pins stuck either to the black side of the ball or pincushion, or the red). Newbery's books perfectly embodied the educational ideas of John Locke, who had advocated teaching through amusement. But Newbery has become known as the 'father of children's literature' chiefly because he was able to show that publishing children's books could be a commercial success. This may have been because he made most of his money from selling patent medicines, and by publishing for adults

Nevertheless, his children's book business flourished, and, following his death in 1767, it was taken over by his descendants, surviving into the 19th century. Newbery was a great innovator too. He produced the first children's periodical for example, called *The Lilliputian Magazine* (1751-52), a miscellany of stories, verse, riddles and chatty editorials. And his most famous work, The *History of Little Goody Two-Shoes* (1765) has a good claim to be called the first children's novel. It tells the story of a poor orphan, Margery, who makes a career for herself as a teacher before, like a less glamorous Cinderella (with no fairy godmother, balls to attend, or glass slipper), she marries the local landowner who she has impressed by her honesty, hard work and good sense.

1.4 A RAPID EXPANSION OF CHILDREN'S LITERATURE

The reasons for this sudden rise of children's literature have never been fully explained. The entrepreneurial genius of figures like Newbery undoubtedly played a part, but equally significant were structural factors, including the growth of a sizeable middle class, technical developments in book production, the influence of new educational theories, and changing attitudes to childhood. Whatever the causes, the result was a fairly rapid expansion of children's literature through the second half of the 18th century, so that by the early 1800s, the children's book business was booming. For the first time it was possible for authors to make a living out of writing solely for children, and to become famous for it. Children's literature, as we know it today, had begun.

1.5 ETHICS AND EDUCATION IN CHILDREN'S LITERATURE

With the emergence and development of literary theories, criticism of children's books also underwent vigorous changes. Following the norms advocated in adult books, various theories were implemented on the so called children's books resulting in multifarious interpretations.

Most authors endeavoured to combine healthy moral lessons with a story. It is deciphered that books that find a place in the canon of children's literature do so, on the basis of two criteria, roughly. The first being literary, inculcating aesthetic pleasure. The second aspect, on the other hand, is educational. Most books propagate certain accepted beliefs and values passed on from one generation to the other, so do the canon of children's literature. The adult authors instill values in children which they believe imminent for their development as disciplined individuals. These books teach their readers obedience, inculcate respect for the adult's world and emphasize and give due consideration to the adult's advice and views. The canon of children's literature at any particular time helps to propagate ideas acceptable to the contemporary society as sufficient amount of exciting interest to render the story attractive to the young, hoping all the while, that the form was not disproportionate; the right proportion being crucial to the success of these influential books.

Most mainstream children's books dogged the adult market as it developed in its many layered variety. If boys were eager to read lurid adventure novels produced for a non-genteel adult readership, then genteel writers would learn to write exciting adventure tales more in harmony with the middle class values. If domestic novels attracted enormous audiences among literate middle class women, then surely the domestic tales could be adapted to serve the reading taste of middle class girls.

Books for children underwent a lot of changes from adventure books in the early nineties, to the fairy tales in the nineteen eighties, and to the recent type of fiction in which a one-sided view is clearly presented, which is usually bourgeois, middle or upper middle class and a typical Western society. Values such as honesty, generosity, sense of dignity, justice, and fair play with a lot of hope and optimism were endorsed through these books, featuring White children, in a clean, comfortable and happy world. Even in the bleakest of worlds, a change for the better is endorsed as portrayed in J. K. Rowling's formulaic novels where each novel ends with a sense of optimism and justice which caters to children's emotions.

The class bias in children's books is convincingly portrayed by excluding all classes except the middle class. The banalities of commonplace concepts of the working class were redeemed to a certain extent. Treated with refinement, they were the privileged devoted servants. Visibly invisible in children's literature is the friction and misunderstanding in families. Perfect families were the tone of the day; unemployment, divorce, separations and death were among other concerns conspicuously unseen in these books. Harry Potter in Rowling's novels strongly endorses today's culture, relegated, neglected, ill-treated and overworked by his aunt, uncle and cousin, confronted by his enemies in his fight against evil and injustice. The last novel relates a change in his uncle, aunt and cousin.

The sexist bias in children's books, clearly portrayed in many novels, with only supportive roles for girls, has aroused the ire of many feminists. But, a novel for girls, elaborated them in two ways; either completely feminine or as tomboys revolting against the restraints imposed upon them by tradition and society. Juxtaposing these two stereotypes within a single book as friends, sisters or classmates was the usual custom; as Anne and George in the Famous Five books by Enid Blyton, and the sisters Meg and Jo March in Little Women. In the above pairs, the former epitomizes femininity with all paraphernalia of good qualities associated with it, which the latter despises in the initial stages and then ardently aspires to. The tomboyish ways are discarded with the development of the text and the tomboy heroines conform to society. This kind of confinement and structuring took place in most children's books and provided a child with his or her initial concepts of 'feminine' roles, games and attitudes.

Literature does not deal with illusions only but with lasting truths too. It depicts life in a universal way, with the reins of power in the adults, even though it is children's literature. Thus, the schooling, their psychology and their upbringing are completely under the control of adults, for if children are left alone to decide for themselves what is good for them; they might become evil and violent as depicted in Golding's *The Lord of the Flies*. That children are capable and independent is true, but the freedom to live according to their whims and fancies with no control or restrictions over them will lead to absolute chaos and confusion. Most children will be happy to live on junk food, watch the idiot box, play video games all the time neglecting studies which will naturally result in a world of obese, lethargic and short-sighted children, an already fast increasing set. As depicted in *The Lord of the Flies,* sometimes children can become cruel and destructive too without the supervision and control of adults. In spite of the criticism by feminist critics, Marxist critics, Post-colonial critics, children's literature has continued to be published without any restriction due to the belief that children's literature and its criticism is one of the basic tools by which dominant ideologies were transmitted and endorsed so as to make them self-perpetuating.

The world of children and their literature is a world of reality and fantasy juxtaposed; a magic kingdom, completely devoid of the obvious control of adults or a world with the control of adults. It communicated various ideologies and values which should be taken into consideration. But children's literature should also be looked into as a source of pleasure and knowledge.

1.6 LEWIS CARROLL'S *THROUGH THE LOOKING GLASS*

1.6.1 Author

Lewis Carroll is the pseudonym of mathematician Charles Lutwidge Dodgson, which he adopted when publishing his famous children's novels and nonsense verse.

The son of a Cheshire parson, Dodgson grew up in a large family which enjoyed composing magazines and putting on plays. In 1851, he went to Christ Church, Oxford. By 1855, he was a fellow (which necessitated celibacy), lecturing in mathematics. He occupied a tower in the college for the rest of his life. He wrote many books on mathematics and logic, and enjoyed inventing puzzles and games and playing croquet.

His love of paradox and nonsense and his fondness for small children led to the writing of *Alice's Adventures in Wonderland* (1865), a story which he began while rowing Lorina, Alice, and Edith, the three small daughters of the College Dean H G Liddell, up the Thames for a picnic near Binsey. A sequel, *Through the Looking Glass* and *What Alice Found There*, appeared in 1871. Interviewed when she was old, Alice remembered him as tall and slender, with blue/grey eyes, longish hair, and 'carrying himself upright, almost more than upright, as if he had swallowed a poker'.

He published *Phantasmagoria and Other Poems* in 1869, *The Hunting of the Snark* in 1876 and *Sylvie and Bruno* in 1889.

Dodgson wrote and received 'wheelbarrows full' of letters (a letter register he started in his late 20s and kept for the rest of his life records more than 98,000 sent and received). Many of these were on religious and political issues while others were full of light-hearted nonsense. He excelled in artfully staged photographs, many of children in costumes and others of friends, including Dante Gabriel Rossetti, Holman Hunt and Alfred, Lord Tennyson. He died, aged 65, of pneumonia.

1.6.2 *Through the Looking Glass*

Through the Looking Glass is Carroll's sequel to Alice in Wonderland. A few of the characters who appeared in Wonderland reappear in Through the Looking Glass, including Alice's cat and the Hatter and the Hare. More significantly, however, is the way in which the sequel mirrors the first book: it begins inside on a snowy November 4, while Wonderland began outside on a sunny May 4; it employs the imagery of chess where Wonderland employs the imagery of playing cards; time and space vary dizzyingly in *Through the Looking-Glass* while size changes drastically in Wonderland. This is all even more significant when considering the main motif of the book, the looking-glass, or mirrors.

Even though both books are considered works of children's literature, and both reflect on the theme of growing-up, Through the Looking Glass approaches this theme in a more abrupt and less playful way. It is as if the troubles associated with approaching maturity are introduced in *Alice in Wonderland* and then met with resignation in *Through the Looking Glass*.

1.6.3 Characters

Alice

Alice is the protagonist of the story. She is a playful, imaginative seven-year-old who was also the main character of Carroll's first book. She is inspired by an actual girl who was in some ways Carroll's ward. She leads the reader through the looking-glass world, which is a metaphor for her journey to adulthood. She is both insightful and ignorant; she often does not understand the characters in the looking-glass world, but often it seems that her thoughts and conversation make more logical sense than theirs. She is persistent in making it through to the eighth square, and she consistently shows her precocious personality through the shameless curiosity and fearless decision-making she engages in while wandering through the looking-glass world.

Alice spends the entire book participating in a game of chess, in which she is a white pawn trying to make it to the eighth square so that she can become a queen. As much as the book emphasizes the necessity of completing that journey, so, too, does it push Alice forward with regret. This tone illustrates the strong paternal feelings the author had for Alice in real life as well as his imagination.

Tweedledum and Tweedledee

Tweedledee and Tweedledum are twin brothers who encounter Alice again in the looking-glass world. They were also present in Wonderland, in Carroll's first book. They are important because they embody proper social behaviour and norms. Even when they engage in fighting, they first decide they are going to do it and then set a time limit so that they can sit down for dinner at the appropriate hour. They impart a message of caution, both through their strict adherence to rules and also through the story of the Walrus and the Carpenter, which they relate to Alice.

There is also a mean streak in these two brothers, for the tease Alice about the idea that she is merely a figment of the Red King's imagination. They claim that she is not real, and that she is only a character in the Red King's dream. Alice is disturbed by this idea, even though she questions at the end of the book whose dream was responsible for the looking-glass world.

Humpty Dumpty

This is also a character who appears not only in this book, but in the author's prequel as well. He is also the subject of a popular nursery rhyme. He is an egg (though he vehemently denies it) with a face and human clothes. Alice is not fond of him, which is not surprising; he constantly interrupts her to instruct her on vocabulary and language. Carroll uses this character to express his view on the ways in which people misabuse language. Humpty Dumpty is nauseatingly confident about his definitions of words, even though most of what he has to say is ridiculous.

He does introduce Alice and the reader to the concept of the portmantaeu word, which is a word that combines two words and their meanings into a new word. He does this in order to explain Jabberwocky in his own terms before his inevitably fall.

White Knight

The White Knight is the protagonist in the last leg of Alice's journey. He saves her from the Red Knight, who wishes to capture "the white pawn." Instead of capturing her, he treats her as an equal and allows her to roam free, although he does express his feelings about her particular journey. He is a disorganized, clumsy character who is interested in bogus inventions. He does, however, have a kind heart.

1.6.4 Chapter 1—Looking-Glass House

Alice, who has been half-asleep and talking to herself, notices that her ball of yarn has come unraveled. She blames the mischief on Kitty, who is not the middle of being cleaned by Dinah. While she scolds Kitty, she imagines that Kitty responds defiantly to all of her accusations.

Alice then becomes distracted by the winter weather, commenting on how the boys were gathering wood for the bonfire but that it soon became too cold for the activity. She muses about the changing seasons, speculating that during the winter, the trees and fields must sleep beneath the blanket of snow, but that in spring and summer, they turn green and dance. The narrator remarks meanwhile that Alice is prone to flights of fancy which often begin with her saying "let's pretend."

Alice, who has been trying to get Kitty to imitate the Red Queen chess piece, turns her attention to the looking glass, in which she imagines that there is another home, very much like her own, but in which some things are reversed. She wishes longingly for the glass to dissolve so that she can step into that other world. Suddenly, the glass becomes misty, and Alice enters the alternate universe that is a reflection of her own world.

Inside, she notices that there is a fire like the one in her hearth. She notices that the clock has the face of an old man which smiles at her. She also sees that the room is not kept as tidy as the one she left, for there are chess pieces all over the floor. When she gets closer to them, she realizes that they are talking and moving.

The White Queen seems to have lost her daughter, Lily, so Alice decides to reunite them by lifting up the Queen and setting her back on the table. The Queen seems to think that she has been relocated by a volcano, as they are near the fire, so Alice concludes that she cannot be seen or heard in this world. She does the same for the King, and also dusts him off, all of which makes him extremely frightened.

She notices a book and tries to read, but at first she does not understand the language. Then she realizes that the text must be reversed since she is in the looking-glass world, so she holds the book up to the glass. The text is revealed to be the poem Jabberwocky, the language of which she still does not understand. Alice, feeling like she will not have time to see everything if she lingers, floats downstairs and out the door to explore the garden.

Analysis

Lewis Carroll was known for his love of contrast, so it makes sense that this book opens with a scene indoors in the middle of winter. Alice in Wonderland, contrarily, opened on a sunny May afternoon. The date is also significant, for when Alice is talking to Kitty, she implies that there is going to be a holiday the following day. She is in fact referring to Guy Fawkes Day, November 5th, the night before which was traditionally celebrated with a bonfire at Christ Church, where Carroll studied, lived, and wrote.

The kitten Snowdrop is an example of Carroll including elements from his own life in his literature. He was good friends with a man named George Macdonald, whose daughter Mary had a kitten named Snowdrop. It is actually this family that played a large role in encouraging Carroll to publish *Alice in Wonderland,* so perhaps the mention of the kitten Snowdrop is a subtle thanks to them.

In this chapter, the reader is introduced to the theme of inversion, which is pervasive throughout the book. Carroll was in fact obsessed with this notion in real life. He wrote some of his letters in mirror writing, and some he wrote starting with the last word and ending with the first. He also drew pictures that turned into other pictures when they were turned upside down.

It is unclear why he nurtured this obsession. One explanation, judged to be inadequate, is that he was left-handed but was forced to use his right, so the inversion techniques were a part of some grand revenge for this travesty. Carroll did do a great deal of work in mathematics and logic, and it is perhaps this passion that encouraged him to explore logical contradiction.

The inclusion of the poem "Jabberwocky" in the book is anything but random. The poem is universally considered to be the greatest nonsense poem in the English language, and it was incredibly popular, especially among schoolboys, during the late 19th century. Carroll originally wanted to put the entire poem in reversed form, but inevitably decided on just the first verse. In a periodical Carroll wrote at the age of 23 to amuse his friends, he provided explanations for all the nonsense words in the first verse, all of which vary from Humpty Dumpty's versions later in the book.

Later work in physics confirmed that there would be dire consequences for the Alice that entered the Looking-Glass world. It is clear that she remained herself when she entered, because she has to hold the book up to a mirror to read it. In this case, her normal matter would clash with all the anti-matter around her, and there would likely be an explosion. This is humorous in light of her speculation about Looking-Glass milk, which is most likely not at all nutritional.

1.6.5 Chapter 2—The Garden of Live Flowers

Alice follows the path she believes will bring her to the garden, but no matter the direction in which she goes, she ends up back at the house. Eventually she runs into a patch of flowers with a tree in the middle. She discovers that the flowers can talk, but they are quite rude, criticizing her lack of intelligence and her strange looks. The flowers think that she must be a flower as well, even if she looks wrong.

The flowers reveal that there is another person in the garden, which Alice surmises from their description of a flower that looks quite like Alice. Alice looks around and sees the Red Queen, who has grown to a little taller than herself. Alice expresses interest in meeting the Queen, even though the flowers advise against it.

But when Alice tries walking toward the Queen, she finds herself in front of the house again. This time, she tries walking in the opposite direction in which she wants to go, and she finds herself walking almost straight into the Queen.

The Queen demands that Alice courtesy and call her "your Majesty" when they speak to each other. Alice tells the Queen that she wants to get to the hill in the distance, and when the Queen calls it a valley, Alice accuses her of speaking nonsense, but the Queen only then claims that she is making sense.

When the pair reaches the hill, Alice notices that the countryside is divided into regular squares. She realizes that the whole world is a chess game, and she very much wants to join the game. All of the sudden, she realizes she and the Queen are running, and when they slow down, the Queen explains that in this world, one has to run to remain in place.

The Queen assures Alice that she can play the game, and that she can even eventually be a Queen if she wants. She will start out as a pawn, however. The Queen gives Alice some instructions as to where she will have to go and whom she will meet, and then she vanishes.

Analysis

There are a couple of examples of allusion in this chapter. The episode of the talking flowers is actually a reference to a the poem "Maud" by Tennyson. Additionally, the Rose and the Violet are meant to represent the two youngest Liddell sisters, Rhoda and Violet, who are otherwise not included in the Alice books.

The theme of inversion appears again when Alice tries to walk toward the Red Queen. Every time she walks in the direction she sees the Red Queen, she ends up closer to the house where she started. But when she suddenly walks in the opposite direction, she ends up right in front of the Red Queen. It also appears within the dialogue between Alice and the Red Queen. The Queen offers Alice a dry biscuit to quench her thirst, and she informs Alice that she must run in order to remain in the same place.

Carrollian scholar Roger Lancelyn Green speculates that the Red Queen is in fact a prototype for the governess of the Liddell children, Miss Prickett. He also argues that their mansion was the original Looking-Glass house, and that the land it looked out upon is the model for the land that Alice viewed as a chessboard when receiving instructions from the Red Queen.

The chessboard/game of chess as a metaphor for life is rather common in literature. Many authors/philosophers employ it, including George Eliot and William James. H. G. Wells opens his book *The Undying Fire* with a conversation between God and the devil, who are playing chess. God is the creator of the game and of the rules and can make as many moves as he likes, and the devil is responsible for introducing "a slight inexplicable inaccuracy into each move, which necessitates further moves in correction."

In *Through the Looking Glass,* Alice apparently has the ability to make her own moves, although it is not clear that the choice is entirely hers. This question is explored throughout the book. Indeed, as soon as the Red Queen tells Alice she is to be the White Queen's Pawn, she begins to run, although she cannot remember starting to run.

1.6.6 Chapter 3-Looking-Glass Insects

Alice tries to survey the land before her, and she notices some elephants tending to enormous flowers like bees. She also notices that there are no rivers and that she is standing on what seems to be the only mountain in the place. Desiring to proceed to the third square, she leaps over the first brook in front of her.

She lands in a carriage and is immediately accosted by a guard asking for her ticket. She does not have a ticket and tries to explain herself, but all the passengers are chastising her for wasting time, breath and money. The passengers are all animals and insects. There is one passenger too small for her to see whispering in her ear.

When the train leaps over the next brook, she finds herself sitting beneath a tree and talking to a large gnat, which had previously been whispering in her ear. She explains to the gnat that she has never known any talking insects, and she proceeds to tell him the names of insects where she comes from. He then responds by telling her the equivalent insects in his world: the rocking horse fly, the snap-dragon fly and the bread-and-butter fly.

The two then discuss whether or not it would be convenient to be able to leave behind one's name. The gnat makes a joke and in so doing makes itself extremely sad. When Alice looks up she finds that it is gone, and wanting to make progress, she walks on. She finds herself in a darker wood with a wood beyond it and assumes this is the wood where things have no names.

Because she is in this wood, she cannot remember her name or the names of things around her. She comes across a Fawn who suffers from the same predicament, and they move on together into the next wood. Here, she remembers, and she proceeds along the path with two finger-posts, both pointing in the same direction, but one for Tweedledee's house, and the other for Tweedledum's.

Analysis

Alice makes the typical two-square leap allowed a Pawn as its initial move. She starts in the second square, but as soon as she leaps a brook she is in a train in the third square. This train takes her over a brook and into the fourth square.

The issue of naming things appears in this chapter twice. The first occasion is in the middle of the conversation between the Gnat and Alice. Alice makes an incredibly astute observation about names, arguing that names are not actually important because they belong to things inherently but because they are useful tags for the person referring to them.

The second occasion involves Alice's short experience in the wood where things have no names. She forgets her name while she is here, although at one point, she believes it begins with an "L", undoubtedly because she has replaced the White Queen's daughter, Lily, in the game. She meets a fawn, with whom she rejoices once they exit the wood and remember their names.

The wood is supposed to represent the universe as well as Alice's observation. Things in the universe do not have signs or labels. Names are a product of the minds that need to organize and refer to them. Otherwise, they would not exist. This falls under the theme of imagination as well, or things merely existing as a part of a separate mind.

Alice's logical observation reveals her as a representation of Carroll, since he was so concerned with formal logic in his studies. Her rationality stands in sharp contrast to the nonsense of the Gnat, and will continue to do so with other characters. This and the consequences of her realization (the excursion in the no-name wood) is also a reminder that Alice is dwelling simultaneously in two worlds: that of the child and that of the adult. Her rationality places her in the world of adulthood, but it tends to get her into trouble in the Looking-Glass world, which might indicate a warning against her swift progress.

1.6.7 Chapter 4—Tweedledum and Tweedledee

Alice comes upon Tweedledum and Tweedledee, and she immediately knows which is which because they have their names on their collars. They chastise her for not beginning a conversation with them, but she is distracted by the poem about the two engaging in a battle. She tries to elicit directions from them, but they continue to advise her on how properly to begin a conversation. When she tries to shake both of their hands at once, they grab her and begin to dance.

Once they stop, they decide to recite poetry for Alice. They recite "The Walrus and the Carpenter," which is basically a tale of a walrus and a carpenter who take a walk on a beach one day and invite some oysters to come along. Many of the young oysters agree and end up getting devoured by the walrus and the carpenter.

After the recitation, Alice admits that she prefers the Walrus because he at least showed remorse for eating the oysters. Tweedledee and Tweedledum argue that even so, he ate significantly more than the carpenter. When Alice changes her mind, they argue that the carpenter ate as many as he could. Alice is left confused about which character she prefers.

Alice hears a rumbling noise and fears that it is coming from some great beast in the woods. The two little men assure Alice that it is just the Red King snoring, and they go to look upon him. Alice is disappointed to see that he is just a rumpled mess. The men then try to convince her that she is just a character in the King's dream and that she is therefore not real. This makes Alice exceedingly upset.

They notice a white rattle on the ground, and this incites the battle between the two men that Alice was originally anticipating. She helps them get dressed in ridiculous outfits for their battle, and when they both complain about injuries, she uses the opportunity to encourage them to save their fighting for another time. At this, they agree to have a shorter fight, but then a monstrous crow flies overhead, and they all run for cover.

Analysis

Tweedledum and Tweedledee are enantiomorphs, which, according to mathematicians, are forms that are mirror images of one another. This is emphasized by the frequent use of the word "contrariwise." It is possible that the original nursery rhyme is an allusion to the rivalry between two composers, Handel and Bononcini.

The poem about the walrus and the carpenter is an important one, especially considering the discussion that follows it. The brothers want to know which Alice thinks is more contemptible, and it appears that she is unable to decide. The question poses a difficult moral dilemma, that involving whether it is right to judge a man by his actions or instead, by his intentions.

This chapter also poses metaphysical problems, for Tweedledum and Tweedledee claim that Alice is only a figment of the Red King's dream. This is more deeply interpreted as the philosophy that things are not real in an of themselves; Bishop Berkeley wrote that things exist only as "sorts of things" in the mind of God. Alice takes the more practical point of view.

Also, this idea of who is dreaming of whom shares an interesting parallel with the idea of mirrors. It is postulated that Alice is dreaming of the King, who is also dreaming of Alice, who still is dreaming of the King, which ends up being an infinite regress. The image is strikingly similar to two mirrors facing one another, reflecting infinitely themselves inside the other mirror. This idea also relates back to Tweedledee and Tweedledum themselves, who have been established as mirror images of one another.

1.6.8 Chapter 5—Wool and Water

Alice catches a shawl that happens to belong the White Queen. The White Queen is just as rumpled as the Red King, and Alice finds that conversing with her is extremely confusing. When Alice comments on the Queen's bedraggled state of dress, the Queen tries to employ her. They get into an argument about the mode of pay; the Queen claims that one gets paid in jam every other day, but never today, though Alice insists that at some point it will have to be today.

The Queen also argues that the backwards way of living is best, because one's memory works in both directions. Alice tries to convince her that prosecuting a crime before it has happened is not right, but the queen argues that the punishment is good for the person apprehended. She puts on a band aid and screams because she anticipates pricking her finger while refastening her brooch, and indeed, after fumbling with it, she pricks her finger.

Alice suddenly becomes sad because she feels so alone in the woods. The Queen tries to console her by getting her to consider something else, anything else, and Alice finds that she is laughing at what the Queen is asking her to think about. The Queen insists that Alice should practice thinking about impossible things, and the two jump across the next brook together.

Alice finds herself in a dark shop with a sheep behind the counter. The sheep encourages her to make up her mind about what she is going to purchase, but Alice asks for time to look around before making up her mind. But when she tries to peruse the shelves, there is never anything on the shelf she is looking at.

She discovers that the sheep is knitting with 14 pairs of needles. The sheep asks her if she can row, and she says that she could only do so in water, and then she finds herself in a boat with the sheep. She notices some beautiful rushes and picks some, but their beauty fades once they are in the boat.

She suddenly finds herself in the shop again with the sheep asking what she wants, and when she asks for an egg, the sheep places it on the shelf. She is convinced that it is not a good policy to put things directly into a person's hand. When Alice reaches for the egg, it just moves farther away from her, and soon everything she approaches becomes a tree.

Analysis

In this chapter, the White Queen proposes the notion of "living backwards." Alice thinks this is a preposterous idea. The White Queen goes on to argue that one who is living backwards has a memory that functions in both directions, and that this is the optimal way of functioning.

This relates to Jan Gordon's hypothesis about Victorian literature and its presentation of childhood. The Victorian era was a difficult one for the notion of childhood. Many laws that previously applied only to adults were applied to children. Additionally, laws that specifically protected children were removed. Further, the thinking that madness was actually a state of perpetuated childhood began to develop.

Gordon proposes that because of this, the line between childhood and adulthood began to blur, especially in literature. The reader notices that the White Queen, and all the other "adult" characters in the book, do not really act like adults. They indulge in childhood fantasies, and Alice is left the burden of providing logical responses and make sensible decisions.

Alice's situation reflects that of children in her era. Carroll was probably attempting in his literature to capture the problem of children being forced to grow up too fast, just like J.M. Barrie in Peter Pan. Alice has not parental role models for guidance on her journey, so she is forced to learn quickly and act the adult herself. Otherwise, she has no chance of reaching the eighth square.

There are a couple of hypotheses about the dream-rushes and

what they are meant to represent. It is possible that they are symbols of the author's child friends. The best are always out of reach. It is also possible that they represent the transience of youth and beauty, because once picked and held in hand, they quickly fade.

Alice's ability to balance an egg on its end on a flat surface alludes to Columbus' supposed accomplishment of the same feat. It might refer to an old gambling game in which the objective was to be the last person to place an egg on a napkin already crowded with eggs. None of the other eggs can be touched, and the winning strategy involves placing the first egg on its end in the very center. Many solutions to the egg-on-its-end problem have been proposed, including cracking it slightly on the bottom, shaking it so that the contents are dispersed and the centre of gravity changes, etc.

1.6.9 Chapter 6—Humpty Dumpty

The egg continues to get bigger and bigger, and it also has acquired human features, and it is sitting atop a rather narrow wall. Alice realizes that this must be Humpty Dumpty. He is offended by her remark that he looks like an egg. Because she is dissatisfied with the conversation, she recites the Humpty Dumpty poem to herself.

Humpty Dumpty asks her not to mutter to herself, and she expresses concern about him being seated so precariously on the wall. He argues that there is nothing to worry about, and before he can explain why, Alice says that it is because the kings men will all come to put him back in his place. He asks her how she knows this, and she says she read it in a book.

Humpty Dumpty then asks her what her name means, and she says that names do not have to have meanings. He argues that her name is stupid because it could mean anything. Alice tries to change the subject by complimenting him on his belt, but he is quite insulted because it is a cravat. He remarks that it was a gift from White King and Queen.

Alice asks Humpty Dumpty to translate Jabberwocky for her, since she observes that he has a way with words. He provides ridiculous definitions for all of the words she does not understand, and when he is done, he offers to recite a poem for her. She does not really want to listen to a poem, but when she hears that he composed it just for her, she figures she should just listen.

He cuts it off rather abruptly and indicates that he thinks they should say goodbye. He remarks that because her face is so ordinary he probably would not realize it if they were to ever meet again. Before she can respond, a great crash shakes the forest.

Analysis

This chapter includes another argument about names that relates to Carroll's interest in formal logic. Humpty Dumpty argues that his name and Alice's and proper names in general should have universal significance, whereas improper names of things can mean whatever he wants them to mean. Obviously, in the real world, this situation is reversed.

This episode in many ways relates back to the original nursery rhyme about Humpty Dumpty. Although it does not proceed in the same way, there are important references to note. For example, Carroll employs the word "proud" rather frequently in this chapter, which is meant to recall Humpty Dumpty's "pride that goeth before his fall."

Carroll is obviously capable of morbid humor, as evidenced by the part of the conversation between Alice and Humpty Dumpty in which they discuss age. Alice remarks that it is impossible for one to stop growing older. This is Humpty Dumpty's reply: "One can't, perhaps, but two can. With proper assistance, you might have left off at seven."

Humpty Dumpty is likely a satire of a certain type of intellectual. He has clear strengths and weaknesses. He of course claims that he is good at everything, but it seems that his most likely specialization is linguistics. The humor is evident because even though Humpty Dumpty can talk extensively about words and language, he is utterly helpless when it comes to mathematics, which was Carroll's own field of expertise.

The story of Humpty Dumpty is also an allegory for the fall of man from grace as well as the fall of the devil for his pride. This also relates to the issue of childhood and the "fall of innocence" that accompanies the progression to adulthood. Perhaps Humpty Dumpty is meant to be a lesson for Alice, though it seems she is already many steps ahead of him when it comes to maturity.

1.6.10 Chapter 7—The Lion and the Unicorn

The rumbling in the forest turns out to be thousands of soldiers and horses that have been sent by the White King. When Alice stumbles upon the White King, he tells her that he is waiting for a messenger. Alice notices a man moving strangely along the road in the distance, and the King attributes his odd movements to his "Anglo-Saxon attitudes."

The man approaches, and when Alice and the White King speak to him, they use words starting with the letter H, since that is the letter that begins his name. He tells the king that "they" are at it again, and when Alice inquires about the situation, she finds out the lion and the unicorn are having a battle. She recalls the relevant rhyme, in which the lion and the unicorn fight for the crown (which is apparently the White King's) while people bring them bread and cake and try to drum them out of town.

The three head into town so they can witness the event. They run into the other messenger, whose name also begins with an H. The King notices the White Queen running in the distance, and when Alice asks why she is running so fast, the King explains that she is probably trying to escape an enemy. Alice wonders aloud why he does not come to her aid, and he explains that she is just too fast for that to be possible.

The unicorn approaches, and it seems that in the most previous round, he emerged the winner. He notices Alice but calls her a monster because he does not know what kind of creature she is. The others tell him that she is a child, and he agrees to believe in her if she will believe in him.

The characters share plum cake, and the lion and unicorn continue to be extremely competitive. All of the sudden, loud drumming interrupts the feasting, and Alice, frightened, jumps over the next brook to escape.

Analysis

The two messengers in this chapter have counterparts in Alice's Adventures. Hatta is the Mad Hatter and Haigha is the March Hare. The illustrations that accompany the story make this clear. Alice has met them before in her previous adventures, but she does not recognize them as characters she already knows.

In this chapter, Carroll emphasizes an important theme in his book. Throughout the work, he has been stressing the arbitrary nature of language. Alice remarks to the king that she sees nobody on the road, and he responds that she must have good eyesight to be able to see "Nobody."

This observation by the King points to the slippery nature of definitions. It plays with the definition of "nobody" and what it means to physically see something. Carroll is playing with his readers' understanding of language and forcing them to think twice about the way in which they use words in everyday speech. None of the characters in the Looking-Glass world speak normally, and most of them question language in an unusual and at the same time insightful way.

The battle between the lion and the unicorn is an episode from a popular nursery rhyme. Carroll is fond of including nursery rhymes within his works; Humpty Dumpty is another example of this tendency.

1.6.11 Chapter 8—"It's My Own Invention"

Alice finds herself alone again, but then she is intercepted by the White Knight, who claims that having come upon her, she is not his prisoner. However, he cannot seem to stay on his horse. Another knight approaches, the Red Knight, and they argue about whose prisoner Alice is. They then have a very clumsy battle to determine the captor.

The White Knight wins, though Alice could not really tell what decided the victory. But when he claims that she is his prisoner, she argues that she wants to be a Queen. He tells her that is not a problem, as he intends to see her safely to the next brook so that she can proceed to the next square and become a queen.

Alice mounts his horse, which the Knight cannot seem to ride properly. He consistently slides off in all directions and lands on his head. While they ride, he tells Alice about all of his inventions: the box turned upside-down so rain won't get in, the beehive attached to his saddle, the pole that keeps hair from falling off, etc. Each of these inventions has a number of problems that Alice contemplates.

The Knight offers to sing Alice a song, and even though she is not interested, she agrees to let him sing to her. He sings about an old man who gives another man advice about how to live. Alice finds that she knows the tune, but the song does not make her cry, even though the knight insisted it would.

They reach the end of their journey, and the Knight requests that Alice see him off. She does, hoping that it encourages him, and then she jumps the final brook into the eighth square. When she lands, she realizes there is a gold crown on her head.

Analysis

At first it seems that the White Knight is a malevolent character in the story, because he tells Alice that he intends to take her prisoner. However, the reader discovers that he is a benevolent force in Alice's world, for he means to help her cross the last brook.

The crossing of this brook causes the White Knight great distress, for it signifies a significant move for Alice on the chess board of her life. She will move to the final square, where she is to become a Queen. While this causes the White Knight great sadness, Alice does not seem to be perturbed, even when he sings his song. The lack of tears from Alice indicates her blissful childhood ignorance.

The Red Knight who battles the White Knight represents a force of evil that means to hold Alice back from pursuing her destiny. Alice is amused as she watches the fight, unable to tell who is winning. This mirrors the ignorance she displays while listening to the White Knight sing; she obviously does not understand the importance of events leading to her destiny.

Some scholars believe that the White Knight is meant to be a caricature of the author. Carroll enjoyed inventing things and toying with odd objects. His physical appearance also mirrors that of the knight's: messy hair, blue eyes and a kind face. It also makes sense considering the role that he plays in Alice's journey. Of all the characters Alice meets, only the White Knight seems to offer her direct help.

1.6.12 Chapters 9-12—Queen Alice; Shaking; Waking; Which Dreamed I?

After realizing that she has become a Queen, Alice finds herself in the company of the Red Queen and the White Queen. The two queens begin questioning her relentlessly, telling her that she cannot be a queen until she passes the proper examination. They ask her strange questions about manners, mathematics, the alphabet, how to make bread, languages, and the cause of lightning. The Red Queen frustrates Alice by correcting every incorrect answer. Alice mistakenly remarks that thunder causes lightning, but when she attempts to reverse her statement, the Red Queen snaps that once she says something, she must live with the consequences. The White Queen changes the subject to a thunderstorm that occurred on the last set of Tuesdays. Confused, Alice listens to a sneering explanation that in Looking-Glass World, days are taken two or three at a time. The White Queen continues her foolish story, while the Red Queen apologizes to Alice for the White Queen's behaviour, explaining to Alice that the White Queen wasn't brought up well.

The Red Queen asks Alice to sing a lullaby to the White Queen, but Alice claims that she doesn't know any. The Red Queen begins singing instead, causing the White Queen to fall asleep on Alice's shoulder. Soon, the Red Queen falls asleep, too, and both queens slump their heads into Alice's lap. The snoring sounds like a song to Alice. She becomes distracted by the music and doesn't notice when the two queens vanish inexplicably. When Alice looks up, she finds herself standing in front of a door emblazoned with the words "QUEEN ALICE." Alice wants to enter but only finds a visitor's bell and a servant's bell, and no bell for guests. She knocks on the door and it flies open. The words "NO ADMITTANCE UNTIL THE WEEK AFTER NEXT!" boom out of the open door. Alice continues to knock to no avail, until eventually an old frog approaches from behind her and asks her what she wants. Alice explains that no one will answer the door. The confused Frog asks what the door has been asking and whether it would need an answer. The door flies open again and Alice hears a song about Queen Alice's grand party.

Alice finds a large table set before her with fifty guests seated around it. She sits down at the head of the table between the White Queen and the Red Queen. A servant brings out food and the Red Queen formally introduces Alice to the food. After the introduction, the Red Queen sends the food back to the kitchen, commenting that it is impolite to eat something after one has made acquaintance with it. Alice becomes frustrated and asks to get the pudding back, which she slices and serves to the guests. As the pudding is passed around, Alice asks the guests why there are so many poems in Looking-Glass World on the subject of fish. The White Queen responds by telling a riddle that asks whether answering the door or uncovering a dish of fish is more difficult. The queens toast Alice, who rises to give thanks to her guests. As she stands up, the room spontaneously erupts into chaos. Candles rise to the ceiling, guests become stuck to their plates, the White Queen tumbles into a soup tureen, and a soup ladle storms around the table. Alice grabs the tablecloth and tugs it off of the table, sending all of the guests flying to the ground.

Alice turns to the Red Queen, whom she considers responsible for the chaos, and grabs her. The Red Queen shrinks down to the size of a doll and Alice begins shaking her. Before Alice's eyes, the Red Queen seems to transform into her kitten Kitty. Alice realizes that she has woken up. She scolds Kitty for waking her up and then grabs the small Red Queen off of the nearby chess table, trying to get Kitty to admit that she had transformed into the Red Queen. Alice addresses Snowdrop, stating her suspicion that the white kitten is the White Queen. Lastly, Alice tries to guess who Dinah might be before deciding that she's probably Humpty Dumpty. She turns back to Kitty and tells her all about the fish-themed poetry she heard in her dream.

Analysis

The chess motif becomes highly pronounced in this chapter, and the various movements of the pieces signify the conclusion of the game. As Alice becomes Queen, the movements and positions of the individual pieces become clear. Flanked by both queens, Alice can see the entire chessboard. As she sits at the head of the table in her castle, all of the guests stretched out before her represent the other chess pieces. The table in this scene represents the table in Alice's house on which the chessboard rests, adjacent to the "real" Alice asleep in her chair. The White Queen's move to the soup tureen sets up the Red King's "checkmate," and when Alice slides over to seize the Red Queen, she puts the Red King in checkmate herself and ends the chess game. Now that the game has ended, Alice wakes up from her dream and finds herself holding Kitty.

Alice seems unsure of herself at the start of the game, but once she exerts her power as a queen, she exposes the façade and liberates herself from the confines of the chessboard. The Red and White Queens' relentless questioning represents an attempt to flatten Alice into submission so that she becomes part of their two-dimensional lives in Looking-Glass World. Alice resists this flattening, which manifests itself literally when the guests at the table become stuck to their plates. Alice rises to give thanks and in doing so becomes three-dimensional, setting off the chaos that allows her to seize the Red Queen and end the chess match.

Some critics see the moment when Alice wins the chess game to be the moment of her sexual awakening. In this reading, Alice's standing up represents a moment of orgasmic realization. The rising candle flames imply erection imagery, while the repetition of the word "moment" in the scene underscores the fleeting sensory intensity that causes Alice to tear away the tablecloth and attack the Red Queen. This orgasmic moment leads to the checkmate of the Red King, so that Alice experiences a sexual awakening. At this point, Alice has nowhere else to go in her dream, and abruptly wakes up. The fact that Dinah continues to wash Snowdrop when Alice regains consciousness supports the fact that the dream has happened in a single "moment." This realization also prompts Alice to wonder whether it was she or the Red King who had had the dream. By leaving off at this moment, Carroll comments that life is nothing but a dream, a blinking moment in God's mind.

Alice's progression across the board

Alice is a white pawn in the game. She first meets the Red Queen in the garden, which is her first move. Her second move is to the third square in the queen's line, and then to the fourth, via the railway. The next move happens when Alice meets the White King. Then she progresses to the fifth, sixth and seventh squares (shop and river, meeting Humpty Dumpty, and the forest). Then the White Knight takes the Red Knight in the battle over Alice. Alice is crowned when she reaches the eighth square, and meets the two other queens. Alice castles when she attends the feast and then wins when she takes the Red Queen and checkmates the King.

1.7 THEMES IN LEWIS CARROLL'S *THROUGH THE LOOKING GLASS*

1.7.1 Chess as Metaphor for Fate

Alice's journey through Looking-Glass World is guided by a set of rigidly constructed rules that guide her along her path to a preordained conclusion. Within the framework of the chess game, Alice has little control over the trajectory of her life, and outside forces influence her choices and actions. Just as Alice exerts little control of her movement toward becoming a queen, she has no power over her inevitable maturation and acceptance of womanhood. At the beginning of the game, Alice acts as a pawn with limited perspective of the world around her. She has limited power to influence outcomes and does not fully understand the rules of the game, so an unseen hand guides her along her journey, constructing different situations and encounters that push her along toward her goal. Though she wants to become a queen, she must follow the predetermined rules of the chess game, and she frequently discovers that every step she takes toward her goal occurs because of outside forces acting upon her, such as the mysterious train ride and her rescue by the White Knight. By using the chess game as the guiding principle of the narrative, Carroll suggest that a larger force guides individuals through life and that all events are preordained. In this deterministic concept of life, free will is an illusion and individual choices are bound by rigidly determined rules and guided by an overarching, unseen force.

1.7.2 Language as a Means to Order the World

In *Through the Looking-Glass,* language has the capacity to anticipate and even cause events to happen. Alice recites nursery rhymes on several occasions, which causes Tweedledum and Tweedledee, Humpty Dumpty, and the Lion and the Unicorn to perform the actions that she describes in her rhymes. Rather than recording and describing events that have already happened, words give rise to actions simply by being spoken. Tweedledum and Tweedledee's quarrel begins only after Alice recites the rhyme about the broken rattle. Similarly, Humpty Dumpty's fall does not happen until Alice describes the events in the classic nursery rhyme. Language covers actions in Looking-Glass World, rather than simply describing them. The flowers reinforce this principle by explaining that a tree can scare enemies away with its "bark." In our language, there is no relationship between the bark of a dog and the bark of a tree, but in Looking-Glass World, this linguistic similarity results in a functional common ground. Trees that have bark are thus able to "bark" just as fiercely as dogs.

1.7.3 The Loneliness of Growing Up

Throughout her adventures, Alice feels an inescapable sense of loneliness from which she can find no relief. Before she enters Looking-Glass World, her only companions are her cats, to whom she attributes human qualities to keep her company. Once she enters Looking-Glass World, she seeks compassion and understanding from the individuals that she meets, but she is frequently disappointed. The flowers and Humpty Dumpty treat her rudely, the Red Queen is brusque, and the Fawn flees from her once it realizes that she is a human. She receives little compassion from others and often becomes sad. The one character who shows her compassion is the White Knight, who must leave her when she reaches the eighth square and must take on her role of Queen. Alice's dreams deal with the anxieties of growing up and becoming a young woman. Since Alice believes that loneliness is an inherent part of growing up, even in her dreams she must face the transition into womanhood alone.

1.7.4 Alienation

Alice is in fact alone through much of the story, though not as much literally as figuratively. She is the only one of her kind in the Looking-Glass world, so even though she is surrounded by creatures pretty much at all times, she has trouble relating to their foreign ways. She is also isolated from the rest of her family due to her imagination; there is a reference to the frustration she causes when she plays pretend. At many points in the story, the reader has the sense that Alice has no place to go to feel at home; she expresses her loneliness while in the Looking-Glass world, but she immediately rebounds and worries about ultimately having to end the game and return to her house.

1.7.5 Adulthood

Carroll's attitudes toward adulthood are not entirely clear in the book, though the book itself can be seen as a motif for the progression from childhood to adulthood, as represented by Alice's journey as a pawn to queenhood. She undergoes many experiences that can be seen as crucial for development, such as the discovery of identity that is demanded by the situation in the woods of forgetfulness. Many of the poems recited focus on the theme of passing youth. However, the incompetence and immaturity of those that may be considered adult characters in the book calls the idea of a progression into question. Alice often proves to be smarter, more thoughtful and more resourceful than the "adults" she encounters in the looking glass.

1.7.6 Moral Choice and Social Etiquette

There are many cases in *Through the Looking Glass* in which the question of control and intentionality come into play. Looming over the entire novel is the question of whether Alice's adventures were really just a figment of the Red King's dream. Additionally, it is unclear whether Alice has any choice about moving from the second to the eighth square, and there are a number of instances during which she seems to question her goal.

Carroll, as a Victorian era author, is concerned about the methodical, logical examination of behaviour. Within almost every conversation Alice has with the characters in the Looking-Glass world is at least one critique of their social norms. But these are not serious critiques, for it has been established by the author that everyone in this world lives backwards, and as Alice has observed, many aspects of living backwards seem impossible. Inevitably, though, this often nonsensical evaluation of rules might indeed be a comment on the burdensome obligations of adulthood and the moral/social responsibilities that accompany it.

1.8 MOTIFS IN LEWIS CARROLL'S *THROUGH THE LOOKING GLASS*

1.8.1 Inverse Reflections

Many of the basic assumptions that Alice makes about her

environment are reversed in Looking-Glass World. Outcomes precede events, cakes are passed out before being cut, destinations are reached by walking in the opposite direction, and characters remember the future and think best while standing on their heads. These strange phenomena challenge the way Alice thinks and in some cases expose the arbitrary nature of her understanding of her own world. Many of Alice's experiences exist as meaningless parodies of aspects of her own familiar world back home. Alice becomes aware of a new, inverted perspective on life as she travels forward and backward through Looking-Glass World.

1.8.2 Dream

Alice falls asleep at the beginning of *Through the Looking-Glass,* just as she did at the outset of *Alice's Adventures in Wonderland,* so that the resulting fantastical adventures occur in her dreams. The story follows Alice through the various episodes of Looking-Glass World so that we experience her adventures through her impressions of Looking-Glass House, the chess game, and her quest to become a queen. The characters and scenes that she encounters exist as a combination of her memories and impressions of the waking world and the random, illogical inventions of her dreaming mind. Carroll emphasizes the dream motif by basing some of the denizens of Looking-Glass World on individuals from the life of his real-life muse, Alice Liddell. For example, the Red Queen is based on Alice's governess Miss Prickett, while the White Knight is closely based upon Lewis Carroll himself.

1.8.3 Chess

The chess game that Alice participates in becomes the organizing mechanism for her adventure in Looking-Glass World. Alice's journey closely follows the rules of a traditional game of chess. The perspectives and movements of the individual characters correspond to the movements of their respective chess pieces. The Red and White Queens have an unlimited view of the board, since queens can move in any direction and as many spaces as they want in a single turn. The Red and White Kings can only move one space at a time in any direction, so while they have the same perspective as the queens, they have limited mobility. This limitation explains why the White King cannot follow the White Queen as she runs away from the other chessmen, since she moves "too fast." As a pawn, Alice can only move forward once space at a time, with the exception of her first move, in which she can move two spaces. Like a pawn, Alice can only "see" one square ahead of her. When she reaches the final square and becomes a queen, she can "see" the whole board because now she has the full mobility of the queen chess piece. Alice's move to take the Red Queen results in a checkmate of the Red King, ending the chess game and causing Alice to wake up.

1.8.4 Train Imagery

Trains and train imagery appear frequently to underscore the feeling of unstoppable forward motion that governs Alice's journey toward womanhood. The Red King's somnolent snoring resembles a train engine, while the White Queen screams like a train whistle before she pricks her finger. Alice skips forward several spaces when she finds herself unexpectedly on a train, shooting through the forest toward her destination and mimicking Alice's forward movement as a pawn in the chess game. The train imagery suggests the irreversible and unstoppable movement toward adulthood that Alice becomes subject to in her journey through Looking-Glass World.

1.9 SYMBOLS IN LEWIS CARROLL'S *THROUGH THE LOOKING GLASS*

1.9.1 The Rushes

The rushes that Alice pulls from the water in Chapter 5 represent dreams. Rushes are plans that grow in riverbeds and poke through the surface of the water. The rapid fading of the rushes' sweet scene after being picked corresponds to the fleetingness of the memory of a dream after a person wakes up.

1.9.2 The Sleeping Red King

Tweedledum and Tweedledee tell Alice that she is only a creation of the Red King's dream, which implies that Looking-Glass World is not a construction of Alice's dream. The Red King becomes a divine figure who dreams up all of Alice's adventures, fostering the idea that she does not actually have any identity or agency beyond what she is allowed in the context of the dream. The idea that we are all just aspects of the dream of a divine power comes from Bishop Berkeley, a philosopher who wrote during Carroll's lifetime and who believed that man and the universe exist as part of God's imagination.

1.10 CRITIQUE ON *THROUGH THE LOOKING-GLASS*

1.10.1 The Critical Reception of *Through the Looking-Glass*

Carroll's *Through the Looking-Glass* is often seen by scholars as a less successful novel than its more celebrated companion piece, *Alice's Adventures in Wonderland* (1865). Critics have interpreted Looking-Glass as the more controlled and less spontaneous of the two works, more the product of Dodgson the mathematical logician and Oxford lecturer than Carroll the story-teller. Thus, although it has been assigned a higher place than either of the critically disparaged Sylvie and Bruno books (1889 and 1893), it has been unfavourably compared with its companion novel since its publication, as Elizabeth A. Cripps notes in her article "Alice and the Reviewers":

There was general agreement, among those who considered the question, that *Through the Looking-Glass* was not so good as its predecessor. The reasons given for this varied. It was perhaps too contrived — "Mr. Carroll makes rather too much use here of the Red and White pieces in the game of chess" — or not so inventive. Possibly the expectations raised by Alice's Adventures were so high that no sequel could hope to meet them adequately. (40)

In "Escape Through the Looking-Glass" (1945), Florence Becker Lennon calls the novel a "masterpiece — only a shade less than Wonderland" (Lennon 66), but then adds that "it already exudes the ripe flavour of approaching decay and disintegration into the cruel (on paper) and unusual Mr. Dodgson and the sentimental-religious Louisa Caroline, as one of the Oxford parodists signed 'The Vulture and the Husbandman'" (66). Harold Bloom takes a similar position in his introduction to Lewis Carroll

(1987): "The movement from 'You're nothing but a pack of cards!' to 'I can't stand this any longer!' is a fair representation of the relative aesthetic decline the reader experiences as she goes from *Alice's Adventures in Wonderland* to *Through the Looking-Glass*. Had the first book never existed, our regard for the second would be unique and immense, which is only another way of admiring how the first Alice narrative is able to avoid any human affect as mundane as bitterness" (5-6). However, the sardonic tone that runs throughout Looking-Glass is central to its thematic complexity, and the notion that it lacks the spontaneity or freshness of its predecessor should not in itself be a source of criticism.

Fortunately, Carroll's *Through the Looking-Glass* has also been recognized for its surprising radicalism despite being very much a literary product of its time. Although it is by no means considered a feminist work in the way that other Victorian novels have been re-appraised by contemporary critics, *Through the Looking-Glass* is nevertheless recognized for its keen understanding of Alice's predicament, most notably in her discovery that "being a Queen... offers neither the security of attachment nor the sovereignty of freedom to which she refers in her opening words to the White Knight: 'I don't want to be anybody's prisoner. I want to be a Queen'" (Rackin 28). As Susan A. Walsh argues in "Darling Mothers, Devilish Queens: The Divided Woman in Victorian Fantasy" (1987), Carroll shows how Alice is ultimately a prisoner of her inability to change the frustrating game in which she finds herself because her only models of behaviour are the helpless but amiable White Queen and the responsible but mean-tempered Red Queen:

> By the end of both Wonderland books a beleaguered Alice has had enough and summarily shatters the dream worlds by withdrawing belief in the system of relationships they espouse... Even though she recognizes the artificial quality of this maddening disorder, that these games... are constructs of culture and not of nature, Alice cannot exert control from the outside because the "inside" dictates the terms of what she must control. As a world-spinner she may exercise the creator's prerogative to destroy her fictions but not, ultimately, to invest them with forms other than those provided by nineteenth-century convention. (34)

The subversive irony of Carroll's novel, of course, is that while it appears to have the happily-ever-after ending of a traditional children's story, Alice's promotion to a Queen only comes to represent the crowning moment of her powerlessness. The bitterness that is engendered throughout Alice's frustrating quest and which culminates during the coronation feast gives the novel its insurgent tone. Indeed, Harold Bloom's earlier criticism of the novel's bitterness is qualified by his admission that this is perhaps what gives the novel its modern appeal: "Bitterness keeps breaking in as we read *Through the Looking-Glass,* which may explain how weirdly and perpetually contemporary this second and somewhat lesser work now seems." (6).

Carroll's novel shows its modernism (and to a certain extent, its postmodernism) in a number of other ways: if the author's mathematical forays into the realm of symbolic logic make his work a natural precursor to Bertrand Russell's and Alfred North Whitehead's *Principia Mathematica* (1910-1913), and his interest in the possibilities of language look forward to Joyce, then his fascination with sign systems in the Alice books makes him a forerunner to contemporary approaches to the field of semiotics:

> Carroll's concerns extend beyond the explication of communication functions to probe the provocative semiotic question argued by Humpty Dumpty: "who is to be master?" we over the signs we manipulate, or the signs over us through the subtle pressures exerted by convention and conditioning? In Carroll's universe, the "masters" of signification are poets, logicians, and madmen. Through his use of imagery and parable to illustrate his humorous exposé of the problems of semiosis, Carroll reveals a profound concern with underlying epistemological issues which anticipate neo-Kantian and Saussurian approaches to that branch of science known as "semiotic." (Mandelker 102)

Finally, Carroll's use of nested structures in making Alice a pawn within a game within a pair of conflicting dreams looks forward to twentieth-century writers like Jorge Luis Borges and Julio Cortazar, who manipulate traditional linear narrative structures and invest them with topological complexity.

All of these things should be carefully considered before unfairly dismissing Looking-Glass as a curious, but essentially derivative, follow-up to Alice in Wonderland.

Unit II
Crime Thiller

Thriller is a genre of fiction, having numerous, often overlapping subgenres. Thrillers are characterized and defined by the moods they elicit, giving viewers heightened feelings of suspense, excitement, surprise, anticipation and anxiety. Successful examples of thrillers are the films of Alfred Hitchcock.

Thrillers generally keep the audience on the "edge of their seats" as the plot builds towards a climax. The cover-up of important information is a common element. Literary devices such as red herrings, plot twists, and cliffhangers are used extensively. A thriller is usually a villain-driven plot, whereby they present obstacles that the protagonist must overcome.

Thrillers are characterized by suspense—a feeling of pleasurable fascination and excitement over what is to come next, mixed in with apprehension, anticipation, and sometimes even, fear. These feelings develop throughout a narrative from unpredictable events that make the reader or viewer think about the consequences of certain characters' actions. The suspenseful feelings build towards a climax that is sure to be memorable.

With suspense and crime, with conspiracies and revenge, the thriller genre has been keeping audiences on their toes with tension and excitement for centuries. When it comes to thrillers, many think of Alfred Hitchcock and his movies, like Psycho (1960) and Frenzy (1972), that contain storylines of embezzlement, murder, wrong accusations, and more. However, the thriller genre began much before these movies ever hit the big screen. Let's take a look at a brief history of the thriller genre.

2.1 DISCOVERING THRILLERS IN ANCIENT EPIC POEMS

Thought to be one of the earliest prototypes of the thriller genre, Homer's *Odyssey* uses similar techniques as today's modern thrillers. The hero of this epic poem, Odysseus, voyages home to be with his wife, Penelope, through extraordinary hardships and trials. He contends with Cyclops, a one-eyed giant, and the Sirens, who sing sailors to their death, all while battling the sea on his journey home from the Trojan War. These encounters contain anticipatory suspense and leave the reader wondering if Odysseus will ever make it home, and if so, how he will do it.

2.2 FAIRY TALES WITH THRILLER-LIKE TENDENCIES

A common convention within the thriller genre is a psycho-stalker storyline. Little Red Riding Hood is an early example of the psycho-stalker theme. This European fairy tale can be traced back to the 10th century and tells the story of a little girl who walks through the woods to bring food to her sick grandmother. She runs into a wolf, the "Big Bad Wolf " in some versions, and tells him where she is going. Long fairy tale short, he runs ahead, swallows her grandmother, and waits for the girl to come, disguised as her grandma, all while the reader wonders if the little girl will survive such an evil nemesis.

In the 19th century, two separate German versions of this fairy tale were retold to the Brothers Grimm, who then turned it into the story commonly read today with a sequel. The story titled Rotkäppchen was included in the first edition of their collection Children's and Household Tales.

2.3 THE EMERGENCE OF THE REVENGE THRILLER

Written by Alexandre Dumas in 1844, *The Count of Monte Cristo* is a daring and adventurous revenge thriller about a man named Edmond Dantès who is betrayed by his friends and is wrongfully imprisoned. There, he meets on old man who teaches him everything and reveals to him the location of a great treasure. Edmond acquires this fortune and seeks revenge on those who destroyed his life and imprisoned him. This literary classic brings readers on a perilous and suspenseful adventure following

Edmond's quest for vengeance, satisfaction, and ultimately, peace.

2.4 INTO THE 20TH CENTURY WITH MODERN DAY THRILLERS

With the 20th century came modern day thrillers. *The Riddle of the Sands: A Record of Secret Service* (1903) by Robert Erskine Childers is an early example of spy fiction and an espionage novel.

The Bourne Identity (1980) by Robert Ludlum tells the story of Jason Bourne, a man who suffers from retrograde amnesia and must seek to discover his true identity. The book starts with a scene of Bourne floating unconscious with gunshot wounds in the Mediterranean Sea—it doesn't get much more "thriller-esque" than that. It is quite the dilemma for readers and viewers alike to figure out.

In recent years, we have seen titles from Vince Flynn, well known for writing political thriller novels, and Dan Brown, an American author of thriller fiction who wrote the 2003 bestselling novel The Da Vinci Code.

Thrillers fit into many different subgenres and categories, and here, we've only scratched the surface. The genre has developed over the years in many different places and stories. Overall, James Patterson said it best when he said in his 2016 book, Thriller: Stories to Keep You Up All Night:

"Thrillers provide such a rich literary feast...this openness to expansion is one of genre's most enduring characteristics. But what gives the variety of thrillers a common ground is the intensity of emotions they create, particularly those of apprehension and exhilaration, of excitement and breathlessness, all designed to generate that all-important thrill. By definition, if a thriller doesn't thrill, it's not doing its job."

2.5 CRIME THRILLER (FICTION)

Crime thrillers, popularly known as Detective Fiction is one of the many branches of popular literature and is arguably one of the most widely read genres. Often denigrated as pulp-fiction, the genre has always been treated as unsuitable for serious literary scholarship. A look back through the pages of world history will speak for the immense popularity that detective fiction has received since its early years of inception. Amidst the continual politics of the literary canon that excludes the genre from literary recognition; detective fiction has come a long way from its nascent days to its modern versions recreating itself with changing times and by drawing inspiration from contemporary life. Though writers in all ages have composed narratives based on crime and detection, this very style of writing evolved as a genre primarily in the nineteenth century. The archetypal story involves a crime, followed by its investigation wherein the detective disentangles the mystery with the aid of his or her extraordinary intelligence, superior reasoning faculty, shrewd observation and an inquisitive mind.

Most detective fiction narratives are seen to focus on a crime of some particular nature, but some stories do not deal with any conventional crime. In many stories the narrative revolves round a mystery often structured as an intricate puzzle, where the narrative is oriented towards solving this central puzzle. This puzzle element require the readers to do more than just a passive reading of the stories and involve their own reasoning faculties to understand the intricacies of the mystery as an ongoing puzzle; that almost appears like a maze. The plot along with various other aspects like the investigator, the mystery involved along with the investigation which follows, are yoked together to generate an exciting puzzle that even challenges the readers to engage their reasoning faculties to solve the mystery along with the investigator.

Despite the genre's continual upsurge on the popularity charts, it has been degraded as less literary and excessively formulaic. It is believed that the popularity which the genre enjoys is due to the thrill and entertainment that the genre provides. However, such criticisms have been outlasted by the genre's widespread popularity that has left critics intrigued by such questions like, what do these formulaic fictions offer that makes them a sustainable as well as compelling addiction for readers. But many critics believe that this addiction spurs the readers away from serious literature. In 1945, American critic Edmund Wilson in his article, 'Who Cares Who Killed Roger Ackryod" degraded the genre and suggested that any indulgence in such stories is wastage of time. This work came as a response to the reviews he received for another article, titled "Why Do People Read Decetative Storis" (1944). In his over simplified review of the genre he finds that most stories are mere duplication of the traditional Holmes model and hopes to read no other book by Agatha Christie as he finds her writing excessively mawkish. This article generated a lot of protest among the loyalist of the genre which included both readers as well as writers. In this response he wrote, "Who Cares Who Killed Roger Ackryod". The following extract from the essay quoted from William W. Stowe's essay "Popular Function as Liberal Art" reveals his attitude towards the genre. He says:

Friends, we represent a minority, but Literature is on our side. With so many fine books to be read, so much to be studied and known, there is no need to bore ourselves with this rubbish. (Stowe 1986: 646)

The archetypal formula based detective fiction still flourishes and continues to appeal to readers. People love reading detective fiction not simply because it provides good entertainment. Detective fiction narratives work on the archetypal notion of the 'right' being triumphant over the "the wrong', which is something that we subscribe to as part of our moral-ethical order.

A close study will reveal that such stories primarily revolve around a set of binaries, highlighting the age old conflict between good and evil. With the victory of the light over darkness it restores notion of righteousness which is something we always conform to. While reading such stories this always mind and thus sustains our interest.

But, still the genre is chiefly viewed as a source of recreation-an activity of leisure. The skepticism associated with the rise of the detective fiction is not only voiced in the title of Edmund Wilson's 1994 essay, "Why Do People Read Detective Stories" but time and again the genre has faced similar questions. In fact, the emergence of the genre and its popularity is primarily seen to be in response to certain social and ideological forces, along with the advent of industrialization, urbanization and creation of the law enforcement figure in England and the United States.

In recent years, our approach towards detective fiction has undergone considerable change. Following years of negligence, the genre now calls for a fresh approach to examine the whole politics of inclusion and exclusion initiated by the proponents of the literary canon. In this regard one must analyze the genre to study the very notions of being non-serious and therefore popular. New age studies have galvanized the genre into a domain of academic respectability by embarking on new studies which explores the complexity of the genre and validates its significance by arguing that the genre deserves serious reading and interpretation. Exploring the various aspects of the genre, theorists of detective fiction have ushered a new wave in the history of the genre, to challenge the harsh criticisms often imposed upon the genre of being limited in scope with its dose of thrill and entertainment. But prior to any serious discussion of the genre, it is fundamental to understand the very idea of what it takes to be a classic detective and how the very notions of crime and detection made their way to literature.

Detective fiction as a genre evolved mainly in the nineteenth century. Although in its nascent years it bloomed in periodicals and full-length novels came much later in the nineteenth century. Interestingly there was no detective, nor was there any idea of detection in the initial years. Prior to the development of printing technology in Europe, accounts of crime saw the light of the day in the form of pamphlets which were circulated with elaborate illustrations and sensational titles. Such pamphlets which started appearing from sixteenth century onwards dealt with various crimes ranging from murder to thefts.

In his book *Crime Fiction since 1800* (2010), Stephen Knight records that Blood and Knavery is an anthology which provides access to such pamphlets including Sundry strange and inhumane Murthers, lately committed (1591). Those which gave detailed descriptions of pick pocketing, gambling etc were known as 'cony catching pamphlet' (Knight 2010: 3), while some others provided detailed accounts of the execution of the criminals. These illustrated narratives were aimed at drawing the attention of the readers in order to disseminate the power of the state and warn its subjects against any acts of crime. Gradually these early crime narratives started appearing in various formats.

Broadside was one such early form of publication which consisted of a single sheet of paper on one side. Usually made of rough paper, these verse or prose narratives were simple narration of the life of the criminal and were light on the pockets of both printers as well as buyers. Another format known as the Accounts provided insights into the lives of the convicted prisoners of London's Newgate Prison. Being published by the Chaplains or the Ordinaries, the religious renderings of such accounts is evident.

They dealt with criminals narrating their lives of crime, their eventual confession and finally their execution. In addition, the stories also ensured authoritative and monetary benefits for the Chaplains. These accounts were expensive than the Broadsides, making it affordable for a particular section of the society. Later in the eighteenth century publishers brought expensive anthologies of such accounts often in the form of a book which came to be known as Newgate Calendars. These accounts were also thought to be based on fact but owing to a chain of constant republishing they ended up as more fiction than fact. The Malefactor's Register on the Newgate and Tyburn Calender (1779), New and Complete Calendar (1795), The New Newgate Calendar (1826) are such editions that were reissued several times. Although they appeared at various times yet these accounts like the Broadside, the Ordinaries Account, the Newgate Calenders mainly emphasized on the criminal's life focusing on his acts of crime and his execution. However, some of the later editions of the Calendars which came in the nineteenth century show the criminals defying the motif of confession, prevalent in the previous versions.

These early narratives of crime laid the foundation stone for the genre and paved the way for what came to be known as Newgate novels.

Detective fiction is one of the most popular and widely read genres of literature and it has undergone a considerable change from its early formats. Owing to the popularity of the genre many detective stories have been adapted to the audio-visual medium catering audiences of both motion pictures as well as cartoon series. Detective fiction as a genre has always been flexible and with changing times it has developed while addressing various contemporary issues. The arrival of psycho-thrillers with serial killers draws our attention to modern concerns. The genre also provides scope to explore issues of gender inequality and eventually there arrived lesbian detective fiction or gay crime fiction. Some stories also focused on racial issues. Pauline Hopkin's *Hagar's Daughter* (1901-02) is regarded as the earliest example of black crime fiction. Though for a major period the genre was thought to be a western phenomenon, but owing to widespread popularity the genre slowly spread its wings to other countries where writers produced their own versions of crime narratives. In many former British colonies the genre found a suitable place to mutate. Writers used the genre as a platform to address diverse but significant issues concerning particular cultures of various nations. Australia has its own tradition of crime narratives which explores Australian issues like the tension between the white colonisers and the indigenous Aborigines. Slowly writers in Russia, Spain, France, Japan, China, South Africa, India *et al.*, have come up with their style of detective stories that focuses on the notions of that particular nation and its culture.

India has always fascinated British authors and writers like Wilkie Collins and Arthur Conan Doyle have made references to the subcontinent in their works *The Moonstone* (1869) and *The Sign of Four* (1890). Later in twentieth century British authors H.R.F. Keating and Leslie Forbes based their crime stories in Bombay (present day Mumbai) and Keatind's detective Inspector Ghote turned out to be so popular that he produced around twenty novels featuring him. However, in India the emergence of the genre is marked by the early works of translation from the English originals to other Indian languages.

Satyajit Ray is a big name in the domain of Bengali detective fiction. The first story featuring Feluda and Tapesh was published in *Sandesh,* a children's magazine started by his grandfather Upendra Kishore Ray Choudhury in 1913. Originally written in Bengali, Feluda stories met with huge success after their launch in 1965 and were later translated into other languages.

Although the genre has become popular, yet it is regarded as non-serious and therefore less literary by the critics of 'high' literature. But detective stories deserve a serious approach since such stories including Feluda stories can be analyzed on the basis of certain premises that help to explore the complexities of the genre.

2.6 AGATHA CHRISTIE, THE MURDER OF ROGER ACKROYD

2.6.1 Author

Agatha Christie is one of the best-known writers of the Golden Age of Detective Fiction, an era in which the popularity of the detective fiction genre blossomed. Agatha Christie was born Agatha Mary Clarissa Miller in Devon, England in 1890. Her father was an American stockbroker. Agatha was the youngest of three children. After working as a nurse during World War I, she married Archie Christie, an aviator in the Royal Flying Corps.

Christie's debut novel, *The Mysterious Affair at Styles,* introduced one of her most famous characters, the detective Hercule Poirot. She began writing the novel during World War I, partly in response to a bet from her sister Madge that she couldn't write a good detective story, and partly to relieve the monotony of her job at a hospital dispensary. The first three publishers she brought the novel to rejected it, and it was almost a decade until she found a publisher in John Lane of The Bodley Head.

While married to Archie Christie, she published six other novels and numerous short stories. Her marriage, however, was turbulent, and she and her husband divorced after she discovered he was having an affair. Soon after her discovery of the affair, Christie disappeared, causing a national uproar. She was found soon after and blamed the disappearance on memory loss.

In 1930, Christie married Max Mallowan, an archaeologist. Her travels to the Middle East with her new husband inspired the settings for several of her most famous novels including *Murder on the Orient Express,* which was written during an extended stay at a hotel in Istanbul, Turkey. During World War II, Christie again worked as a pharmacist and nurse. Her knowledge of medicine influenced her mysterious characters, many of whom died from lethal injections.

Christie received numerous awards and critical honours for her work. She was honoured as the Commander of the Order of the British Empire in 1956 and Dame Commander of the Order of the British Empire in 1971. Her husband was knighted for his work as well. Her work generally received warm critical praise, though some, including the journalist Christopher Hitchens, criticized Christie for her conservative political and social views.

Christie remains the bestselling author in the world. Her 80 books and numerous stories have sold over a billion copies in English and another billion in foreign translation. Her play, *The Mousetrap,* is the longest running play in history with over 23,000 shows. Only the *Bible* has sold more copies than Christie's books. She is also the author of several romance novels, written under the pseudonym Mary Westmacott, and one autobiography chronicling her travels with her husband.

Recent scientific study of her notes and writings has suggested that, towards the end of her life, Christie began suffering from Alzheimer's disease. She died from natural causes in 1976 and is buried in the churchyard of St. Mary's, Cholsey. During World War II, Christie wrote two novels, *Curtain* and *Sleeping Murder,* both of which she locked away and intended to be published after her death. They were to be the closing chapters for her two greatest characters, Hercule Poirot and Mrs. Marple. Poirot is the only fictional character to have received an obituary in the *New York Times*.

Encompassing the 1920s and 1930s, the Golden Age was dominated by British female writers including Agatha Christie, Dorothy L. Sayers, and Margery Allingham, as well as Scottish writer Josephine Tey and New Zealander Ngaio Marsh. Although detective fiction enjoyed heightened popularity in the early 20th century, the roots of the genre reach into the 19th century. The focus on a particular detective, whose investigation provides the forward motion of the story, can be seen in several 19th-century works. These include, Edgar Allan Poe's *"The Murders in the Rue Morgue"* (1841) and *"The Purloined Letter"* (1844), short stories that feature detective Auguste Dupin; Arthur Conan Doyle's famous Sherlock Holmes stories (1880s–1920s); Charles Dickens's *Bleak House* (1853), featuring detective Inspector Bucket; and Wilkie Collins's *The Moonstone* (1868), featuring Sergeant Cuff and considered by many to be the first mystery novel.

These early examples of detective fiction focused on detectives who, often with the help of a sidekick, assembled clues into solutions to complex crimes, revealing the full solution at the end of the story.

Golden Age detective fiction used many elements of these early detective stories, developing them into a conventional formula typically including the following characteristics:

- a believable plot and characters grounded in the real world, or at least a realistic world
- a crime that seems unsolvable by everyday police, or is "impossible" (for example, a door locked from the inside)
- a criminal presented to readers early in the narrative, among other ordinary characters
- events and suspicious behaviour that provide misdirection

- use of stereotypical characters to fill out the cast
- unsympathetic murder victims
- a brilliant detective (amateur or professional) whose powers of deduction far exceed those of ordinary detectives
- a solution that does not introduce new clues but often focuses on insignificant details the reader easily passes over
- a presentation of the case that concludes the narrative in a satisfying way, leaving no clue unexplained.

2.6.2 *The Murder of Roger Ackroyd*

The Murder of Roger Ackroyd adheres to many of the conventions of Golden Age detective fiction. The crime occurs toward the beginning of the novel, and the first police officers on the scene are clearly inept. Although Roger Ackroyd is well liked in the village, members of his family agree he is controlling. The cast of characters is populated in part by eavesdropping butlers, gossiping spinsters, and sniffling maids. Although crucial clues to the solution of the crime are mentioned as the story unfolds, they do not attract readers' attention, while secret relationships and schemes unrelated to the murder provide misdirection. Brilliant detective Hercule Poirot is able to notice these seemingly unimportant details, fit them together like the pieces of a puzzle, and present the solved case to characters and readers at the end of the story.

However, *The Murder of Roger Ackroyd* departs from the conventional ending of a Golden Age detective story, which typically ends when the detective lays out the solution. In this novel Poirot presents an incomplete solution to the assembled characters, refusing to name the criminal at all. Only after all the characters exit the scene do readers learn the true solution—the narrator, who has been describing events in a seemingly objective and admiring Watson-ish way, is actually the murderer. The novel readers have been reading is not the objective account at all, but a manuscript carefully curated to pass over the narrator's true involvement in the crime. Some readers have felt this "twist" ending was a bit devious, as a reliable narrator was a convention they had come to expect and using an unreliable narrator was not "fair play." Fellow detective novel author, Dorothy L. Sayers, defended Christie by saying, "It is the reader's job to suspect everybody."

2.6.3 Characters

Dr. James Sheppard

The novel's narrator is a physician in the town of King's Abbott. He serves as a companion-chronicler to Hercule Poirot, the brilliant detective who will eventually crack the very complicated case. Although Sheppard appears to be a genial, straightforward character, his complicity in the mystery will prove one of the great plot-twists of all time. Ultimately, Dr. Sheppard is revealed to be a shrewd, duplicitous, detached villain.

Caroline Sheppard

Dr. Sheppard's older spinster sister is a voracious gossip who uses a network of servants as informants to gather all sorts of information on anyone who piques her interest. She is unsatisfied unless she knows about all the goings-on in the town, and usually interjects her opinions on things, especially when unprovoked. Agatha Christie later admitted that Caroline served as a model for her famous Miss Marple character, the spinster detective who pokes her nose in everyone else's business.

Hercule Poirot

Perhaps Agatha Christie's most famous character, Poirot appears in 33 novels and over 60 short stories. A retired Belgian detective, Poirot is small in stature but full of self-importance. He is a brilliant detective, relying on his own logic and critical thinking skills (rather than an obsession over physical facts and clues) in order to determine the truth of the crime. He treats everyone as a suspect, and takes no statement or allegation for granted. Instead, he painstakingly verifies all testimonies while privately forming his own hypotheses, only revealing the truth when he is sure of his suspicions.

Mrs. Ferrars

Although she never appears as a living character in the novel, Mrs. Ferrars nonetheless plays an important role in the plot. A nervous woman who, according to Caroline, couldn't stand her alcoholic husband, she poisoned him in order to escape from his abusiveness. However, the financial strain of being blackmailed for this crime, as well as the guilt over the crime itself, led her to kill herself, but not before asking her close companion Roger Ackroyd to avenge her against the blackmailer.

Roger Ackroyd

A genial widower, Ackroyd is the central figure in King's Abbott. A wealthy businessman, Ackroyd's influence as well as the intrigue surrounding his stepson, family, and himself, make him a constant subject of gossip and speculation. Sheppard describes Ackroyd as being a proper man, who believed heavily in society's rules for rightness as well as its class divisions. He is murdered at the beginning of the novel, providing the mystery that Poirot will so brilliantly solve.

Ralph Paton

Ackroyd's stepson, Paton is handsome and charming, but constantly getting into trouble with debts and financial obligations. His disappearance, as well as several major clues (including how well he stood to benefit from Ackroyd's death), make him the major suspect in the crime. He is described as having a "weak" character, which leads him to fall constantly into debt, and look for easy ways to discharge it (such as agreeing to marry Flora when he is already committed).

Mrs. Cecil Ackroyd

Ackroyd's sister-in-law, she and her daughter Flora came to live at Fernly Park after her husband (Ackroyd's brother) died. Shallow and garrulous, Mrs. Ackroyd is prone to episodes of self-involved drama, and admits to falling into debt in an effort to sustain her upper class lifestyle. She complains of the difficulty of relying financially on her miserly brother-in-law.

Flora Ackroyd

Mrs. Ackroyd's daughter, Flora is young, fair, and beautiful. Like her mother, she is burdened by the strain of being financially dependent on her uncle, and longs for freedom from this frustrating reliance. Although she agrees to be engaged to her step-cousin Ralph Paton, she does so because she sees the opportunity for more independence and a new life, not out of love. She claims to have a weak character (particularly with regards to money) just like Ralph, and she claims that an understanding of this mutual weakness brought them together.

Geoffrey Raymond

Ackroyd's young, charming secretary, Geoffrey Raymond is buoyant and debonair, maintaining a relaxed attitude throughout the investigation. Although Ackroyd's death upset him, he is nonetheless laid back and confident throughout the novel. He admits to being in a bit of debt, which the money he got from Ackroyd's will takes care of, but insists that he has an alibi for the time of the murder, and thus should not be considered a suspect.

Major Blunt

A big game hunter and old friend of Ackroyd, Blunt is taciturn and, when he does speak, direct. Blunt's secret love for Flora Ackroyd seems out of character with his moderate, reserved personality, but his ultimate decision to express this love allows him to win her over in the end.

Miss Russell

Ackroyd's housekeeper, Miss Russell is efficient and no-nonsense, with a proficiency that renders her intimidating to many of the characters she encounters, even those in a higher social class than she. Although she is reserved to the point of inaccessibility, she ultimately demonstrates emotion when confronted after her son, Charles Kent, faces suspicion for Ackroyd's murder. Miss Russell distanced herself from her son because she gave birth to him out of wedlock – although she provided for him financially, she refused to acknowledge him publicly for fear of what it would do to her reputation. Her respectability is of the utmost importance to her.

John Parker

Ackroyd's butler, Parker, is a professional and competent servant. Poirot suspects there is something corrupt about him, and eventually discovers that Parker blackmailed his former employer, and was snooping around for the means to blackmail Ackroyd, as well. Although Parker is greedy, Poirot nevertheless deems him too cowardly to be Ackroyd's murderer.

Ursula Bourne

Born a "lady" but forced to make her own living when her parents could not provide for her, Ursula decided to become a parlormaid. Although it represented a step-down in class, it allowed her to support herself, and she knew she was a competent maid. After falling in love with Ralph Paton and secretly marrying him, Ursula was furious when he announced his engagement to Flora and is distraught when he disappears after his uncle's murder.

Charles Kent

Miss Ackroyd's disowned son, Kent shows signs of having been a strong, capable, smart man, but an addiction to alcohol and heroin has caused him to become a seedy, paranoid criminal. Although Miss Russell wants to believe he can recover from his addiction, he does not show any signs of being motivated to cure himself. He does not, however, reveal his mother's identity when questioned by the police, helping to preserve her reputation in town.

Inspector Raglan

The main inspector into Ackroyd's murder, Raglan immediately identifies Ralph as a potential suspect. Raglan's reticence to welcome Poirot onto the investigating team is softened only by Poirot's adept flattery. He is proud of his investigative method, although he lacks the critical thinking skills and brilliance that allow Poirot to analyze the many clues the crime provides.

Inspector Davis

The local police officer, Davis is the first on the scene when Ackroyd is found murdered. He is self-important and blundering, and obsessed with physical clues that will ultimately not prove to be useful to solving the murder. His initial incompetence only serves to demonstrate the brilliance of Poirot.

Colonel Melrose

A local, Colonel Melrose is initially reluctant to believe in Ralph's guilt. He is fond of Ralph and unwilling to consider the possibility that Ralph could be the murderer. However, as the evidence against Ralph mounts, he hesitatingly begins to be convinced that Ralph is the killer.

Mr. Hammond

Roger Ackroyd and Mrs. Ferrars' lawyer, Mr. Hammond is a small, "dried up" man who Dr. Sheppard describes as "having lawyer written all over him" (p. 111). However, he does willingly provide Poirot with some key details about the terms of Ackroyd's will as well as the money Mrs. Ferrars was paying her blackmailer.

Elise Dale

The housemaid, Elise Dale is a simple, straightforward girl, and quickly dismissed by Poirot as a potential suspect.

Miss Gannett

A good friend of Caroline Sheppard, Miss Gannett is, like Caroline, a busybody and town gossip, who adores speculating with Caroline about the crime.

Colonel Carter

A friend of Caroline and Dr. Sheppard, Colonel Carter is a

somewhat pompous man who likes to exaggerate the details of his "exotic" and "impressive" past.

Mrs. Folliott

Ursula Bourne's sister, Mrs. Folliott pretends to be her former employer in order to help Ursula get a job. A kind woman unused to lying, she becomes incredibly uncomfortable when Dr. Sheppard asks her about Ursula.

2.6.4 Chapter 1—Dr. Sheppard at the Breakfast Table

Dr. Sheppard, the narrator, begins the story by noting Mrs. Ferrars, local resident, died on the night of September 16–17. He was summoned in the morning, but she was already dead when he arrived. At breakfast with his gossipy sister, Caroline Sheppard, Dr. Sheppard reluctantly reveals Mrs. Ferrars's death, only to find out Caroline has already heard the news from Annie, the parlourmaid, with details supplied by the milkman. Caroline believes Mrs. Ferrars poisoned her own husband about a year ago. So when Dr. Sheppard tells her the cause of death—an overdose of the insomnia drug Veronal—Caroline immediately assumes it was suicide out of remorse for murdering her husband. When Dr. Sheppard says this idea is nonsense, Caroline asks her brother if he is personally satisfied it was not a suicide. He does not answer.

Analysis

Chapter 1 introduces two of the main characters—Dr. James Sheppard and his sister Caroline Sheppard—as well as the first death in the story. Because the title of the novel indicates Roger Ackroyd as the murder victim, starting off with a different death may cause readers a little surprise. It is just one of several such surprises in the novel and a taste of the author's enjoyment in challenging reader expectations. The first chapter could, after all, lead to an entirely different murder mystery in which Mrs. Ferrars is poisoned in a way that looks like an accident, or at worst, suicide. Christie uses this initial bit of misdirection to put readers off balance and cause them to begin asking questions and speculating answers. She also creates a character who will both echo and stoke the reader's impulse to speculate and come up with theories based on feelings and limited knowledge: Caroline Sheppard, the gossip.

The use of first-person point of view places the focus on Dr. Sheppard, who, as the physician in a small village, has access to the private lives of its inhabitants. This role, with the authority and access it provides, is an essential ingredient in the novel. Dr. Sheppard is in a position to know things others do not know. Perhaps the respected nature of Dr. Sheppard's position makes the idea that he is an unreliable narrator more shocking at the end.

This opening chapter employs foreshadowing, adding to the suspense created by talk of murder and suicide. The use of first-person point of view allows this foreshadowing to take the form of the narrator's instincts, feelings, and intuitions. Within the first few paragraphs of the novel, before he even arrives home for breakfast, Dr. Sheppard already feels "upset and worried," though he does not explain why. "I am not going to pretend that at that moment I foresaw the events of the next few weeks," he writes, and adds he felt instinctively "there were stirring times ahead." At this point, the only event he can logically be reacting to is Mrs. Ferrars's death. The reader may deduce—correctly or not—that he simply suspects the death was suicide and is unsettled by it. The breakfast conversation seems to support this conclusion.

Caroline is introduced as a terrible gossip, but almost an admirable one. She has the ability to arrive at the correct conclusions with few or no actual facts. For example, Dr. Sheppard says she "has constantly asserted, without the least foundation for the assertion" that Mrs. Ferrars poisoned her husband. Of course, she does have something of a foundation, as she notes Mrs. Ferrars is not the kind of person who can endure suffering, and "there's no doubt that the wife of a man like Ashley Ferrars"—later revealed as a drunkard—"must have had to suffer a good deal." And Caroline turns out to be quite correct.

2.6.5 Chapter 2—Who's Who in King's Abbot

Dr. Sheppard interrupts his narrative to give some background on the village of King's Abbot. The village is nine miles from the "big town" of Cranchester and boasts a population "rich in unmarried ladies and retired military officers" all of whom love to gossip. Roger Ackroyd, who lives in a large home called Fernly Park, is "a man more impossibly like a county squire than any country squire could possibly be" but had little success in marriage. Eighteen years ago Ackroyd had married a young widow with a son, Ralph Paton, but she died soon after their marriage. Ralph, now 25, is known as a wild, but good-looking, young man. A great deal of town gossip concerns the love life of Roger Ackroyd.

As he goes on his rounds, Dr. Sheppard recalls having seen Ralph Paton—whom he did not expect to be in the village—and Mrs. Ferrars walking and talking intently just yesterday. His recollection is interrupted by an unexpected meeting with Roger Ackroyd, who acknowledges he's heard the bad news about Mrs. Ferrars. "It's worse than you know," Ackroyd tells Dr. Sheppard, inviting him to his home that evening at 7:30 for an explanation of this enigmatic statement. Dr. Sheppard also learns Ackroyd believes his stepson, Ralph, is still in London. After making his rounds, he sees several patients in his surgery, or medical office, located in his home. The last of these patients is Miss Russell, Ackroyd's housekeeper. Claiming pain in her knee as the purpose of the visit, she asks about how to help a cocaine addict kick the habit.

Analysis

Chapter 2 introduces Roger Ackroyd, a wealthy man much admired in the village but with a tragic past. His wife, a widow when he married her, ended up an alcoholic and died of an alcohol-related affliction shortly after their marriage. This event is important in introducing a theme in the novel—moral weakness. Her son, Ralph Paton, is wild and a "continual source of worry and trouble." His behaviour is attributed to a "weakness" inherited from his mother.

Chapter 2 also gives more insight into Dr. Sheppard's bad feeling, which serves as foreshadowing and heightens suspense. Thinking about whether Mrs. Ferrars's death was suicide, as he does admit suspecting, he notes that women who "reach the determination to commit suicide, usually wish to reveal the state of mind that led to the fatal action." He thinks it likely she would have told someone what was in her mind. He recalls having seen

Ralph Paton and Mrs. Ferarrs in deep conversation the previous day, leaving him with a "foreboding of the future." But only after readers reach the end of the novel does the reason for Dr. Sheppard's anxiety become clear: he fears the possibility Mrs. Ferrars has told someone why she was in distress.

2.6.6 Chapter 3-The Man Who Grew Vegetable Marrows

At lunch Dr. Sheppard tells his sister he will be dining with Roger Ackroyd. She shares some gossip: Ralph Paton is staying at the Three Boars, the local inn, and went on a date—perhaps with Flora Ackroyd, Roger Ackroyd's niece. Caroline also mentions a new neighbour—a foreigner named something like Mr. Porrott who is interested in growing vegetable marrows (or summer squash).

A short time later, Dr. Sheppard is outside when a vegetable marrow flying through the air narrowly misses him. Mr. Porrott's egg-shaped head appears over the wall, and he apologizes for hurling the vegetable. He tells Dr. Sheppard he is retired from his profession, which was the "study of human nature." He also mentions he is old friends with Ackroyd, who told him his stepson Ralph is engaged to Flora Ackroyd. As the men converse briefly, Dr. Sheppard reveals he lost a large inheritance in a bad investment—and Hercule Poirot quickly figures out what it was. In the meantime, Caroline has run into Ackroyd, told him Ralph was staying at the Three Boars, and overheard Ralph telling a woman "the old man will cut me off with a shilling" and "I don't want him to go altering his will."

Concerned, Dr. Sheppard goes to the Three Boars to have a chat with Ralph. Ralph tells him he's in a "devil of a mess" and hasn't "the least idea what to do next." He says the source of the problem is his stepfather and what he is likely to do. When Dr. Sheppard offers to help, Ralph rejects his help, claiming, "I've got to play a lone hand."

Analysis

Chapter 3 introduces Christie's most famous detective, but not yet by his correct name. Readers familiar with her novels would have encountered Poirot in two previous works and would recognize his trademark egg-shaped head, "suspiciously black" hair, elaborate and immaculately groomed moustache, and foreign accent. There is always something comical about Poirot—from his love of hot chocolate to his self-appreciation—that leads characters in the novels to underestimate his ability. These eccentric qualities also make him a memorable and well-loved character for readers. Although the murder named in the title has not yet occurred, this chapter paints Poirot (or "Porrott") as a man who has some regret about going into retirement. "We work to attain an object, and the object gained, we find that what we miss is the daily toil," he explains to Dr. Sheppard.

Ralph Paton's appearance in King's Abbot, his secretive meeting with an unknown woman, and his conversation with Dr. Sheppard about needing to "play a lone hand" are used to cast suspicion on Ralph, even though the murder has not yet occurred. Surely he is in some trouble, and that trouble concerns his uncle and his uncle's will in some way. His presence in town, when he is supposed to be in London, and his worry that his uncle might write him out of his will already give Ralph motive and opportunity to kill Roger Ackroyd.

Chapter 3 also includes information that might easily be passed over, but which becomes relevant later. Dr. Sheppard had received an inheritance about a year before and lost it in a risky investment in a gold mine.

2.6.7 Chapter 4-Dinner at Fernly

Just after 7:30 Dr. Sheppard arrives at Fernly Park. Parker, the butler, lets him in. Sheppard takes off his overcoat and sets down his doctor's bag. Just before he enters the drawing room, he hears a sound from inside, like a window being shut. As he opens the door, the housekeeper, Miss Russell, is just leaving, flushed and breathing hard. She claims she was checking the flowers in the room.

Inside the drawing room, Dr. Sheppard sees there are no windows, only a large set of French doors. He considers what could have made the sound he heard. In the room is a small display table, known as a silver table, with a transparent lid containing jade and silver objects and some African knickknacks. He lifts the lid to see one of the objects more closely, but it slips. He recognizes the sound as the one he heard. Just then Flora Ackroyd enters the room, followed shortly by her mother, Mrs. Ackroyd. A few minutes later Hector Blunt, a well-known big-game hunter and friend of Ackroyd, enters. Ackroyd and his secretary, Geoffrey Raymond, arrive, and all go in to dine. Uncharacteristically, Ackroyd is subdued and preoccupied during dinner.

After dinner Ackroyd invites Dr. Sheppard to his study. He asks the doctor for some medicine for his stomach pains and sends Parker to get the doctor's bag. He has Dr. Sheppard close and lock the window, and then reveals Mrs. Ferrars confessed to him she poisoned her husband. She also told Ackroyd, to whom she had been secretly engaged, she was being blackmailed by someone who knew the truth. She did not disclose the identity of the blackmailer but hinted the person was a member of Ackroyd's household. Ackroyd feels responsible for her suicide because he reacted with horror, not sympathy, to her confession.

Parker enters with the evening's mail on a tray, and then leaves again. In the stack of mail is a letter from Mrs. Ferrars, posted just before she died. Ackroyd reads part of it aloud. It is a suicide note, full of regret for her wrongs and asking him to find the blackmailer: "I would not tell you the name, this afternoon, but I propose to write it to you now." Suddenly, Ackroyd refuses to read more, despite Dr. Sheppard's urging, saying he will read it later. As Dr. Sheppard leaves, Parker is near the door, as if he had been listening.

As the doctor walks home, he passes through the gates near the lodge of Fernly Park and encounters a stranger with his face obscured by a hat and an upturned collar. The stranger asks the way to Fernly Park. Once at home, Dr. Sheppard winds the clocks, and at 10:15 he starts up the stairs to bed. Suddenly the phone rings. Dr. Sheppard answers, and then tells Caroline, "They've just found Roger Ackroyd murdered."

Analysis

Chapter 4 introduces the household of Roger Ackroyd—his housekeeper Miss Russell, his butler Parker, his personal assistant Geoffrey Raymond, his widowed sister-in-law Mrs. Cecil Ackroyd, his niece Flora, and his friend Major Hector Blunt. It also includes important information concerning the death of Mrs. Ferrars—the murder, blackmail, and suicide—that serves to confirm and expand on Caroline's assessment of her death.

As the chapter that includes the time in which the murder takes place, it is narrated in careful detail to expose readers to all the details that may become important clues later. Because some important information appears in passing, its relevance can be easily missed, such as the presence of Dr. Sheppard's black doctor's bag. And some details are not at all relevant to the crime, though they are important parts of Christie's subplots and misdirection. One detail that seems highly suspicious is Miss Russell's flustered condition, especially when her explanation of checking the flowers is an obvious lie. This detail, however, is unrelated to the murder of Roger Ackroyd. Instead, it is part of a subplot about Miss Russell and her illegitimate son, a cocaine addict she is trying both to hide and to help. Parker's suspicious eavesdropping is another misdirection. He behaves suspiciously as if he is trying to hear the name of the person blackmailing Mrs. Ferrars, perhaps because he wants to know if he is going to be caught as the blackmailer himself. But later Poirot concludes he was only hoping to hear something juicy that would allow him to blackmail Ackroyd. Parker turns out to be a blackmailer, but not the blackmailer of Mrs. Ferrars, thus muddying the waters of the case still more.

In addition, because of Christie's choice to use an unreliable narrator, some details are used as misdirection and later revealed as relevant to the crime. For example, the sound Dr. Sheppard hears—of the silver table being shut—seems an important detail because it suggests the murderer opened the silver table to steal the dagger before Dr. Sheppard heard the lid being closed. However, it later becomes clear Dr. Sheppard's attention was drawn to the silver table because he heard it being closed, and it was then he noticed, and stole, the dagger to use as a weapon.

2.6.8-Chapter 5—Murder

Dr. Sheppard drives quickly to Fernly and rings the bell. Parker answers the door, but when the doctor asks if he has phoned the police, the butler is taken aback. Dr. Sheppard says, "If, as you say, your master has been murdered—"but Parker is shocked, insisting he made no such call. The two go together to Roger Ackroyd's study. The door is locked, and Ackroyd does not answer when called. They break down the door and find Ackroyd sitting in his chair. He is stabbed dead, with the dagger left in the wound.

Dr. Sheppard sends Parker to alert the police and the household. Then he does "what little had to be done," carefully leaving the dagger undisturbed. Raymond and Blunt arrive. Raymond suggests there was a burglary, and Blunt agrees, because no one would want to murder Ackroyd. The letter from Mrs. Ferrars is missing.

Just then, the local police inspector, Inspector Davis, and the constable, Jones, arrive. Dr. Sheppard and the others explain what happened, the doctor claiming Ackroyd had been dead half an hour or more when they found him. Outside the window, now wide open, the police find footprints indicating a person went in and out that way. Dr. Sheppard suddenly remembers the stranger he encountered the night before and describes him to the police.

Dr. Sheppard says he left the house at 8:50 and arrived home by 9:15. Raymond says he heard Ackroyd talking to someone in his study at 9:30 and saying, "The calls on my purse have been so frequent of late... that I fear it is impossible for me to accede to your request." Parker claims he saw Flora exiting the room at 9:45 and telling him Ackroyd did not want to be disturbed. The inspector sends Raymond to fetch Flora and asks her about her interaction with Ackroyd. She replies that when she went in to say goodnight, he said he was busy and complimented her dress. Then she left. When pressed, she says he told her to tell Parker not to disturb him. Immediately after they inform Flora her uncle is dead, she faints and is taken upstairs.

2.6.9 Chapter 6—The Tunisian Dagger

With Flora settled, the inspector again questions the doctor about the mysterious stranger. Dr. Sheppard says he didn't get a good look at the man's face. The inspector then tells him Parker mentioned something about blackmail, and Dr. Sheppard says Parker must have been listening at the door. The doctor then tells the inspector everything Roger Ackroyd divulged during their earlier conversation. Both men agree Parker has been acting suspiciously, and the inspector seems to think Parker is the culprit.

Then, after the inspector removes the dagger from the body, the doctor examines the body, concluding, "the blow was delivered by a right-handed man standing behind him, and death must have been instantaneous." When they ask Raymond about the dagger, he says Major Blunt gave Mr. Ackroyd the knife from Tunis. Blunt confirms this fact. Raymond notes it is usually kept in the silver table. The doctor reveals he heard the lid of the little table being closed the evening before. Miss Russell is questioned, and she claims she shut the open lid when she was checking the flowers. The inspector floats a theory: someone reached in the open window near the table and took the dagger.

When Dr. Sheppard gets home, he tells Caroline about the murder but not the blackmail. Caroline thinks the idea of Parker being the prime suspect is ridiculous.

Analysis

In these two chapters the evidence of the time of death is established by several witnesses. One important piece of evidence is that Ackroyd's voice was heard coming from within his study at 9:30. Another is that Flora said good night to her uncle at about 9:45. Dr. Sheppard received the phone call at 10:15, and the body was discovered a few minutes later. Dr. Sheppard declares Ackroyd had already been dead at least 30 minutes by this time. This timeline leaves very little time for the murder to take place. More important, an accurate time of death is important for confirming alibis. For example, when Dr. Sheppard says he was home by 9:15—a fact Caroline can corroborate—it essentially places him above suspicion. If the time of death were shown to be incorrect, solid alibis would come into question.

The inspector is a typical character in an Agatha Christie novel: the hapless police inspector. He is overenthusiastic and jumps to conclusions that sometimes contradict each other. This trait makes him easy to manipulate. The inspector immediately considers two potential suspects: Parker and the mysterious stranger. It is interesting to note that Dr. Sheppard calls attention to the suspicious behaviour of both men. Dr. Sheppard is the one who saw Parker listening at the door and reveals this information to the inspector. Dr. Sheppard is the one who meets the mysterious stranger, and thus he is the one who brings up the man's presence and suspicious demeanour. These observations and revelations are all natural, given the circumstances, but they draw attention to how many details of the case are details only Dr. Sheppard knows and can divulge—such as the letter about the blackmail, the reason for Mrs. Ferrars's suicide, the words spoken by the man on the telephone, and the window that he locked during his conversation with Ackroyd. Because these are details no other living character knows, no one can prove or disprove them.

The aftermath of the crime and the beginning of the police investigation provide a window into social assumptions made during the time of the novel. First, the lower classes are often viewed with suspicion, and when a crime is committed, the police naturally consider them among the first suspects. The inspector is quick to suspect Parker, partly because he is acting suspiciously and partly because he is a servant. "Butlers can creep about as soft-footed as cats," notes the inspector. Second, women are considered too weak to handle much stress. The inspector doesn't want Flora to be told of the murder before he questions her, for fear she will be too distraught to answer questions. "She can answer my questions better without being upset by knowing the truth about her uncle," he states.

2.6.10 Chapter 7—I Learn My Neighbour's Profession

The next morning Dr. Sheppard completes his rounds and, returning home, learns from his sister that Flora has arrived and wants to see him. She asks Dr. Sheppard to go with her to the Larches, Mr. Porrott's home, to ask him to look into her uncle's death. She reveals Mr. Porrott is really Hercule Poirot, the famous private detective. Flora says the police—especially Inspector Raglan from Cranchester—suspect Ralph, but Flora doesn't believe he is the murderer. When they visit the Larches, Poirot agrees to take the case, though he warns them he won't stop until he finds out the truth. Dr. Sheppard briefs Poirot on the facts of the case.

Poirot and Dr. Sheppard go to the police station to let the police know Poirot will be working on the case. Inspector Raglan is less than enthusiastic about this news. He lists the evidence against Ralph. On the previous evening he went out at 9:00, was observed near Fernly Park about 9:30, and hasn't been seen since. He is rumoured to have money problems, and his shoes match the footprints at the crime scene.

Poirot takes the opportunity to examine the crime scene and asks Dr. Sheppard to describe the position of the body and other details about the room. He also asks Parker about the state of the fire in the room when the body was discovered. Parker notes it had burned very low and adds a few other differences between the room in its present state and the room the previous evening: the curtains were drawn, the light was on, and a chair was drawn out more. Poirot then explains why the matter of the fire is important. When the doctor left Roger Ackroyd at 8:50, the window was shut and locked. At 10:15, when the body was discovered, the door was locked and the window open. Because the fire had burned low, Ackroyd obviously did not open the window to cool down the room. So he may have opened the window to let someone in.

Colonel Melrose, the chief constable, enters to say the phone call supposedly from Parker was actually placed from a public phone booth at the train station at 10:15 the previous night.

2.6.11 Chapter 8—Inspector Raglan Is Confident

Colonel Melrose wonders aloud why the person placed the telephone call. Hercule Poirot answers that "when we know that, we shall know everything" and then asks Dr. Sheppard about the stranger he encountered at 9:00 the previous evening. They determine it would take only between two and five minutes to go from the place near the lodge where Dr. Sheppard saw the stranger to Ackroyd's window.

Parker and Raymond are both summoned to speak with Poirot, who asks Raymond if he pushed the chair back into its correct place after the body was found. Raymond says he did not. Both Raymond and Parker are asked about any strangers that might have visited Ackroyd. They agree the closest thing to a stranger would have been a young man who came to sell Ackroyd a Dictaphone. But this man does not match Dr. Sheppard's description of the stranger he saw.

Poirot asks to see the silver table in the drawing room, and Dr. Sheppard shows it to him. Afterward they exit the drawing room through the French doors. Inspector Raglan walks by, boasts of his superior investigative method, and reveals Ralph Paton was seen going up toward Ackroyd's house at 9:25. He concludes Ralph had enough time to steal the dagger, stab his stepfather, and get back to the inn.

Poirot investigates a small summerhouse on the grounds,

taking along Dr. Sheppard. Inside, Poirot discovers two clues: a scrap of a white material and a small goose quill.

Analysis

Chapter 7 develops Poirot's obsession with finding the truth, as well as his method for doing so. He has an intense exchange with Flora when she asks him to solve the case, explaining he won't stop investigating once he starts, and she might come to regret his dedication to the truth: "You may wish that, after all, you had left it to the local police," he advises. She insists she wants "all the truth," so he accepts the case, but not without ominously warning her "I hope you will not regret those words." In Poirot's view, finding the truth is a worthy goal and one he will pursue like a dog on the scent. But it also has a dangerous side. For those with something to hide, or who do not want to face the truth, the truth can be devastating. His warning to Flora suggests he suspects she either has something to hide or would not want to find out the real truth.

After Poirot makes clear his dedication to finding the truth, he immediately begins to demonstrate the systematic, methodical way he will arrive at it. His astute questioning of the witnesses shows he is considering aspects of the case and details of the scene others have not considered. Some details (such as the position of the chair) go unexplained although they are important to the solution of the crime. Some details Poirot explains. For example, he quickly fixes on the state of the fire and of the window, connecting these two details (a low-burning fire and an open window on a cool night) to suggest the window must be open for some purpose other than comfort. He also shows his mind can easily construct a timeline of events and extrapolate from it to reach a logical conclusion—an ability that eventually helps him use a small time discrepancy in Dr. Sheppard's narrative to solve the case.

Chapter 8 continues to showcase Poirot's unusual brilliance in finding the truth, as he goes about the grounds looking for additional clues. Inspector Raglan's "confidence" and method of detection are contrasted with Poirot's, and in a device Christie uses often in her novels, the inspector's method and conclusions are found wanting while Poirot's seem portentous. Like other police officials in the Christie universe, Inspector Raglan is useful mostly for making Poirot look good. However, Inspector Raglan's presence serves another purpose here. While readers are distracted by the rather comical overconfidence of Raglan and amazed by Poirot's intellect, Christie drops seemingly unimportant details into the narrative. Like the presence of the doctor's black bag at the murder scene, these details are mentioned in a way that allows them to avoid reader focus. In this chapter the short discussion of the young man selling Dictaphones is just such a detail.

2.6.12 Chapter 9—The Goldfish Pond

On the way back to the main house, Hercule Poirot and Dr. Sheppard discuss who might stand to inherit the estate. They also overhear a conversation between Major Blunt and Flora. Blunt says he intends to go back to Africa, because he's too rough for refined society. When Flora is distressed, Blunt asks if she'd prefer he stay, and she says she does. She also reveals the family lawyer, Mr. Hammond, has informed her Roger Ackroyd left her a sizable inheritance. She is happy and suggests the money leaves her free not to do something, but won't say what.

Poirot then makes his presence known, and the two eavesdroppers join Blunt and Flora. In response to Poirot's questioning, Blunt says when he was outside for a smoke about 9:30 he heard Ackroyd's voice coming from inside. He also tells them he thought he saw a woman disappearing into the bushes. Poirot asks if he moved the pulled-out chair in the room back to its correct position. Blunt says no. Then Poirot asks Flora if the dagger was in the silver table when she was examining it before dinner. She says she thinks it was not there.

Poirot sees something bright in the pond and attempts to fish it out. Pretending to be unsuccessful, he actually retrieves the object and quickly hides it. On the way back to the house, he shows the object to Dr. Sheppard. It is a woman's wedding ring with the inscription "From R., March 13th."

2.6.13 Chapter 10—The Parlourmaid

Back at the house, money matters are discussed. Poirot asks Mr. Hammond if Ralph needed money. Mr. Hammond notes that shortness of funds is a perpetual state for the young man. When asked about the terms of Ackroyd's will, Hammond reveals 1,000 pounds was left to Miss Russell, 50 pounds to the cook, 500 pounds to Raymond, 10,000 pounds to Mrs. Ackroyd, and 20,000 pounds to Flora. The rest of the large estate goes to Ralph. In addition, it is discovered that 40 pounds are missing from Ackroyd's bedroom. Ursula Bourne, the parlourmaid, is summoned and asked about the money. She says Ackroyd's bedroom was not hers to tidy. Elsie Dale, the housemaid, is similarly summoned and questioned, but she, too, denies knowing anything about the money.

Poirot and Sheppard discuss Ursula Bourne, who also reported being treated rudely the evening before and who planned to leave Ackroyd's service as a result. Poirot notes she does not have an alibi for the time of the murder. Sheppard recalls the letter from Mrs. Ferrars did not specify the gender of the blackmailer. Poirot is intrigued by this bit of information.

Poirot observes that a good deal of evidence points to Ralph as the murderer—"motive, opportunity, means." But since Flora seems so convinced of Ralph's innocence, he intends to keep investigating, just to be sure.

Analysis

Chapters 9 and 10 develop the possibility of a financial motive for the murder, which is, after all, a frequent motive in crime fiction. Flora is overjoyed to receive enough money to be free of some course of action she was clearly dreading. Blunt lost money in some speculative investment and plans to go back to Africa to hunt. Ralph, known often to be in need of funds, stands to gain considerable wealth. The missing 40 pounds underscores the possibility that someone in the household is desperate enough to steal from Ackroyd's own bedroom.

Money is such an obvious motive, given Ackroyd's wealth, that Poirot is curious about why Dr. Sheppard finds it a surprising possibility to consider. Dr. Sheppard "truthfully" admits he wishes he had thought of inheritance as a motive. The word truthfully here is interesting, for it introduces the question of whether Dr. Sheppard is always truthful. Poirot is intrigued by Dr. Sheppard's surprise and his truthful comment, saying thoughtfully, "I wonder just what you mean by that." Again Poirot shows his knack for asking the right questions. Why is the possibility of a financial motive surprising to Dr. Sheppard? Perhaps he has been focusing on a different motive. When Poirot warns Dr. Sheppard "it is not easy to hide things from Hercule Poirot," it seems he already has his suspicions.

Dr. Sheppard is more focused on the blackmailer as a person of interest and hints at a narrative in which the blackmailer murdered Ackroyd because he believed Ackroyd would be able to identify him or her. In Chapter 10 he seizes on Miss Russell's suspicious behaviour and suggests she might be the blackmailer by noting the letter from Mrs. Ferrars to Ackroyd did not specify the gender of the blackmailer.

Chapters 9 and 10 also develop two of the misdirection subplots—subplots Christie uses to cause characters to conceal information, thereby making them seem as if they might be hiding their own involvement in the murder. Secret keepers seem suspicious, even when their secrets are unrelated to the crime at hand. One of these subplots is Flora's need for money and her involvement in some course of action she finds unpleasant enough that she is glad to be free of it. Another is the mystery of Ursula Bourne's leaving service at Fernly, which seems a harsh reaction to simple rudeness or disarranged papers.

2.6.14 Chapter 11—Poirot Pays a Call

Hercule Poirot has given Dr. Sheppard the task of visiting Mrs. Folliott, one of Ursula Bourne's references. On Sunday he travels to Mrs. Folliott's home, where he is shown into the drawing room. When asked about Ursula Bourne, however, Mrs. Folliott becomes upset and refuses to say anything about her. Sheppard leaves and arrives home about 6:00 pm. Caroline tells him excitedly she had a visit from Poirot and relates the conversation to her brother. Poirot was flattering toward her, gave her some juicy gossip about various celebrities, and got some gossip from her, too: the story of overhearing Ralph talking to an unknown woman in the woods. Poirot also asked about the patients Dr. Sheppard saw the day of Roger Ackroyd's death. Caroline recalls Miss Russell was one of them, and this recollection jogs Dr. Sheppard's memory of the odd questions Miss Russell asked. Considering this event, he puts a log on the fire and goes in to dinner.

2.6.15 Chapter 12—Round the Table

On Monday Dr. Sheppard gives evidence at the inquest, which Ralph Paton does not attend. In fact, he cannot be found, an absence the inspector finds suspicious. Dr. Sheppard, Poirot, and the inspector again discuss the phone call the doctor received the night of the murder. Poirot still maintains, "when we find the explanation of that telephone call we shall find the explanation of the murder." Poirot cautions the inspector against putting too much importance on the fingerprints found on the dagger, suggesting they are likely to be Ackroyd's own, placed there by the murderer after Ackroyd was dead.

Returning to Fernly a short while later, Poirot assembles a "little reunion" of Mrs. Ackroyd, Flora, Major Blunt, Raymond, and Dr. Sheppard around the dinner table. He begins by asking Flora, as Ralph's fiancée, to persuade him to come forward. She swears she has no idea of his whereabouts. He then puts the question of Ralph's whereabouts to the whole group. No one speaks up. Poirot assures them he intends to get to the truth, though he knows every person at the table is hiding something.

Analysis

Chapter 11 gives the unmistakable impression that Poirot sends Dr. Sheppard to see Mrs. Folliott in part to have time alone to talk with Caroline. In response to Poirot's strategic flattery and a sense of transacting gossip for gossip, Caroline offers Poirot information Dr. Sheppard knew but did not reveal. The chapter also reminds the reader of the odd interaction between Miss Russell and Dr. Sheppard, an interaction that seems to take on greater importance given the developments in the Miss Russell subplot.

Despite the sense that the doctor's visit to Miss Folliott is a wild goose chase, or diversion, it does increase the suspense around Ursula Bourne. But unanswered questions about Ursula Bourne are not the only outstanding questions. There is still the matter of the phone call. As Poirot states again in this chapter, "When we find the explanation of that telephone call we shall find the explanation of the murder." The telephone call seems completely unnecessary—the body certainly would have been found without it.

In Chapter 12 readers are reminded that despite the fascinating twists and turns of Poirot's investigation, the normal procedures of a suspicious death must continue. The inquest is completed in a matter-of-fact manner, though once again Dr. Sheppard is in a position to control the flow of information, as he is the medical expert on the case. The notable absence of Ralph is the only oddity, since his continued absence serves to make him look guilty. Poirot is clearly puzzled by Ralph's absence because it is so illogical, and he calls several characters together to find out Ralph's whereabouts and/or have Flora convince him to come back.

Chapter 12 ends with an unexpected event: Poirot accuses the assembled group of keeping secrets from him. "Every one of you in this room is concealing something from me," he tells them. This interaction highlights an important theme in the novel: secrets. Nearly everyone in the novel has them—some big, some insignificant. Most of the secrets have no bearing on the murder case at all, but concealing information makes it difficult for Poirot to untangle the relevant from irrelevant and find the truth he seeks.

2.6.16 Chapter 13—The Goose Quill

Monday evening Dr. Sheppard has dinner at Hercule Poirot's house. Poirot chides his guest about holding back the information on Ralph's rendezvous in the woods and says he finds Miss Russell quite interesting. Dr. Sheppard expresses curiosity about what Poirot really thinks of the whole matter, but Poirot tells him he is "like the little child who wants to know the way the engine works" and declines to enlighten the doctor.

However, Poirot does give Dr. Sheppard a little lecture on how he ascertains characters' movements and double-checks them, using the doctor's evidence about his encounter with the mysterious stranger as an example. Poirot also explains that the quill he picked up in the summerhouse is used for taking heroin, and the path the stranger was headed toward would have taken him to the summerhouse as well as to the main house.

Poirot also notes his serious doubts about the parlourmaid's story. Then he invites Dr. Sheppard to share his own theories. The doctor says he believes the person with Ackroyd at 9:30 was Ralph, but since Ackroyd was alive at 9:45, Ralph is not the murderer—the mysterious stranger must be. Also, he thinks the stranger was in league with Parker, who was trying to blackmail Mrs. Ferrars. Poirot says this theory does not account for telephone call, the pushed-out chair, the missing 40 pounds, or Blunt's belief that Raymond was the person with Ackroyd at 9:30. Also, Poirot observes the case against Ralph is a little too neat, suggesting he is actually innocent.

2.6.17 Chapter 14—Mrs. Ackroyd

Dr. Sheppard observes the investigation has now entered "a different phase." Poirot continues his investigation, but Dr. Sheppard no longer plays "Watson to his Sherlock." Their paths have diverged, though Sheppard follows the investigation from village gossip.

On Tuesday morning Mrs. Ackroyd summons Dr. Sheppard. Thinking she is ill, the doctor goes to see her in a professional capacity. She is in bed and claims to be sick with shock over Roger Ackroyd's death. After she accepts a tonic as medicine for this dubious illness, she gets to her point. Complaining that Poirot insinuated she is hiding something, she insists she is not. But then she admits to having a number of unpaid bills, adding that Ackroyd was not generous in covering her debts, despite his wealth. After taking her time getting to the point, she tells the doctor that Friday afternoon she rifled through Ackroyd's papers to see if she could find his will and have a peek. Ursula Bourne interrupted her at this task, and then Ackroyd, too, arrived in his office. Mrs. Ackroyd made an excuse and left, while Bourne remained to talk with her employer.

Dr. Sheppard senses Mrs. Ackroyd is still holding something back and asks if she was the one who left the silver table open. She admits it, saying she was looking at one of the pieces and considering having it appraised by an expert. However, Miss Russell interrupted her, and then Dr. Sheppard arrived. Sheppard considers this new information, thinking Miss Russell must have come in to the drawing room quickly, thus explaining why she seemed out of breath. He connects this information to Poirot's discovery of the white fabric in the summerhouse. On his way out, he notices Ursula Bourne has been crying and inquires as to why. She says if he knows where Ralph is, he should tell him to come home.

Back at home, the doctor learns Poirot has given Caroline a task: to find out if Ralph Paton's boots were black or brown. Dr. Sheppard does not understand, but he says, "I see now that I was unbelievably stupid about these boots. I failed altogether to grasp the point." Caroline has a friend who works at the Three Boars find out. She discovers the boots are black.

Analysis

There is a noticeable shift in Chapters 13 and 14 as Poirot draws away from Dr. Sheppard and keeps him at arms' length, while beginning to use Caroline as a replacement "Watson." Dr. Sheppard seems slightly annoyed that Poirot went to see Caroline privately, complaining Poirot has given her a swelled head now full of gossip both "true and untrue." After all, Dr. Sheppard likes to be in charge of the flow of information about the case and has until now been in the position to have this control easily. Now that he knows Dr. Sheppard has withheld information about Ralph, Poirot is less likely to trust the doctor's information to be complete and objective.

Poirot lets Dr. Sheppard know in several ways that the situation has changed. He asks seriously, "Why not have you told me the truth?" To Poirot, truth is of the utmost importance, and by using the word truth in particular he communicates clearly his disappointment in Dr. Sheppard's not being truthful. When Dr. Sheppard tries to undermine Caroline's information by suggesting it is imagined or frivolous gossip, Poirot calls Caroline an "expert" and suggests her conclusions—even those built on intuition—may contain a great deal of truth. He even elaborates on why he has reason to trust Caroline's conclusions, suggesting that "intuition" is really just a sort of subconscious logic. "Women observe subconsciously a thousand little details," he explains. "Their subconscious mind adds these little things together—and they call the result intuition." So as Poirot has begun to question the truthfulness of Dr. Sheppard, he gives Caroline high marks for using intuition to discover the truth.

But what Poirot says after these first exchanges in Chapter 13 is even more significant. Dr. Sheppard is naturally interested in how close Poirot is getting to the truth. When he inquires what Poirot thinks of the whole case so far, Poirot refuses to indulge him. Instead, he reminds Sheppard he (Poirot) has the "eye of a detective who knows and cares for no one—to whom they are all strangers and all equally liable to suspicion," adding he always keeps in mind that "the person who speaks may be lying." To illustrate, he uses several examples, the first being Dr. Sheppard's own testimony about the night of the murder. Furthermore, Poirot uses exactly those facts that become significant in the solution to the mystery—Dr. Sheppard's statement he left the house at 8:50 and ran into the mysterious stranger at 9:00.

Later in the conversation, after giving Dr. Sheppard a chance to float a theory and then pointing out all the clues it does not account for, Poirot circles back to the question of Ralph Paton's strange disappearance. Dr. Sheppard comes up with a "medical" explanation that Ralph's nerves went "phut." The doctor is clearly interested in keeping the case against Ralph afloat, even if it means filling in holes with dubious medical explanations. However, Poirot thinks the case against Ralph is too tidy and is therefore an indication of his innocence after all. This conclusion means, of course, Poirot will be looking more closely at other potential suspects—an uncomfortable prospect for the real murderer.

In Chapter 14, Dr. Sheppard acknowledges Poirot has cooled toward him, and their paths diverge from here on in the story. However, it is not only the relationship between Poirot and Dr. Sheppard that changes in Chapter 14. The narrative voice also shifts, including interesting shifts in verb tense. Dr. Sheppard begins the chapter by saying "the whole thing can be divided into two parts, each... distinct from the other. Part I ranges from Ackroyd's death... to the following Monday night. It is the straightforward narrative of what occurred, as presented to Hercule Poirot." The words straightforward and as presented well describe the style and content of the narrative thus far. The events described are exactly as Dr. Sheppard presented them to Poirot.

However, all that changes in Chapter 14. After this point, the narrator's voice becomes increasingly noticeable, as Dr. Sheppard interjects more personal commentary, using the present tense: "As I know now, I failed in this latter task," he says. And then, indicating Poirot has already solved the case: "To Poirot alone belongs the renown of fitting those pieces into their correct place." These present-tense comments imply some of the text of the narrative is written at a time after Poirot has revealed the truth of the case to Dr. Sheppard. Because in Chapter 23, Dr. Sheppard gives Poirot a draft of the first 20 chapters, this sense of looking back over the case from a future point suggests Dr. Sheppard both finishes the final chapters and also revises previous chapters of manuscript with commentary in the present.

2.6.18 Chapter 15—Geoffrey Raymond

Later Tuesday afternoon Dr. Sheppard visits Hercule Poirot at the Larches, encouraged to do so by Caroline on the pretext of bringing him some jam. He relates his conversation with Mrs. Ackroyd, and Poirot notes this supports Miss Russell's claim that she closed the lid of the silver table. Now they know for certain she was outside—probably meeting someone. Sheppard also delivers the message that Ralph's boots were black, not brown. Poirot seems "crestfallen" and soon changes the topic.

Geoffrey Raymond arrives and is shown in. He has a confession to make: "I was in debt ... and that legacy came in the nick of time." He hadn't wanted to mention it at first because he thought it made him look bad. After Raymond leaves, Poirot hints Blunt may be concealing something about his love life.

Dr. Sheppard then suggests the blackmailer of Mrs. Ferrars is not necessarily the same person who murdered Roger Ackroyd. Poirot agrees it is possible, but he points out the letter naming the blackmailer has disappeared. Then Poirot suggests Parkermay be the blackmailer, since he could easily have taken the letter. He then suggests a little experiment. The two go together to Fernly and tell Parker they want to test whether voices inside could have been heard from the terrace. Major Blunt is told to stay on the terrace, and Parker and Flora re-enact their meeting outside Ackroyd's room. Parker, carrying a tray with two whiskey glasses on it, speaks to Flora. After Parker leaves, Flora confirms she thinks there were two glasses on the tray. Poirot seems satisfied. When the two are alone again, Dr. Sheppard asks Poirot what was the point of the question about the glasses. "One must say something," Poirot says, adding, "that particular question did as well as any other." Sheppard is perplexed, but Poirot does not explain further, though he indicates he has gained important information.

2.6.19 Chapter 16—An Evening at Mah Jong

That night Dr. Sheppard and Caroline invite Miss Gannett and Colonel Carter for a mah jong party. Mah jong is a game more "peaceful" than bridge, according to the doctor. Once the game starts, the gossip soon follows. They discuss the case for a time, focusing on the meaning of Poirot's boot question, the money stolen from Ackroyd, and how the parlourmaid is heard crying every night. As the game continues, gossip turns toward Ralph Paton. Caroline expresses displeasure that her brother, who is often with Poirot, isn't contributing to the gossip.

Suddenly Dr. Sheppard realizes he has "The Perfect Winning," a rare event in the game of mah jong, when a player wins on their original hand. "I had never hoped to hold the hand myself," he says. Feeling triumphant, he shows his winning hand. Then, in the giddiness of victory, he parts with one small piece of information about the case: the gold wedding ring with the inscription. Several theories emerge as to who was secretly married to whom.

After the party, Dr. Sheppard and Caroline go up to bed. Caroline mentions she knows Flora does not care at all about Ralph Paton and never has.

Analysis

Chapter 15 contains answers to some questions, but raises others. Raymond reveals the information he was hiding, making him the latest of those accused of concealing information to come forward. Miss Russell's questions about drug addicts seem to be related to an article about cocaine smuggling. On the other hand, Poirot's strange reaction to the colour of Ralph's boots goes unexplained, as does his purpose for staging the re-enactment of Flora and Parker's meeting outside Ackroyd's study door the night of the crime.

The chapter develops themes related to keeping secrets and searching for truth in subtle ways. Caroline, shown to have an instinct for truth, tells her brother "You're not so honest, that's all. You always have to pretend." She says this in context of her own love of gossip, but since she has an uncanny ability to correctly sum up a person, the statement can also be seen as a generalization of Dr. Sheppard's overall truthfulness. Poirot, too, seems to doubt Dr. Sheppard's truthfulness, noting after Raymond comes to confess his little secret that "two of the people I accused have given me the truth." Unless Poirot doubts Mrs. Ackroyd's story or Raymond's, he is suggesting Dr. Sheppard is still concealing information.

It is not unusual for Christie to include games in her novels, especially because dinner parties and evening entertainment at the time often included card games, such as bridge. As a narrative device they provide a chance for characters to summarize the case thus far, comment on its outstanding questions, or provide exposition in the form of chitchat and gossip. In Chapter 16, however, the game takes on a more symbolic meaning, as Dr. Sheppard's "Perfect Winning" can be read as a representation of his sense his plan is going to come out perfectly. His triumph in winning at maj jong reflects his triumph over having outwitted Poirot and the police and gotten away with his well-planned crime. This reaction shows Dr. Sheppard does not know how close Poirot is to the truth.

2.6.20 Chapter 17—Parker

The next morning at 11:00 the joint funeral of Mrs. Ferrars and Roger Ackroyd takes place. Afterward Hercule Poirot invites Dr. Sheppard back to his home. Poirot asks for help in interrogating a witness—Parker, who is supposed to meet him at the Larches at noon. Poirot says, rather enigmatically, he hopes Parker is the blackmailer.

Poirot begins the meeting with Parker by asking him if he has "made many experiments in blackmail?" Although the butler acts shocked, it turns out Poirot has learned Parker was blackmailing his previous employer, Major Ellerby. Parker confesses and admits he eavesdropped on Ackroyd after he heard the word blackmail through the study door. After Parker leaves, Poirot observes the butler believes "it was Ackroyd himself who was the victim of blackmail" and thus "knows nothing at all about the Mrs. Ferrars business."

Next, Poirot takes Dr. Sheppard to see Mr. Hammond. Poirot asks the doctor to explain what Ackroyd said about Mrs. Ferrars being blackmailed. Mr. Hammond, also the lawyer for Mrs.

Ferrars's estate, confirms she paid out 20,000 pounds from her estate during the last year of her life.

Dr. Sheppard invites Poirot to dinner. After they have eaten, Poirot, Caroline, and the doctor discuss the case. Caroline tells Poirot she thinks he's wrong for believing someone in the Ackroyd household is the murderer. She maintains Flora wouldn't kill anyone and Ralph isn't a murderer. She also has a theory that Ralph is hiding in Cranchester, a theory Poirot does not confirm. Then he describes how an ordinary man might become a murderer. He might have a weakness, and when the opportunity of easy money by blackmail presents itself, the temptation is too great. But the woman he is blackmailing decides to reveal the truth, and so the blackmailer becomes a murderer.

After Poirot's hypothetical scenario concludes, the phone rings. The police in Liverpool have detained Charles Kent, the man believed to be mysterious stranger. They ask Dr. Sheppard to identify him.

2.6.21 Chapter 18—Charles Kent

Dr. Sheppard, Poirot, and Inspector Raglan travel to Liverpool. On the way, Inspector Raglan admits Poirot was correct about the fingerprints on the dagger being Ackroyd's own.

Dr. Sheppard identifies Charles Kent as the man he met near Fernly. Then Poirot shows Kent the small goose quill he found in the summerhouse, saying Kent dropped it that night. Kent admits he was at the house that evening. But he adds he was at a pub by 9:25 and thus couldn't have done the murder. Poirot suggests Kent was born in Kent, noting "under certain circumstances" a person named Kent would come from Kent. Kent becomes angry.

Later Dr. Sheppard and Poirot have lunch together. Sheppard notes, "I know now that the whole thing lay clearly unraveled before him." But things are still unclear to the doctor. When he asks why Kent was at Fernly, Poirot answers "because he was born in Kent." But this answer does not illuminate the issue for Sheppard.

Analysis

Once again, questions are answered, and new ones are raised. In

Chapter 17 the issue of Parker's suspicious behaviour outside the door of Ackroyd's study the night of the murder is resolved. Indeed he had been eavesdropping and was flustered to be caught behaving suspiciously and with blackmail on his mind. But he is not the murderer. The importance of Charles Kent and the part he plays in the case, if any, comes to the fore.

These two chapters hold several other items of interest. Although in Chapter 14 Dr. Sheppard makes it clear he felt a distancing between him and Poirot, in these chapters the two certainly seem to spend considerable time together—interviewing witnesses, performing experiments, seeing Ackroyd's lawyer, having dinner, and the like. Yet Chapter 18 contains one of those fascinating uses of Dr. Sheppard's present-tense narrative interruptions, as he seems to look back from the end of the story and see events more clearly: "I know now that the whole thing lay clearly unraveled before him ... But at the time I had no suspicion of the fact."

As the puzzle pieces of the case continue falling into place, there is a sense of approaching the climax of the narrative, even though readers will not learn the full story for several chapters. Chapters 17 and 18 intensify this sense, not only because Dr. Sheppard indicates, "the whole thing lay clearly unraveled." There are other moments that both heighten suspense and develop themes central to the story. One such moment is a brief interaction between Poirot and Caroline in which she expresses her theory that Ralph Paton is in Cranchester—a theory based partly on Poirot having been observed driving to Cranchester. Poirot "looks bewildered" and laughs heartily as he explains he went there to see the dentist. It seems as if Caroline's intuition has failed her, but the truth is she is quite correct (as revealed in Chapter 24). Two lessons emerge from this. One is that Caroline is, once again, right. Another is that Poirot is, despite his commitment to the truth, quite capable of lying and willing to do so in its pursuit.

A second moment occurs a few minutes later, as they discuss Ralph Paton, whom everyone in the village agrees has a "weak nature"—a weak character or moral weakness—but whom everyone likes and cannot imagine as a murderer. Poirot wonders aloud where "weakness" might lead. Caroline interjects that her brother is "weak as water" and addresses him directly: "I've always considered it my duty to look after you. With a bad bringing up, Heaven knows what mischief you might have got into by now." On its surface this statement seems like mild teasing among siblings or from an older sister used to her overprotective role. But Poirot returns to this concept of "weakness" moments later in the conversation, painting a hypothetical picture of an ordinary man who has a "strain of weakness" that, in the right circumstances, leads that person to make wrong choices. A man with this weakness, Poirot says, may stumble accidentally on a secret and be unable to resist the temptation to make a great deal of money by blackmail. Repeated misdeeds could then result, because by doing wrong the person's "moral fibre is blunted." As Poirot outlines this hypothetical case, Caroline takes it to mean Poirot believes Ralph Paton is the killer, when in reality it is Dr. Sheppard he is describing.

2.6.22 Chapter 19—Flora Ackroyd

Just after his rounds the following morning, Dr. Sheppard encounters Inspector Raglan. The inspector informs him the barmaid at the Dog and Whistle, Sally Jones, has confirmed Kent's alibi. Sheppard and Inspector Raglan go together to Hercule Poirot's home to deliver this news. Poirot advises Raglan not to release Kent just yet.

Poirot also explains he believes Flora took the 40 pounds from Roger Ackroyd's bedroom. Then, as she was coming down the staircase, she saw Parker approaching Ackroyd's study door with the tray of whiskey, and she pretended to be exiting the study. Poirot explains how he used his "little experiment" to demonstrate how this sequence of events could have happened.

The three men then drive to Fernly, where they discuss the scenario with Flora. Major Blunt is with her. Flora confirms Poirot's version of events, saying she is "weak" and that noticing a similar weakness in Ralph made her willing to marry him. Major Blunt contradicts her, claiming Ackroyd gave him the 40 pounds, but Poirot does not believe his confession. Speaking privately to Blunt, Poirot says he knows the secret Blunt has been concealing: he is in love with Flora. Poirot tells him not to worry, for Flora is not really in love with Ralph—she's being loyal to him simply because he's under suspicion. Blunt rushes outside after Flora.

2.6.23 Chapter 20—Miss Russell

Inspector Raglan is confused and discouraged by the new developments in the case. He complains that the alibis are now worthless and that he has to start from scratch, with a new focus on 9:30 instead of 9:45. The inspector is still puzzled by the telephone call to Dr. Sheppard, and Poirot continues to maintain it is an important clue. The inspector considers the possibility that Ralph went to see Roger Ackroyd, found him attacked and nearly dead, left quickly thinking he'd be blamed, but called the police in case Ackroyd could be saved.

Back at Dr. Sheppard's house, the doctor sees a few patients, and then goes to his workshop to repair a broken alarm clock. Poirot arrives to talk to Dr. Sheppard, and Caroline shows him to the workshop. It turns out Poirot would like Dr. Sheppard's help interviewing Miss Russell, an interview that will take place in Dr. Sheppard's surgery. Dr. Sheppard agrees.

In the interview, Poirot informs Miss Russell that Flora lied about seeing her uncle at 9:45. This time discrepancy means Charles Kent's alibi is no good. Miss Russell breaks down, admitting Kent is her illegitimate son who had been living in Canada and returned to England. A drug addict, he came to see her, asking for money. She met him in the summerhouse about 9:20 or 9:25, spoke with him, and gave him some cash. Poirot notes that Kent could not have been the person with Ackroyd at 9:30.

Analysis

The revelation that Flora did not go into her uncle's study at 9:45 on the night of the murder changes the case significantly. It is now possible Ackroyd was already dead by 9:45. The effects are explored through the comical reaction of Inspector Raglan. His confusion and need to go back through the facts of the case, trying to reassemble a coherent theory, reflect the reaction enthusiastic readers might have as they take in this new information. The inspector is still trying to make the facts fit his previous idea of the criminal. This way of thinking is a mistake he continually makes, and here it serves to highlight the wisdom of Poirot's method of suspecting everyone and doubting every unverified fact.

One interesting fact to note is Poirot's observation that Dr. Sheppard "should be an inventor by trade, not a doctor." This statement shows Poirot has observed Sheppard's aptitude for mechanical things, but it also suggests a deeper meaning. Had Dr. Sheppard been an inventor, rather than a doctor, he would not have stumbled upon Mrs. Ferrars's secret and been tempted to blackmail and murder. The "weakness" described in Chapter 17 would perhaps not have emerged.

These chapters develop the idea Poirot's commitment to the truth has both a benefit and a cost. The price of truth—an important theme in the novel—is featured in Chapter 19 not only as Poirot reveals Flora's secret thievery but as he reveals Major Blunt's love for Flora and Flora's real motive for defending Ralph. It was to Flora that he said, "You may wish that, after all, you had left it to the local police" before getting her assurance she wanted him to discover the whole truth.

The related theme of secrets is also developed in these chapters. As Miss Russell's secrets are revealed in Chapter 19, it becomes clear that secrets are often interconnected. They lead to other secrets and overlap with and reinforce other characters' secrets. Here Miss Russell's illegitimate child, kept secret, leads her to conceal information about the mysterious stranger at Fernly the night of the murder. Flora's original lie became an alibi for Charles Kent, among other people, so when her statement is proved false, Kent's alibi also falls apart. And so Poirot must untangle lies unrelated to the crime because even seemingly unconnected lies can hinder his ability to solve the case. If Flora's thievery had remained secret, her lie would have been believed and used as an alibi for Kent. If Kent's alibi had not disappeared, Miss Russell would not have had reason to divulge her own secret. The search for truth involves "all the truth," not mere parts of it.

2.6.24 Chapter 21—The Paragraph in the Paper

The next morning an announcement written by Hercule Poirot appears in the newspaper. It says Ralph Paton was found and arrested in Liverpool, where he was preparing to leave for America. As expected the news sparks a fresh round of speculation and gossip, led by Caroline. Caroline also reveals she saw a mysterious man arrive at Poirot's house, but when she asks Poirot about it, he says only, "Soon you must make his acquaintance."

Poirot asks Dr. Sheppard to come to his home that evening at 9:00 and to bring along Mrs. Ackroyd, Flora, Blunt, and Raymond. It will be a "little reunion," he says. Dr. Sheppard goes to Fernly to issue this invitation. There Mrs. Ackroyd tells him Flora is engaged to Hector Blunt.

Back at home, Dr. Sheppard is surprised by the arrival of Ursula Bourne, who is distraught and demands to see Poirot. Poirot goes to her at once, sympathetically saying, "It is not Ursula Bourne, is it, my child—but Ursula Paton? Mrs. Ralph Paton."

Chapter 22—Ursula's Story

Ursula Bourne reacts to Poirot's question with sobbing and admits she and Ralph have been secretly married. Having seen the paragraph in the paper, she wants Poirot to help save Ralph, who she insists is innocent. Poirot urges her to tell him everything, and she does. She is poor, but a gentlewoman by birth. When her father died, she had to make a living. Her sister, Mrs. Folliott, gave Ursula a reference so she could find a job as a parlourmaid. After obtaining employment at Fernly, she met Ralph Paton, fell in love, and married him. Ralph had told her they could make it public when he paid off his debts and had enough money to support her. However, getting out of debt was easier said than done, so when Ackroyd told Ralph he would pay his debts if he married Flora, he agreed. But Ursula was upset when she found out. She approached Roger Ackroyd and told him the truth—a conversation that did not go well and resulted in her preparing to leave his employ. Ursula and Ralph later met in the summerhouse. Poirot then asks what time the meeting took place. She says it was 9:33 when she met Ralph there, and they argued for about 10 minutes. Poirot assures her the newspaper announcement is false and asks her to trust him to sort everything out.

Analysis

In these chapters Poirot is seen working behind the scenes to push the case to a conclusion. He already has a "little idea" (a solution he believes is correct) and has scheduled a "reunion" for 9:00 that evening. He refuses to give away any of this solution until the time is ripe: "I much dislike to have to explain my little ideas until the time comes," he declares in Chapter 21. Agatha Christie fans will recognize an important part of her Hercule Poirot formula—the moment he assembles all the characters and solves the mystery in a dramatic fashion, giving a detailed explanation of each clue and each step in his process. This final meeting usually ends with Poirot identifying the real murderer and often contains more than one surprise, such as a secret identity or relationship. Before the "reunion," however, Poirot must wrap up his work of getting to the heart of all the concealed information. To that end, in Chapters 21 and 22 the strange behaviour of Ursula Bourne is finally explained. The reason for her decision to leave Ackroyd's employment was not rudeness, or papers in disarray, but her secret marriage to his stepson. Her nightly weeping stems from her heartbreak and worry about Ralph's safety as the primary suspect in the investigation.

Meanwhile, Poirot's arrangements for the reunion go on behind the scenes. He has a mysterious guest, whom Caroline saw arriving in the early morning with his face hidden. Poirot has said she will meet this mysterious guest when the time is right, suggesting he will play a part in the revelation of the mystery's solution.

The themes of secrets, the price of truth, and moral weakness are all touched upon in these chapters. Poirot again shows his ability to keep secrets and tell lies when convenient. He conceals the identity of his mysterious guest and conceals his "little idea." His paragraph in the paper was a lie. And Ursula Bourne's honesty with Ackroyd about her relationship with Ralph shows the price of truth, as revealing it brought her misery. Her upright and inherently honest disposition is contrasted with Ralph's "innate weakness" in grasping "at the easy, the immediate solution" of agreeing to marry Flora to get money from Ackroyd.

2.6.25 Chapter 23—Poirot's Little Reunion

Hercule Poirot tells Caroline to take care of Ursula Bourse because the young woman is needed at his "little reunion." Poirot recalls with nostalgia that his friend Hastings used to keep a written record of Poirot's cases. Dr. Sheppard admits he has actually been writing about the case all along and gives Poirot the first 20 chapters of his manuscript. After reading the manuscript, Poirot congratulates Dr. Sheppard on his modesty and reticence in keeping his "personality in the background" and for his meticulous approach to the case. He notes, "You have recorded all the facts faithfully and exactly—though you have shown yourself becomingly reticent as to your own share in them."

The two men and Ursula Bourne leave for Poirot's home, where the reunion will take place. Caroline is sad to be left out of the excitement, but Poirot tells her everyone at the reunion is a suspect, so she is not invited.

At his home, Poirot arranges the chairs and fusses over the lighting. The guests arrive. Poirot begins by introducing Ursula as Mrs. Ralph Paton, surprising everyone. He then begins to tell the story, beginning from the time he agreed to take the case. He outlines how he figured out there were two separate meetings in the summerhouse on the night of the murder. One was between Ursula Bourne and Ralph Paton. The meeting in the woods between Ralph and an unknown woman, plus the wedding ring inscribed "from R." and a date, rounded out the picture of secret spouses. Another meeting was between Charles Kent and Miss Russell.

Poirot mentions a most interesting aspect of the case: the question of who was with Roger Ackroyd at 9:30. It could not have been Ralph, who was in the summerhouse at the time. Charles Kent had already left. Poirot, therefore, considered the possibility no one was with Ackroyd at all. He points out that the words spoken by Ackroyd are not conversational. Rather they sound like dictation for a letter given to a secretary. He has his guests recall the young man who visited the previous Wednesday—from the Dictaphone company. Poirot reveals he asked the company if Ackroyd purchased one, and it turns out he did.

Raymond mentions it would have been better for Ralph if he'd come forward. As the group speculates about where Ralph might be, Poirot points dramatically to the doorway, where Ralph Paton is standing.

2.6.26 Chapter 24—Ralph Paton's Story

Hercule Poirot observes that even after he accused everyone of concealing information and several people came forward with their secrets, Dr. Sheppard did not. But Poirot figured out Dr. Sheppard must have met with Ralph and told him the case looked pretty bad for him. Dr. Sheppard admits he thought suspicion would fall on Ralph, whose money trouble and secret marriage would make him look guilty. He encouraged Ralph to go into hiding and helped him hide in a nursing home for the "mentally unfit."

Poirot comments quietly to Dr. Sheppard that his manuscript of the case was truthful "as far as it went." But "it did not go very far."

Ralph says he left the summerhouse about 9:45 and walked all over town, thinking about what to do next. Raymond notes this activity doesn't give him an alibi. Agreeing, Poirot explains that the real murderer needs to come forward to save Ralph from arrest. A message arrives, and Poirot reads it. Then he says he knows the identity of the murderer and intends to send it to Inspector Raglan in the morning.

Analysis

Poirot's preference for the dramatic is part of his character, which is an endearing mixture of self-satisfaction, comical fussiness, and intellectual brilliance. Some of Poirot's appeal is the way characters underestimate him because of his eccentricities. But even though the characters seem skeptical of Poirot's little party and amused at the way he fusses over seating arrangements and lighting choices, they are ultimately amazed at his ability. His dramatic flair—arranging lamps "to throw a clear light on the side of the room where the chairs were grouped ... leaving the other end of the room, where ... Poirot himself would sit, in a dim twilight"—is part of the Poirot charm. But it does not get in the way of his true purpose: "I discover all the little secrets," he says. "It is my business."

Poirot's sense of the dramatic increases the novel's suspense by creating a theatrical backdrop for the revelations to come. The seats are arranged as if the group of suspects is in fact an audience attending a show. Poirot sits in shadow so that he can step out as if from behind a curtain onto the stage. Poirot unfolds his narrative (inside Christie's narrative) with its own plot structure: rising action to climax to resolution.

As he begins the exposition of his little drama, he first hooks the audience with the revelation of Ursula Bourne's identity and a short explanation of the clues that led him to it. Then the rising action increases in intensity as he drops a bombshell: the presence of the Dictaphone that raises the question of Ackroyd being with another person at 9:30. He continues to build the case, as he reveals three outstanding questions that have led him to the truth: "the telephone call ... the footprints on the windowsill ... the hiding-place of Ralph Paton." The question of Ralph Paton's whereabouts becomes another important event in the rising action and is made all the more dramatic when Poirot produces the man himself, reuniting husband and wife. Poirot explains how he found Ralph, despite Dr. Sheppard's "discretion," that is, lying. Finally, Poirot comes to the climax of the evening as he declares he knows the identity of the murderer. He bows like an actor exiting the stage and leaves the audience to wonder.

While the characters in the novel are forced to be satisfied by this ending, Agatha Christie's audience would not be. And so the novel moves into its own climax.

2.6.27 Chapter 25—The Whole Truth

Hercule Poirot gestures to Dr. Sheppard to stay behind after the others leave. "What did you think of it all?" Poirot asks him. Dr. Sheppard replies he's not sure why Poirot didn't go to the police instead of giving an elaborate warning and wonders if Poirot really believes one of the people present at the reunion committed the murder. In answer, Poirot walks through the case to show that "all the facts point indisputably to one person." Two facts and one time discrepancy led him to the truth. The first fact is the telephone call, which Poirot deduced must have been made by an accomplice. The motive for the call had to be that Roger Ackroyd's body was discovered at a certain time, allowing the murderer to be there. Dr. Sheppard, Parker, Blunt, and Raymond were the only people present when the body was found. In addition, in his position as butler Parker would have been on the scene whenever the body was found and thus had no need of the phone call.

The pulled-out chair was the second fact. Pulled out, it would have been directly between the door and the window and positioned to hide completely the small table just in front of the window. Poirot concluded there must have been something on the table the murderer did not want seen. So the murderer moved the chair to block it from view and then shortly after the body was discovered, removed the mystery object and moved the chair back into position. The presence of the Dictaphone salesman gave Poirot the idea that the object on the table was a Dictaphone. Because no Dictaphone was found at the scene, the murderer must have removed it in some kind of receptacle.

Poirot suggests that by 9:30 Ackroyd was already dead, and a Dictaphone had been rigged up to play back his voice, possibly using some kind of mechanical timing device, like an alarm clock. Then Poirot comes to the matter of the footprints. He notes Ralph had two similar pairs of shoes—one pair that was being cleaned at the time of the crime (and was taken by the police) and one that the murderer must have taken to make the footprints. Ralph, then, was not wearing either of these but must have owned a third pair of shoes, perhaps a pair of boots—a fact Poirot had Caroline confirm.

Poirot sums up his analysis of the murderer. It had to be someone who was at the Three Boars that day, knew Ackroyd had bought a Dictaphone, had mechanical skill, had the opportunity to take the dagger from the silver table before Flora arrived, brought a receptacle for hiding the Dictaphone—such as a black bag—and was briefly alone in the study after the crime was discovered and while Parker was telephoning for the police. Dr. Sheppard, in fact.

2.6.28 Chapter 26—And Nothing but the Truth

Poirot tells Dr. Sheppard the time discrepancy in his story drew his attention. If it took five minutes or less to walk from the gates by the lodge to the house, and Dr. Sheppard left Fernly at 8:50, why was it 9:00 when Dr. Sheppard passed through the gates. Poirot suggests the doctor killed Roger Ackroyd before leaving at 8:50 and then faked the footprints, locked the study door from the inside, headed toward the gate, and passed it at 9:00. The Dictaphone, timed to begin at 9:30, would provide an alibi, for Sheppard was already home then.

Poirot then explains the motive: Dr. Sheppard was the one who blackmailed Mrs. Ferrars. When it was clear she had confessed to Ackroyd, the doctor killed him to hide his secret. The phone call was arranged to ensure Dr. Sheppard was on the scene immediately to retrieve the Dictaphone and place it into his black bag. Dr. Sheppard had asked a steward of an American ship to call him with some message about a patient. Dr. Sheppard pretended the call was about Ackroyd.

Poirot suggests Dr. Sheppard finish his manuscript with its former reticence and perhaps make use of an overdose of sleeping medicine in order to clear Ralph's name. Dr. Sheppard thanks Poirot for an entertaining evening and goes home.

Analysis

Chapter 25 provides the shocking plot twist that stunned the novel's original readers and brought the literary technique of the unreliable narrator into the crime drama mainstream. Like a doctor, a novel's narrator is usually assumed to be trustworthy, and readers often imagine the author as narrator, even when an identifiable character tells the story in first person. Modern readers may not be as trusting as those first reading the novel, to which this ending was both shocking and controversial. The unreliable narrator was not the convention in crime novels of the time.

Between the two chapters, Poirot lays bare Dr. Sheppard's crime and explains how large issues, such as the strange phone call, and small ones, such as Ralph's boots and five minutes unaccounted for, pointed him in the right direction—of the "whole truth." As Chapter 25 begins, Dr. Sheppard is still unsure where Poirot is going and seems to hope Poirot will name someone else. The doctor plays along, offering possible theories for various clues and gasping with shock when Poirot reveals that by 9:30 Ackroyd was already dead. Poirot, too, keeps up the game, telling Dr. Sheppard, "You take it for granted that what was heard at nine-thirty was Mr. Ackroyd's voice speaking into a Dictaphone." Dr. Sheppard knows full well this assumption is incorrect, and Poirot knows he knows. Eventually Poirot accuses Dr. Sheppard in no uncertain terms, and Dr. Sheppard begins to lose control. He notices his own voice has become "strange and forced" and tries to "rally" as Poirot lays out the evidence.

However, the meeting ends in a strangely unemotional way, as detective and murderer wish each other polite good nights, and Dr. Sheppard thanks Poirot for an interesting evening. The failure to show remorse even when confronted with the truth suggests Dr. Sheppard has little "moral fibre" left.

2.6.29 Chapter 27—Apologia

At 5:00 the following morning, Dr. Sheppard finishes his manuscript. In it, he explains a few more details about the crime: how he decided to substitute the dagger from the silver table for the one he'd brought along and how he knew he'd have to kill Roger Ackroyd as soon as he heard of Mrs. Ferrars's death. On the pretense of making a minor repair to the Dictaphone, Dr. Sheppard had brought it home and made a timing device for it in his workshop.

Dr. Sheppard points out the places in his written account of the murder where he omitted important details, such as "I hesitated with my hand on the door handle, looking back and wondering if there was anything I had left undone" and "I did what little had to be done."

Reflecting on Hercule Poirot's statement that there is "only one way out," Dr. Sheppard considers what drug to use. He decides on Veronol, the same drug Mrs. Ferrars took. He writes he is taking this way out because he doesn't want Caroline to know what he's done and believes Poirot will keep it from her. He ends the manuscript wishing "Hercule Poirot had never retired from work and come here to grow vegetable marrows."

Analysis

The final chapter serves as a confession, suicide note, and narrative analysis. Written in the present tense—"Five a.m. I am very tired—but I have finished my task"—it effectively brings readers into the mind of the murderer.

The need to keep up appearances gone, Dr. Sheppard reveals much more of his personality in this chapter. In a resigned way, he admits his weakness, as if he had little control over his own impulses: "I suppose I must have meant to murder him all along," he confesses. And, as Poirot postulated, an ordinary man with a weakness might, in the right circumstances, become a murderer. Unfortunately, being a doctor enabled Sheppard to know secrets and closely observe human nature. Learning Mrs. Ferrars's secret, he was unable to resist the temptation this knowledge posed. He also knew enough of human nature to see clearly that Mrs. Ferrars probably confessed the truth before killing herself.

Although he accepts his weakness, Dr. Sheppard's arrogance displays itself in this final chapter. He discusses how he felt "quite satisfied" with his perfect execution of his careful plan and expresses pride in his writing abilities: "I am rather pleased with myself as a writer." His pride stems from his careful word choice, which revealed some of the truth but carefully omitted the whole truth. Thus, "I did what little had to be done" meant hiding the Dictaphone and moving the chair. However, bits of truth were not what Hercule Poirot was after. Poirot was interested in "all the truth"—the whole truth. And that is what he found, to the disappointment of Dr. Sheppard.

2.7 SYMBOLS IN AGATHA CHRISTIE, *THE MURDER OF ROGER ACKROYD*

2.7.1 Mah Jong

The game of mah jong, played by Dr. Sheppard and Caroline along with Miss Gannett and Colonel Carter, functions as a symbol of strategy—of both Hercule Poirot and Dr. Sheppard. Like a game of mah jong, in which tiles turned face down are revealed during play by turning them face up, Poirot reveals the hidden secrets of the characters. His revelations are systematic and strategic, as if he were assembling pairs of tiles in mah jong. But the game also works as a symbol of Dr. Sheppard's well-executed strategy for committing murder and getting away with it. During the evening, Dr. Sheppard is startled to realize he has "The Perfect Winning—going mah jong on one's original hand." At this point in the novel, readers have no reason to think he will be found out as the murderer. He has a solid alibi, and no one seems to suspect him. His feelings of triumph over the "Perfect Winning" channel his feeling of having arranged everything so perfectly as to keep him beyond suspicion.

2.7.2 Letters and Manuscripts

Through two prominent examples in the novel, the written word is shown to have the ability to both hide truth and reveal secrets.

First, the letter written from Mrs. Ferrars to Roger Ackroyd represents writing's ability to reveal secrets, as it identifies her blackmailer and solidifies her own confession of murder and suicide. Yet the secrets contained in the letter are easily hidden again by destroying it. Second, the book itself is a manuscript written by Dr. Sheppard, which he intended to publish at some point "as the history of one of Hercule Poirot's failures" and which becomes his confession and suicide note. In the final chapter Dr. Sheppard demonstrates how his written words could misrepresent the truth. He notes the sentence "I did what little had to be done!" which is included in the original account of finding the body. The reader is meant to assume he did what doctors do—examine the body. But in his confession he explains how these words are misleading. He actually did what needed to be done to execute his plan for murder, which "was quite little—just to shove the Dictaphone into my bag and push back the chair against the wall in its proper place."

2.8 MOTIFS IN AGATHA CHRISTIE, *THE MURDER OF ROGER ACKROYD*

2.8.1 Gossip

In the village of King's Abbot, Dr. Sheppard tells readers, residents' "hobbies and recreations can be summed up in the one word, 'gossip.'" This description proves apt over the course of the novel. Juicy news travels quickly from servant to servant, from elderly lady to elderly lady, and along all paths in between. Dr. Sheppard often finds some piece of information he thought was known only to him has already traveled along the gossip paths to his sister Caroline Sheppard or to Hercule Poirot. The giving and receiving of gossip becomes a narrative device in the story—one by which Poirot learns important details of the case and one by which readers follow along with new clues and discoveries. Most important, however, is that the reckless curiosity, speculation, suspicion, and occasional moments of truth of the gossiping villagers reflect and validate those feelings experienced by the reader. This chain of gossip, or information spreading, has the effect of drawing the reader into the novel as one of the villagers, not as an outsider.

2.8.2 Eavesdropping

Eavesdropping is an important motif in the novel, allowing Hercule Poirot to learn information character's would prefer to keep hidden. In a number of instances clues are revealed when someone overhears a conversation, or part of one. Caroline Sheppard overhears Ralph Paton talking to a woman she can't see but who turns out to be Ursula Bourne, his secret wife. Poirot and Dr. Sheppard overhear Major Blunt and Flora Ackroyd in a conversation in which Flora admits her need for money, and Blunt is clearly in love with Flora.

Eavesdropping also provides plot points and leads to important misdirection. One important example is Parker's eavesdropping outside Ackroyd's door the night of the murder. When he is caught obviously eavesdropping, he becomes a suspect—the stereotypical crime-novel butler. Not until much later does he admit he was eavesdropping in the hope of finding out some information to use for blackmail. And characters' overhearing of Ackroyd's Dictaphone playing back his own recorded voice provides the false alibi Dr. Sheppard needs to escape suspicion.

2.9 THEMES IN AGATHA CHRISTIE, *THE MURDER OF ROGER ACKROYD*

2.9.1 Secrets Breed Secrets

The novel begins and ends with secrets. The first event in the narrative is the suicide of Mrs. Ferrars—a suicide prompted by her secrets. She was guilty of murdering her husband and was being blackmailed by someone who discovered her unpunished crime. Ralph Paton is secretly engaged to Flora and even more secretly married to Ursula Bourne. Flora secretly stole money from her uncle. Miss Russell keeps her illegitimate son, Charles Kent, a secret. Parker hides the fact that he previously blackmailed an employer and was considering blackmailing Ackroyd as well. Major Blunt is secretly in love with Flora. Yet Dr. Sheppard keeps the biggest secret of all: concealing his guilt from the reader as well as from Hercule Poirot and the police. However, only some of these secrets are relevant to the murder of Roger Ackroyd. But because people are keeping so many secrets, their deliberate concealment—which sometimes includes lying—poses formidable obstacles to Poirot's search for the truth.

Unfortunately for all secret-keepers, Poirot is adept at ferreting out concealed information. Poirot's investigation is hindered by the commitment of the characters to keep their skeletons in the closet, but Poirot perseveres. When he first takes the case, he states, "Everyone ... has something to hide" (Chapter 7). Yet later he observes "it is not easy to hide things from Hercule Poirot." After spending time and effort hunting down answers to questions unrelated to the murder, Poirot finally gives a handful of people the opportunity to come clean. "Each one of you has something to hide" he says to those assembled (Chapter 12). One by one, the characters give up their secrets or have them revealed by Poirot.

Not only do the characters keep secrets, large and small, but secrets seem to breed secrets. Mrs. Ackroyd secretly attempted to find out the terms of Roger Ackroyd's will but only because, she says, he was secretive about money in the first place: "In dear Roger's place, I should have not objected to revealing the provisions of my will. But men are so secretive. One is forced to adopt little subterfuges" (Chapter 14). Mrs. Ferrars's secret crime leads to Dr. Sheppard's secret crime, and Dr. Sheppard commits suicide partly because he wants to keep his guilty secret from his sister Caroline.

2.9.2 The Price of Truth

Although Hercule Poirot is interested in bringing the guilty to justice, he is even more a seeker of truth. When he is on a case, his pursuit of the truth is relentless and single minded. Poirot rather comically compares himself to a hound following a scent to describe this aspect of his personality: "The good dog, he does not leave the scent" (Chapter 7). And he isn't after truth just because it is his job, or for the satisfaction of solving a puzzle, although these are certainly among his motivations. He finds the truth beautiful, elevating it to a work of art rather than something more akin to scientific knowledge. In Chapter 12 Poirot tells Flora quite seriously, "I mean to arrive at the truth. The truth, however ugly in itself, is always curious and beautiful to the seeker after it."

Hercule Poirot might love the truth beyond all else, but the novel demonstrates truth has a dangerous side. If one discovers the truth, one might regret it. Poirot tells Flora that in the end she may wish she had left the case to the police rather than bring him into the matter—implying the police are inept and will be unsuccessful. When she insists she does want the truth, he responds ominously, hoping she "will not regret those words." The characters also seem to agree generally that women in particular need to be shielded from the truth. The police suggest delaying telling Flora her uncle is dead because she will be too upset to answer questions. Indeed, when they do tell her, she faints. In Chapter 10, Flora's mother prefers to believe Ackroyd's death was so dreadful she "can't help feeling that it must have been an accident of some kind." She doesn't want to think it could have been murder. And Dr. Sheppard commits suicide in part because he doesn't want Caroline to find out what really happened: "I should not like Caroline to know. She is fond of me, and then, too, she is proud."

Finally, the truth can be a weapon against the secretive and guilty. Once Poirot knows the truth, he uses it to force the murderer to confess and even encourage the murderer to end his own life. Gathering all the suspects together in Chapter 24, he announces, "Tomorrow the truth goes to Inspector Raglan." And when he confronts Dr. Sheppard with the whole truth, Dr. Sheppard sees, as Poirot puts it, there is only "one way out." Ultimately the truth Poirot discovers leads the way to justice.

2.9.3 Moral Weakness

Throughout the novel, individuals' moral failures and bad choices are blamed on weakness of character, or moral weakness. Ralph, known as a wild young man, has his poor life choices blamed on his mother passing down a moral weakness, a "victim of heredity. He had not inherited his mother's fatal propensity for drink, but nevertheless he had in him a strain of weakness." Flora, who knows Ralph well, refers to this weakness when she asks Hercule Poirot to investigate and clear Ralph of suspicion: "Ralph may be weak," she explains. "He may have done foolish things ... but he wouldn't murder anyone" (Chapter 7). In Chapter 17, Ralph's weakness is again the topic of conversation as Dr. Sheppard notes the young man's "weak nature ... But not a vicious one." Ultimately

Ralph's weakness comes through in his relationships with money and with women. He is constantly in need of money, likely a result of poor self-discipline and self-indulgence. He decides to marry Flora to stay in his uncle's good graces (and his will). Poirot describes Ralph's pattern of poor decisions as a product of "innate weakness" and desire for "the easy, the immediate solution" (Chapter 22).

Ralph and his mother are not the only ones described as having weak character. As she admits to stealing her uncle's money, Flora also attributes both Ralph's and her own bad decisions to moral weakness. Indeed "that's what brought us together ... I understood him ... I'm the same underneath ... We're weak, miserable, despicable things" (Chapter 19).

Dr. Sheppard, too, shares this moral weakness, which leads to his becoming a blackmailer, then a murderer. Caroline brings up her brother's weakness when she tells Poirot the doctor is "weak as water, if I weren't about to look after him." Later in that chapter, Poirot poses a hypothetical situation revolving around this kind of moral weakness—describing it as a tendency to give in to temptation when one is placed in certain situations. He tells a little story about an ordinary man with no "murder in his heart" but with a "strain of weakness—deep down." If that man faced difficulties or came upon a secret, he might realize his opportunity to make a great deal of money and so become a blackmailer. Of course, Poirot's hypothetical story is not hypothetical at all: it is Dr. Sheppard's own story.

2.10 CRITIQUE ON AGATHA CHRISTIE, *THE MURDER OF ROGER ACKROYD*

2.10.1 Relying on the Unreliable: *The Murder of Roger Ackroyd*

The Murder of Roger Ackroyd was Agatha Christie's sixth novel, first published in the United Kingdom in 1926. Considered as "Christie's masterpiece", it embodies the most daring, witty and controversial use of the detective story genre conventions by any writer of her time and thus became one of the landmarks of mystery writing. Great part of its innovation lies in the fact that the narrator of the whole story, Dr. Sheppard, turns out to be the murderer. This identification between narrator and murderer14 carried out by a talented and unforeseen plot-twist will make Sheppard's unreliability as narrator the crucial and (i)logical path in reader's interpretation of events.

In their *Dictionary of British Mystery Writers* (1989), Stanley and Benstock highlight the fact that "even though this narratological device may seem to flout the conventions of the genre, in fact it merely takes advantage of their existence to create a puzzle that is a peak of the genre's art" (74).

The narrator of this novel and the key figure of my analysis is Dr. Sheppard, a new acquaintance of Hercule Poirot and his neighbour in the city were the action is set, the fictional little town of King's Abbot. The story is told completely in his words, and Christie manages herself to make Sheppard's narrative discourse in such a way that nothing he says is untrue. Contrarily, in a second reading of the novel readers would realize that the voice we are listening to does not even tell a lie; he just disguises and hides the truth all through a smart mixture of words, actions and thoughts that make him look the most innocent and loyal character from a vast and diverse range of suspects the author offers in her novel.

In this way, although the author leaves a number of subtle clues and nods to the reader to make us figure out the murderer's identity, these remain secret and unnoticed and will eventually come to light when we begin to distrust the narrative voice we are listening to.

As I will analyse in the subsequent sections, several examples are found throughout the narration that contribute to the reader's trust in the narrator. One of the most outstanding and explicit ones is the emphasis the author gives on the positive traits of Sheppard's characterisation. For instance, a clear case is found in his respected and appreciated position in the small town due to his job as a doctor, and consequently his social status, high morals and his belonging to the upper-middle classes.

The way Christie describes both Poirot and Dr. Sheppard also enriches the readers' confusion and provides them with another reason to fall in Sheppard's trap, since it forces us to wonder about the stranger's identity. In fact, it becomes Poirot, whose description is told from the apparent reliability of the doctor's perspective, and not the murderer who is portrayed as being the peculiar outsider. Thus, Poirot's weird appearance, his foreignness, the way he talks, and his unfamiliarity for Kings Abbot's inhabitants all define his portrayal.

In *The Gentle Art of Murder*, the American Professor Earl F. Bargainnier proposes an interesting comparison between Captain Arthur Hastings and Dr. James Sheppard. According to him, Christie began by following Conan Doyle, with Hastings as Watson to Poirot's Holmes. As a dense narrator, Hastings is reliable only as to facts—what is seen and what Poirot tells him. In like manner, he represents an unreliable character as to the interpretation of those facts. Sheppard shares this unreliability as well as the same as he represents the character that accompanies the Belgian detective in his crime investigation, thus transcribing every step and the evolution of the murder in his own way. Then, Sheppard's role as Hercule Poirot's assistant, together with his apparent desire to solve the mystery and to uncover clues rather than dispel us from them, also represents two of the multiple narrative strategies Christie uses in her novel to divert the reader's suspicious and to create a kind of honesty facade recreated by his responsibility both as narrator and as character.

Agatha Christie's decision to portray the narrator as a most reliable character and later to make us realise that it has been the main element of our deception makes *The Murder of Roger Ackroyd* an original and innovative work. This subverts the previous narrative device that perceived the narrator as the omnipresent voice who, eager to discover the truth, was always right and "who takes the reader by hand from the first page and accompanied him through the comforting English environment, in which all people seem incapable of doing harm to others". (GUTKOWSKILY 2011: 52).

We will now analyse the narrative entity in Christie's novel following the theoretical principles that Rimmon-Kenan proposes. In terms of the narrative level, the narrator of *The Murder* of *Roger Ackroyd* is intradiegetic, meaning he does not occupy a 'superior' position in the story he narrates, but rather he is a diegetic character in the first narrative who tells other's characters stories and concerns. As far as the extent of his participation in the story, our narrator is a homodiegetic one telling his narration in first person and he is also what R. Kenan has coined "intradiegetic-homodiegetic" (autodiegetic in Genette's terminology) since he not only actively takes part in the story, but he can be even considered as its protagonist together with the detective. As regards the degree of participation in a story, Dr. Sheppard is an intrusive voice since he is constantly involved throughout the action and his interventions are very relevant because they reveal great amounts of information about the central enigma that surrounds the story. As happens with Pip, the narrative voice in Charles Dickens' *Great Expectations* (1860), Dr. Sheppard in Christie's novel is not, in principle, an omniscient narrator as such, however the detachment and position towards the story he narrates is highly authoritarian, since he knows everything about it, like the extradiegetic narrator (intradiegetic opposed narrative level): obviously, he knows the solution to the final enigma, he has knowledge of simultaneous events happening in different places and in different times, he is aware of the characters' innermost thoughts and feelings, etc.

As mentioned in the introduction, in traditional detective stories the reader feels fulfilled when he reaches the solution of the initial enigma using his logical capabilities; the author, contrarily, has a kind of "responsibility" to astonish him with an end that is unexpected but plausible at the same time. But, how can these two opposite requirements of making up a plausible but misleading world be combined? As Gutkowski points out, "the trick lies in the capability of the author to create, through a cunning narrator, a deviation from reader's expectations" (51). In the previous section I tried to draw my attention in the fact that having an unreliable narrator does not strictly mean having a liar, but there are many other factors that contribute to that assimilation. Henceforth, I start the analysis of the main narrative techniques and strategies Christie uses to deceive readers by leading us to a false conclusion, to "rely on the unreliable".

From the factors and characteristics that shape narrative unreliability, the strategies I am going to focus on are those related with the language he uses and the way he uses it, paying attention to double meanings and multiple interpretation of his speeches, the ellipsis, the changes and slips in the narrative discourse, and the way his characterization contributes to his reliability.

2.10.2 Opposition of two methods of reaching the truth

In *The Murder of Roger Ackroyd*, as mystery fiction, the truth turns out to be the main goal. However, in this case Agatha Christie manages to make this task a challenge, both for the characters and for the reader, so, throughout the novel, she proposes a dual way to reach it. Thus, one of the most delicate and facetious narrative strategies the author uses in her novel is the sharp and antithetical sense that is provided by the two characters that seem most interested in finding out the murderer's identity: Hercule Poirot and Caroline Sheppard. With this narrative approach, what Christie is eventually achieving is, first, contributing to the reader's discovering the murderer, and secondly, it makes the figure of the narrator even more trustworthy and reliable for the readership.

The Belgian detective firmly follows an evidence-based methodology, there is always a reason in his actions: "I admit nothing that is not-proved!" (RA 234). Accordingly, he gradually advances the investigation by tying up loose ends, considering each of the circumstances of the case, interviewing the characters involved in the drama, until in a final blow he invariably gathers all the suspects and eventually unmasks the murderer. Sometimes, and as happens with our novel, his ethical standards are not orthodox enough, and he does not hesitate to push a man to commit suicide: "I am willing to give you the chance of another way out. There might be, for instance, an overdose of a sleeping draught. You comprehend me?" (RA 307). We are, then, clearly shown some of Poirot's deductive systems: thus, once he has examined the characters appearing in the story, he takes a series of notes about each of them in a systematic way: motive, alibi, contradictory evidences and suspicious circumstances: "Everything is simple, if you arrange the facts methodically" (RA 93). Unlike Poirot, a city man who likes to move in urban environments and hates the countryside because of its excessive heat (and cold), Caroline Sheppard is an elderly woman who lives in a small town, King's Abbot. Her weaknesses are a small garden, and her long conversations with friends and neighbours, who have been living in the village almost as many years as she has. Despite being a little "nosy" Miss Sheppard is a nice lady and also very intelligent.

In comparison with his sister, the doctor at first sight appears to be the rational, down-to-earth and sensible part of the family, which makes us more easily get carried away by what he tells. However, although James also tries to earn the reader's trust by means of his displays of affection towards his sister, we eventually come to realize that another reason for this abhorring Caroline's talent for gossip and rumours lies in the fact that she may stumble upon the truth: "it is all wrong that Caroline should arrive at the truth simply by a kind of inspired guesswork" (RA 6). In fact, there are times he has to face some dangerous situations because of Caroline's ability to make uncomfortable comments about the crime, all of them on the right track for solving the enigma: "I saw the opportunity of further questioning gleaming from her eye. I saw the chance to escape into the garden" (RA 20).

At the end of the novel, we realise that what he has feared most throughout the course of the investigation, has been that Caroline may have discovered him: "My greatest fear all through has been Caroline. I have fancied she might guess." (RA 311). Though Caroline is a standard character of the sort that could have been treated stereotypically, she is portrayed so carefully that she takes on a vivid life of her own: "He (Poirot) said I had the makings of a born detective in me- and a wonderful psychological insight into human nature" (RA 145). Caroline's intuitive spirit was what encouraged Christie to create a female detective who devoted her intuition in rural environment. It is said that Caroline Sheppard was the seed that eventually gave life to the acclaimed and adorable Miss. Marple.

The same antithetical situation we see in the Sheppard's siblings can be extrapolated in the two main detectives that build Christie's literary output: Hercule Poirot and Miss Marple. Thus, whereas the Belgian detective is an embodiment of many eccentricities, sometimes make him seem unreal and a kind of mental superhero, the lovely Miss Marple has a credibility touch derived in part from her predecessor, Caroline Sheppard, and in part from being modelled to some extent on Christie's grandmother.

Where Poirot works on logic and reasoning, Miss Marple works essentially on intuition. She depends for her success on five qualities (STANLEY and BENSTOCK 1989: 75): an extensive knowledge of people garnered over years; her belief that gossip is true more often than not; her intuition; a gift for making connections between people's minor misdemeanours and their capacity for greater ones; and finally her consistent, pessimistic lack of trust, which prevents her from taking any one she meets at face value.

UNIT III
LGBT Fiction

The LGBT community or GLBT community, commonly referred to as the gay community, is a loosely defined grouping of lesbian, gay, bisexual, and transgender (LGBT) and LGBT-supportive people, organizations, and subcultures, united by a common culture and social movements. These communities generally çelebrate pride, diversity, individuality, and sexuality. LGBT activists and sociologists see LGBT community-building as an antidote to heterosexism, homophobia, biphobia, transphobia, sexualism, and conformist pressures thought to exist in the larger society.

Homosexuality is a feeling or desire involving sexual attraction to people of one's own sex. In common usage, the term homosexual is used to refer to both same-sex oriented males and females. The word 'Gay' is often used as a synonym for male homosexual behaviour while the term 'Lesbian' is referred to a woman who is sexually attracted to another woman. In terms of sexual orientation of individuals, a bisexual person is sexually attracted to both men and women. Transgender is another category who is neither a complete man nor a complete woman and are called 'Hijras' in Hindi and jovially referred to as 'neither here nor there'. Gays and lesbians emphasise the cultural, social and identity aspects of homosexuality.

Sexologists and sociologists are becoming increasingly aware that society cannot be divided into compartments such as homosexual and heterosexual, gay and lesbian, male and female. There is an entire sexual spectrum out there including bisexuals, transsexuals and transgendered people. In fact, sexuality is turning out to be a complex mix of biology, behaviour and identity.

Although homosexuality has a long history in India, the gay movement is relatively nascent. Until recently, most homosexuals in India did not have many social and cultural avenues to express their sexuality. This is changing now, thanks to greater awareness and education. Many men of homosexual orientation are choosing to identify themselves as 'gay' and embracing a lifestyle that resists marriage and other conventions of an otherwise heterosexual society. They remain largely invisible and form networks that shy away from the public glare for fear of social and familial backlash.

The word 'Gay' is associated with several stereotypical images and ideas, like the way they act and dress. Thus, whether correct or not, we have a certain awareness of gays in our consciousness, like feminine men wearing tight, leopard prints. However, there is no real image of lesbians in our consciousness. They are denied any kind of identity and it could just as well be that they don't exist at all. This is another kind of silencing that we see taking place. Lesbian women cannot speak for themselves, because according to society, they don't exist at all. Female sexuality has always been as taboo-something not to be discussed, something which is a matter of the "domestic sphere". This new angle to female sexuality will obviously be hard to accept. Furthermore, this also punctures male supremacy as the need for the males get rejected here. Women are forcibly married off to men so as to "cure" them. They are suffocated by ideological discourses and glorified expectations of women as custodians of "morals, tradition and culture".

With this environment and backdrop, the Lesbian movement has crawled along with the gay initiatives for its sustenance and growth. For a better understanding of the different facets of homosexuality, there is a need to visit the conceptual, cultural, social and legal aspect of homosexuality as well as to ascertain its acceptance status in various countries.

3.1 CONCEPTUAL AND HISTORICAL ASPECTS

The shift in the understanding of homosexuality from sin, crime and pathology to a normal variant of human sexuality occurred in the late 20th century. The American Psychiatric Association, in 1973, and the World Health Organisation in 1992, officially accepted its normal variant status. Many countries have since decriminalised homosexual behaviour and some have recognised same-sex civil unions and marriage.

The new understanding was based on studies that documented a high prevalence of same-sex feelings and behaviour in men and women, its prevalence across cultures and among almost all non-human primate species. Investigations using psychological tests could not differentiate heterosexual from homosexual orientation. Research also demonstrated that people with homosexual orientation did not have any objective psychological dysfunction or impairments in judgement, stability and vocational capabilities. Psychiatric, psychoanalytic, medical and mental health professionals now consider homosexuals as a normal variation of human sexuality.

Human sexuality is complex. The acceptance of the distinction between desire, behaviour and identity acknowledges the multidimensional nature of sexuality. The fact that these dimensions may not always be congruent in individuals suggests complexity of the issues. Medicine and psychiatry employ terms like homosexuality, heterosexuality and trans-sexuality to encompass all related issues, while current social usage argues for lesbian, gay, bisexual and transgender (LGBT), which focuses on identities.

The prevalence of homosexuality is difficult to estimate for many reasons, including the associated stigma and social repression; the unrepresentative samples surveyed and the failure to distinguish desire, behaviour and identity. The figures vary between age groups, regions and cultures.

Anthropologists have documented significant variations in the organisation and meaning of same-sex practices across cultures and changes within particular societies over time. The universality of same-sex expression coexists with variations in its meaning and practice across cultures. However, recent research argues that psychological and interpersonal events throughout the life cycle explain sexual orientation. It is unlikely that a unique set of characteristics or a single pathway will explain all adult homosexuality.

The argument that homosexuality is a stable phenomenon is based on the consistency of same-sex attractions, the failure of attempts to change and the lack of success with treatments to alter orientation. There is a growing realisation that homosexuality is not a single phenomenon and that there may be multiple phenomena within the construct of homosexuality.

Anti-homosexual attitudes, once considered the norm, have changed over time in many social and institutional settings in the west. However, heterosexism, which idealises heterosexuality, considers it the norm, denigrates and stigmatises all non-heterosexual forms of behaviour, identity, relationships and communities, is also common.

In addition to the challenges of living in a predominantly heterosexual world, the diversity within people with homosexual orientation results in many different kinds of issues. Sex, gender, age, ethnicity and religion add to the complexity of issues faced. The stages of the life cycle (childhood, adolescence, middle and old age), family and relationships present diverse concerns. In most circumstances, the psychiatric issues facing gay, lesbian and bisexual people are similar to those of the general population. However, the complexities in these identities require tolerance, respect and a nuanced understanding of sexual matters. Clinical assessments should be detailed and go beyond routine labelling and assess different issues related to lifestyle choices, identity, relationships and social supports. Helping people understand their sexuality and providing support for living in a predominantly heterosexual world is mandatory. People with homosexual orientation face many hurdles including the conflicts in acknowledging their homosexuals feelings, the meaning of disclosure and the problems faced in coming out.

Gay-affirmative psychotherapies have been developed, which help people cope with the awareness of being same-sex oriented and with social stigmatization. There is no evidence for the effectiveness of sexual conversion therapies. Such treatments also raise ethical questions, In fact, there is evidence that such attempts may cause more harm than good, including depression and sexual dysfunction. However, faith-based groups and counsellors pursue such attempts at conversion using yardsticks, which do not meet scientific standards. Clinicians should keep the dictum "first do no harm" in mind. Physicians should provide medical service with compassion and respect for human dignity for all people irrespective of their sexual orientation.

There are a few small case series in psychiatric literature detailing homosexuality in males and its treatment with aversion therapy. It places the responsibility on the individuals without critically examining the social context, which is stigmatising and repressing. The medicalization of sexuality and the political impact of labelling and its role in social control are often discounted. The ubiquitous use of disease models for mental disorders is rarely questioned.

There is a dearth of Indian psychiatric literature that has systematically investigated issues related to homosexuality. Data on prevalence, emotional problems faced and support groups and clinical services available are sparse.

Research into these issues is crucial for increasing our understanding of the local and regional context related to sexual behaviour, orientation and identity in India.

Despite medicine and psychiatry arguing that homosexual orientation is a normal variant of human sexuality, mental health fraternity and the government in India are yet to take a clear stand on the issues to change widely prevalent prejudices in society. The fraternity needs to acknowledge the need for research into the context-specific issues facing LGBT people in India. The teaching of sexuality to medical and mental health professional needs to be perceptive to the issues faced by people with different sexual orientations and identities. Clinical services for people with such issues and concerns need to be sensitive to providing holistic care. A positive and a non-judgemental attitude will go a long way in relieving distress. Professional societies need to increase awareness of these issues, transfer knowledge and skill and provide opportunities to increase the confidence and competence of mental health workers in helping people with different sexual orientations and identity. Psychiatrists and mental health professionals need to be educated about the human rights and possible abuses. The emphasis should not just be on education but also on a change of attitude.

The American Psychological Association is urging mental health professionals not to shun the assumption that gays and lesbians can change their sexual orientation through therapy or other treatments, insisting that it will not work.

A new resolution adopted by the group states that parents guardians, young, people, and their families would also be wise to avoid sexual orientation treatments that portray homosexuality as a mental illness or developmental disorder.

The group adds that people should instead seek psychotherapy, social support, and educational services "that provide accurate information on sexual orientation and sexuality, increase family and school support and reduce rejection of sexual minority youth.".

Researchers have not firmly concluded to what extent homosexuality is genetically inherited, but many think it is a mix of nature and nurture.

However, a number of studies have suggested the involvement of genes in homosexuality. Glassgold said that though conflicting research on the therapy issue is cited by some, studies have found that "sexual orientation was unlikely to change due to efforts designed for this purpose."

Based on this review, according to a statement issued by the APA, the task force suggested that mental health professionals better avoid misrepresenting the efficacy of sexual orientation change efforts (SOCE) when providing assistance to people distressed about their own or other sexual orientation.

The task force examined 83 peer-reviewed journal articles on the topic of SOCE written from 1960 to 2007, along with other recent studies on the psychology of sexual orientation.

'Therapy can't turn gays and lesbians straight'.

Analysing the studies conducted in the past, the task force could not reach any conclusion on whether SOCE is effective, or on whether the methods might be safe or harmful.

Without such information, psychologists cannot predict the impact of these treatments and need to be very cautious, given that some qualitative research suggests the potential for harm. Practitioners can assist clients through therapies that do not attempt to change sexual orientation, imposing a specific identity outcome.

The Task force also identified some clients seeking to change their sexual orientation may be in distress because of a conflict between their sexual orientation and religious beliefs.

It suggested that licensed mental health care providers treating such clients help them "explore possible life paths that address the reality of their sexual orientation, reduce the stigma associated with homosexuality, respect the client's religious beliefs, and consider possibilities for a religiously and spiritually meaningful and rewarding life."

Homosexuality as a cultural phenomenon is not new. Sappho, a Greek poet and teacher of arts, who lived between 630 and 612 BC in the Greek city state of Lesbos, was known for her preference for women and had affairs with several of her female protégés at her Centre for Arts. Yet she was highly respected, both for her artistic sensibility and her poetry, which combined reference to lesbians love. Plato extolled her as the tenth Muse and the coins of her times were embossed with her image.

It was with the advent of Christianity that homosexuality came to be stigmatized and segregated to the borders of the mainstream sexuality. The meta narrative of Christianity demonized homosexuality. Later, in the early twentieth century, the sexological discourses pathologised it in the West. The Biblical account of destruction of Sodom and Gomorrah is well known across the Christian world. Sexologists, such as, Karl Westphall, Karl Ulrichs, Richard von Krafft-Ebbing and Havelock Ellis considered homosexuality as inversion. Gays and lesbians were, therefore, scorned, discriminated against and victimized. Surprisingly, therefore, lesbians and gays remained 'closeted', and there was hardly a gay/lesbian literature.

Since the middle of twentieth century, the attitudes towards homosexuality have undergone a change. Gayism/lesbianism has not only been de-bounded and decriminalized but also a large number of countries, such as, Netherlands, South Africa, Canada, Hungary, Iceland, Belgium, Spain, Germany, France, Mexico, a few federal units of the United States and several others have legalized gay marriage.

In India the situation has been paradoxical. The stigmatization and circumvention of homosexuality are considered of the colonial import. So is homosexuality—this is what the Right wing forces believe. According to them, homosexuality is alien to Indian culture and is a source of moral corruption. The British colonial government introduced Article 377 in the Penal Code in 1868 criminalizing homosexuality and laying down stringent punishment of fine and/or life imprisonment for sexual acts against 'the order of nature'. Earlier than that in Indian culture, lesbianism and gayism were acceptable forms of sexuality—the most ancient sculptural art of Khajuraho caves and the architecture of some of the Hindu temples in Orissa bear testimony. Influenced by colonial thinking, the non-heteronormative sexual identities came to be objected and outlawed in India.

The cultural environment has, therefore, been hostile to gays and lesbians in India. They are afraid to cross to boundaries and 'come out' for fear of physical violence, and social opprobrium and there is not much literature dealing with same-sex love. Any cultural expression of lesbianism/gayism engenders anger and retaliation, especially among the Right wing forces, who display abhorrence and complete intolerance of homosexuality, in art and literature. It must also be mentioned here whether in films or literary works, the representation of gays/lesbians projects them as borderline bugs, criminals, mentally sick, or deprived of heterosexual coition.

In the nineties, the issue of identity assumed great importance both in the realm of lesbians and gay theory and the Movement. The idea of biological essentialism was found to be limiting and exclusionary as other nonheteronormative sexualities like transgenders, transsexuals, hijras, kothis, and panthis, who are women trapped in men's bodies were ignored. Therefore, the overarching umbrella term 'Queer' came to be used for all these categories. Judith Butler's theory of 'performativity', using post-structuralist tools of Jacques Derrida, Michel Foucualt and Jacques Lacan, conceptualized gender/sexuality as 'performative, that is, a role performed by the subject, according to her/his choice which resulted in (i) pluralism of gender identities and (ii) considering gender/sex as fluid and a matter of choice. Its effect can be seen in India where the Gay Pride Marches in Delhi, Kolkata, Bangalore and Chennai include lesbians, gays, hijras, transgenders, and others who come together as 'Queer' to forge coalitional politics against the homophobic Indian society.

Homosexuality has an ancient history in India. Ancient scriptures like *Rig-Veda* which dates back around 1500 BC and sculptures and vestiges depict sexual acts between women as revelations of a feminine world where sexuality was based on pleasure and fertility. The description of homosexual acts in the *Kamasutra*, the Harems of young boys kept by Muslim Nawabs and Hindu Aristocrats, male homosexuality in the medieval Muslim history, evidences of sodomy in the Tantric rituals are some historical evidences of same sex relationship.

However, these experiences started losing their significance with the advent of Vedic Brahmanism and, later on, of British Colonialism. Giti claims that Aryan invasions dating to 1500 B.C. began to suppress homosexuality through the emerging dominance of patriarchy. In the *Manusmriti* there are references to punishments like loss of caste, heavy monetary fines and strokes of the whip for gay and lesbian behaviour. Manu's specifications of more severe punishments for married women can suggest either a wide prevalence of such relationships among married women or a greater acceptance of these practices among unmarried women. In either cases, these references point to the tensions in the norms of compulsory heterosexuality prescribed by Brahmanical partite. Both sexual systems coexisted, despite fluctuations in relative repression and freedom, until British colonialism when the destruction of images of homosexual expression and sexual expression in general became more systematic and blatant.

Various explanations of the origin of homosexuality have been proposed. Some of these explanations invoke biological factors, where as others invoke social factors. Some argue that homosexuality is a chosen lifestyle, some believe that sexuality is socially constructed, and some make a case for homosexuality being multiple determined. Homosexuals are more likely than heterosexuals to manifest non-right handedness. Therefore, one could say that homosexuality has a possible prenatal origin in some homosexuals. On the other hand, the majority of homosexuals are right-handed.

Recent studies on the concordance for homosexuality among identical twins have shown that identical twins are highly discordant for homosexuality; these studies have also consistently implicated the non-shared family environment but not the shared family environment in the genesis of homosexuality.

Several environmental factors have been implicated in homosexuality for instance, male homosexuals are more likely to report a dominant mother than male heterosexuals. On the other hand, not all male homosexuals report a dominant mother and some heterosexuals men have a dominant mother. Additionally, in a sample of homosexual men with borderline personality disorder, their fathers were more affectionate and their mothers was more emotionally distant, which is the opposite of the dominant mother, absentee father paradigm. Another environmental factor associated with homosexuality is childhood molestation. Homosexuals appear more likely to have been molested or raped by men in childhood than heterosexuals. However, several homosexuals molested or raped in childhood recall experiencing same sex attractions before their molestation or rape. Additionally, how is it that whereas boys molested by men are more likely to be homosexual as adults, even girls molested by men are likely to be lesbians as adults?

Social constructivism as applied to understanding the origin of homosexuality is better known as 'Queer theory', though queer theory does not strictly concern itself with homosexuality; it aims to undermine any explanation that goes against the social constructionist paradigm. Queer theorists argue that "The Homosexual" is a 19th century social construction, and a product of medical discourse, an idea initially made famous by "Michel Foucult". Queer theorists argue that prior to this date, some people engaged in homosexual acts but had no homosexual identity. Queer theorists also emphasize the instability of erotic targets in some individuals and the cross-culture variability of homosexuals expression to argue that homosexuality is socially constructed. The notion that the concept of a homosexual is a recent social reconstruction has been thoroughly debunked. Throughout recorded history, several European and non-European cultures have been aware of Individuals who sexually prefer partners of the same sex or both sexes. Such awareness has also often corresponded to a taxonomy of the types of people with sexual interest in the same sex, and such taxonomy has often classified both the receptive and the active partners in a male homosexual act. Middle-Eastern cultures have even had terms for a different kinds of boy prostitutes. Some cultures have not developed a taxonomy of non-heterosexual types or lack the concept of homosexual. However one can still find homosexuals among such cultures. Indeed a cat by any other name or by no name is still a cat.

The claim of the social constructionists that there are social sources of human sexuality cannot be easily dismissed. Surely, those who favour a biological explanation of homosexuality need to account for the cross-cultural variability in the tolerance and expression of various homosexual behaviours.

Since time immemorial and within all cultures of the world

gays, lesbians, Transgendered and intersexed people have been described, acknowledged and even accommodated within society. From the "mahu" and "aikane" of Polynesia to the "berdache" of Native America Tribes; from the "sekhet" of prehistoric Egypt to the "eunuchs" of ancient Greece and Rome; from the "sares" to the Isralites to the 'mu omin' or trusted men of the Syrians, from the traditional third gender roles of aboriginal tribes in Africa such as among the Mbo people of Zaire to the place and harem guards of the Arabs and Chinese; from the cross-dressing entertainers of Manila and Bangkok to the "Hijra" and "Jogappa" dancers and temple priests of north and south India; right down to our own modern gay and transgendered communities in San Francisco, London and Sydney—persistent and unmistakable "third" or alternative gender subcultures have always naturally existed in one form or another. The existence of same sex romance and sexual desire in the past has been reported since ancient times.

Ancient Greece has long been portrayed as a homosexual paradise for today's modern gays and lesbians. The most famous historic gay culture, Greek society normalized same sex love among its male and female members. Homosexual relations were believed to be above the lower-classes, reserved for the middle class and aristocracy.

3.2 HOMOSEXUALITY IN INDIA

Homosexual people were somehow excluded or left unnoticed by Indian ancient Vedic civilization and its Sanskrit texts is neither reasonable nor fair to that great culture. India's ancient literatures are comprised of voluminous texts and their priestly authors were all known for their detailed accounts of all sciences, both godly and mundane. It is highly unlikely that they would omit or overlook any aspect of human nature. Rather we see in the Kama shastra full accounts of both men and women who had "Tritiya-prabriti" or "third-sexed" by nature and described as homosexuality.

The present day "hijra" or "eunuch" class of Northern India is unquestionably comprised largely of homosexual and transgendered people, with only very few who are truly intersexed. This has been documented through years of research and personal interviews conducted by professionals like Dr. Serena

Nanda, the professor of Anthropology for the city University of New York, in her book *"The Hijra of India"*. Sinhas (1967) study of hijra in Lucknow, in North India, acknowledges the hijra role as performers, but view the major motivation for recruitment to the hijra community as the satisfaction of the individuals homosexual urges.

Anyone familiar with modern GLBTI (gay, lesbians, bisexual, transgender, intersexed) communities people will immediately recognize the correlation between them and the Vedic descriptions of the third sex. This is because their gender qualities and behaviours are universal and especially now-a-days quiet well known.

Homosexuality is generally considered a taboo subject by both Indian civil society and the government. Public discussion of homosexuality in India has been inhibited by the fact that sexuality in any form is rarely discussed openly. In recent years, however, attitudes towards homosexuality have shifted slightly. In particular, there have been more depictions and discussion of homosexuality in the Indian news media and by Bollywood. On **2 July, 2009,** Delhi High Court, decriminalised homosexual intercourse between consenting adults and judged **section 377** of the Indian Penal Code to be conflicting with the fundamental rights guaranteed by the Constitution of India.

Religion has played a significant role in shaping Indian customs and traditions. While homosexuality has not been explicitly mentioned in the religious texts central to Hinduism the largest religion in India, some interpretations have been viewed as condemning homosexuality. Scholars differ in their views of the position of homosexuality within India's main religious traditions. There have been arguments that homosexuality was both prevalent and accepted in ancient Hindu society.

The **Manusmriti,** which lists the oldest codes of conduct that were proposed to be followed by a Hindu, does include mention of homosexual practices, but only as something to be regulated. Though homosexuality was considered a part of sexual practices, it was not always well accepted. There were punishments prescribed for homosexual behaviour, For instance, the verse referring to sexual relations between an older woman and a virgin (woman) reads "**....** a woman who pollutes a damsel (virgin) shall instantly have (her head) shaved or two fingers cut off, and be made to ride (through the town) on a donkey", suggesting a severe punishment. However, the verse referring to sexual relationship between two virgins suggests a relatively milder punishment "... a damsel who pollutes (another) damsel must be fined two hundred (panas), pay the double of her (nuptial) fee, and receive ten (lashes with a) rod". These provisions, quoted out of context, seem homophobic, but in fact they are concerned not with the gender of the partners but with the loss of virginity that rendered a young woman unworthy of marriage. For instance, the punishment for a forced sex act between a man and a woman states ... "If any man through Insolence forcibly contaminates a maiden, two of his fingers shall be instantly cut off, and he shall pay a fine of six hundred (panas)", which seems more severe in comparison to the punishment prescribed for the same act between two virgins. There is also no penalty prescribed for two non-virgins who have sex together.

The skewed treatment may have been due to gender bias, considering that the *Manusmriti* is the same scripture that has stated that the status of woman in the society is the same (or even lower than) that of a man's land, his cattle and other possessions.

The unabridged modern translation of the classic Indian text Kama Sutra deals without ambiguity or hypocrisy with all aspects of sexual life including marriage, adultery, prostitution, group sex, male and female homosexuality and transvestism. The text paints a fascinating portrait of an India whose openness to sexuality gave rise to a highly developed expression of the erotic.

Actually, in classical India, the disparagement for the homosexuals was not devoid of compassion. The homosexual belongs to a deficient class of men called *Kliba* in Sanskrit, deficient because he is unable to produce male offspring. The word (which has traditionally been translated as eunuch, but almost certainly did not mean eunuch) was a catch-all term to include someone who was sterile, impotent, castrated, a transvestite, a man who had oral sex with other men, who had anal sex as a recipient, a man with mutilated or deficient sexual organs, a man who produced only female children, or finally, a hermaphrodite. In short, *Kliba* is a term traditional Hindus coined to describe a man who is in their terms sexually dysfunctional (or in ours, sexually challenged). *Kliba* is not a term that exists any longer, but some of its remnant—the perception of a deficiency, and the combination of pity, dismay and a degree of disdain toward a man who is unable to marry and produce children—continues to cling to the Indian homosexual.

In ancient texts, folktales and in daily conversations, mismatched lovers, generally these with vast differences in status (a fisherman or an untouchable falling in love with a princes), are reluctantly absolved of blame and the union gradually accommodated, because it is viewed as destined from a former birth. When a brave homosexual couple defies all convention by openly living together, its tolerance by the two families and the social surround generally take place in the framework of the rebirth theory. In 1987, when two policewomen in the state of Madhya Pradesh in central India got "married", a cause in Indian media, the explanation often heard from those who could no longer regard them as "just good friends sharing living accommodation" was that one of them must have been a man in a previous birth and the couple prematurely separated by a cruel fate.

In ancient India homosexual activity itself was ignored or stigmatized as inferior, but never actively persecuted. In the Dharmashastras, male homoerotic activity is punished, albeit mildly: a ritual batch or the payment of a small fine was often sufficient atonement. This does not change materially in spite of the advent of Islam, which unequivocally condemns homosexuality as a serious crime. Muslim theologians in India held that the Prophet advocated the severest punishment for sodomy. Islamic culture in India, though, also had a Persian caste where in homoeroticism is celebrated in literature. In Sufi mystical poetry, both in Persian and later in Urdu, the relationship between the divine and humans was expressed in homoerotic metaphors. Inevitably, the mystical was also enacted at the human level. At least among the upper classes of Muslims, among "men of refinement", pederasty became an accepted outlet for a man's erotic promptings, as long as he continued to fulfill his duties as a married man. Emperor Babur's autobiography is quite clear on his indifferent love for his wife and his preference for a lad. We also know that until the middle of twentieth century, when the princely states were incorporated into an independent India. There was a strong tradition of homosexuality in many princely courts in north India. The homosexual relationships were much safer than relationships with mistresses whose children could be the source of endless divisive rivalries.

It seems that the contemporary perception of homosexual activity, primarily in images of sodomy, can be traced back to the Muslim period of Indian history. As we saw, the classical Hindu image of homosexual activity is in terms of fellatio. In the *Kamasutra,* for instance, the fellatio technique of the closeted man of "third nature" (the counterpart of the *Kliba* in other Sanskrit texts) is discussed in considerable sensual detail.

In Ancient India lesbian activity is described in the *Kamasutra* at the beginning of the chapter on harems, where many women live together in the absence of men. What the queens have is just one king, preoccupied with affairs of state, to go around. The women use dildos, as well as bulbs, roots or fruits that have the form of male organ. The implication is that lesbian activity took place only in the absence of the "real thing". There are hints on other kinds of lesbian activity in the ancient law books: The harsh punishment is not for the activity itself but for the "deflowering", the heinous crime of robbing a young girl of her chastity. Not surprisingly, it seems that female homosexuality was punished more severely than homosexuality among men; out of concern for the protection of women's virginity and sexual purity, traditionalists would say; to exercise control over women's sexual choice and activity, modern feminists would counter.

It is ironical that reactionaries, both Hindu and Muslim, who reject homosexuality as a decadent western phenomenon subscribe to the same foreign code that is so alien to the Indian tradition. The Indian tradition of indifferent or deliberate ignorance is also incompatible with the model of the western gay movement, which is beginning to make inroads into our metropolises. In its insistence on the politics of a gay identity, of a proud or at least defiant assertion of homosexual identity, this movement is beginning to compel the rest of society to confront the issue publicly.

Unlike the West, the Hindu society does not have the concept of 'sexual orientation' that classifies males on the basis of who they desire. However, there is a strong, ancient concept of third gender, which is for individuals who have strong elements of both male and female in them. According to Sanskrit texts such as the *Naradasmriti, Sushruta Samhita,* etc., this third sex or gender includes people we call today homosexuals, transgenders, bisexuals and the intersexed (LGBTI). Third genders are described in ancient Vedic texts as males who have a female nature—referring to homosexual men or feminine gendered males. The gender/sexual role of third genders has for long been predominantly associated with receiving penetration from men, just like the gender/ sexual role of manhood has been to penetrate men, women or third genders. However, the *Kamasutra* clearly describes third-gender men assuming both masculine and feminine identities as well as both receptive and dominant sexual roles.

Although Hindu society does not formally acknowledge sexuality between men, it formally acknowledges and gives space to sexuality between men and third genders as a variation of male-female sex (i.e., a part of heterosexuality, rather than homosexuality, if analysed in Western terms). In fact, Hijras, Alis, Kotis, etc.—the various forms of third gender that exist in India today—are all characterized by the gender role of having receptive anal and oral sex with men. Sexuality between men (as distinct from third gender) has nevertheless thrived, mostly unspoken, informally, within men's spaces, without being seen as 'different' in the way it's seen in the West. As in other non-western cultures, it is considered more or less a universal aspect of manhood, even if not socially desirable. It is the effeminate male sexuality for men (or for women) which is seen as 'different,' and differently categorised. Men often refer to their sexual play with each other as *'masti'*.

A significant fallout of this has been that sexual desire between men, which was near universal earlier, is now become more and more isolated from the mainstream, as men are distancing themselves from it because of the stigma of effeminacy or third gender attached to the notion of 'gay'.

In her book, *Love's Rite*, Ruth Vanita examines the phenomena of same-sex weddings, many by Hindu rites, which have been reported by the Indian press over the last thirty years and with increasing frequency.

In the same period, same-sex joint suicides have also been reported. Most of these marriages and suicides are by lower middle class female couples from small towns and rural areas across the country; these women have no contact with any LGBT movements. Both cross-sex and same-sex couples, when faced with family opposition, tend to resort to either elopement and marriage or to joint suicide in the hope of reunion in the next life. Vanita examines how Hindu doctrines such as rebirth and the genderlessness of the soul are often interpreted to legitimize socially disapproved relationships, including same-sex ones. In a 2004 survey, most—though not all—swamis opposed the concept of a Hindu-sanctified gay marriage. But several Hindu priests have performed same-sex marriages, arguing that love is the result of attachments from previous births and that marriage, as a union of spirit, is transcendental to gender.

Many Indian and Hindu intellectuals now publicly support LGBT civil rights. Some liberal Hindu reform movements, especially those in the West, also support social acceptance of gays, lesbians and other gender minorities. Psychoanalyst Sudhir Kakar writes that Hindus are more accepting of "deviance or eccentricity" that are adherents of Western religions, who typically treat sexual variance as "anti-social or psychopathological, requiring 'correction' or 'cure'". Hindus, he argues, believe instead that each individual must fulfill their personal destiny (svadharma) as they travel the path towards moksha (transcendence).

Commenting on the legalisation of homosexuality in India; Anil Bhanot, general secretary of The United Kingdom Hindu Council said: The point here is that the homosexual nature is part of the natural law of God; it should be accepted for what it is, no more and no less. Hindus are generally conservative but it seems to me that in ancient India, they even celebrated sex as an enjoyable part of procreation, where priests were invited for ceremonies in their home to mark the beginning of the process.

The third gender (South Asia) Hindu philosophy has the concept of a third sex or third gender (*tritiya prakriti*—literally, "third nature"). This category includes a wide range of people with mixed male and female natures such as effeminate males, masculine females, transgenders, transsexuals, the intersexed, androgynes, neutrois and so on. However, the original nature of third gender has nothing to do with "sexual-orientation" as is reported by the sects of modern LGBT and contemporary west. Third-genders have no connection with sex among men (which is universal). Third-genders are of a different gender from males and females because they have a female inside regardless of who they are sexually attracted to. Even though, "homosexuality" refers to a third-gender's sexuality for men, many MTF third-genders are not "homosexual" and are attracted either exclusively to women or are 'bisexual' and likewise, many FTM transgenders are attracted to men. Such persons are not considered fully male or female in traditional Hinduism, being a combination of both. They are mentioned as third sex by nature (birth).

3.3 ACCEPTANCE OF HOMOSEXUALITY—A GLOBAL PERSPECTIVE

A study of acceptance of homosexuality at global level is interesting, enigmatic and at times defies logic. Globalisation tends to bring consensus and uniformity by smothering rough edges and makes human beings as well as nations move in a positive direction of understanding, peace, cordiality and enlarging areas of cooperation. This does not apply to homosexuality where standpoints are irreconcilable and poles apart. At one end of the spectrum is total acceptance with connotations of normal human behaviour while at the other end it is viewed as a sin/crime to be crushed ruthlessly. There is no dialogue and reconciliation between the two extreme ends. A historical study of the subject shows that homosexuality was never accepted by state as well as religion till the Twentieth Century and was always regarded as a crime by the state and a sin by the religion. However with the march of time the negative view of homosexuality has been eroding with more and more states accepting it as a normal human behaviour and have been treating homosexuals as equal citizens with the same rights and privileges as enjoyed by other citizens. This metamorphosis is attributable to human rights movements and a relook at religious concepts. The Roman Catholic Church, once in the forefront of oppositions is gradually moving towards permissiveness and conciliations. The acceptance of homosexuality as a part of society has made giant strides. No country in Europe has a law against homosexuality. Although Russia has no laws against homosexuality, yet it enacted an anti-gay propaganda law in 2013 prohibiting any positive mention of homosexuality in the presence of minors including online transmissions.

3.4 *FUNNY BOY* BY SHYAM SELVADURAI

3.4.1 Author

SHYAM SELVADURAI was born in Colombo, Sri La[illegible]
and is of a Tamil and Sinhala mixed backgro[illegible]

openly gay, which is a problematic issue for a Sri Lankan resident. At the age of nineteen, he moved to Canada with his family after the 1983 ethnic riots. He studied creative writing and theatre and has a Bachelors degree in Fine Arts from York University. He currently lives in Toronto. *Funny Boy* his first novel was published to acclaim in 1994 and won the W.H. Smith/Books in Canada First Novel Award and in the U.S. The Lambda Literary Award and was named a Notable Book by the American Library Association. His second novel *Cinnamon Gardens* has been published in Canada, the U.K., and the U.S. and translated into 6 languages—Italian, French, German, Danish, Spanish and Hebrew. It was shortlisted for the Canada's Trillium Award, as well as the Aloa Literary Award in Denmark and the Premio Internazionale Riccardo Bacchelli in Italy. Shyam Selvadurai is the editor of an anthology, Story-wallah! A Celebration of South Asian Fiction, published in Canada and the U.S. His young-adult novel, *Swimming in the Monsoon Sea,* was short-listed for the Governor General's Award but won the Lambda Literary Award in the Children's and Youth Literature category in 2006.

3.4.2 Characters

Arjie

Arjun Chelvaratnam, called "Arjie" by his friends and family members, is the narrator and protagonist of *Funny Boy*. A Sri Lankan Tamil raised in Colombo with his sister Sonali and brother Diggy, Arjie is clearly unlike other boys from his earliest years. Barely interested in traditionally masculine pursuits, Arjie is more fond of acting out weddings and reading Little Women than playing cricket or rugger. He develops a long-standing mix of curiosity and shame about this difference, and as he grows up throughout the book, he begins to discover his attraction to men. But when he sees Radha Aunty marry Rajan instead of Anil and Amma reunite with Daryl Uncle while Appa is away, Arjie begins to lose faith in the storybook image of romantic love he learned from Janaki's Sinhala comic books. Ironically, he finds love only after his father sends him to the prestigious Queen Victoria Academy to make him more of "a man"; he meets a boy at the school named Shehan, although they eventually grow apart while

Arjie waits to leave Sri Lanka for Canada. He has to make this move at the end of the book because his Tamil family is under persecution during the early days of the Sri Lankan Civil War; throughout the book's earlier sections, he also gradually learns about Sri Lanka's ethnic tensions and begins to recognize the racism in his community and his own family. Although he is Tamil, he only speaks Sinhala and English, and so feels relatively disconnected from the nationalistic sentiments that lead people like Jegan and Ammachi to support the Tamil Tigers, although he intimately understands the oppression his Tamil minority faces. As he watches his family members and acquaintances suffer violence because of their ethnicity, gender, or commitment to justice, Arjie also develops a more complex moral outlook during the book. Although the book ends with Arjie's move to Canada at a relatively young age, he sees and experiences a lifetime's worth of turmoil and injustice during his youth, which clearly instills in him both a sense of moral purpose and an instinct for pursuing that moral purpose carefully and realistically.

Amma

Arjie's Amma (the Tamil word for "mother") is loving and close to her son; although she has a strong sense of right and wrong, she often chooses not to voice it, but she is also anything but passive. Instead, she tends to hold the family together emotionally in times of crisis. When Arjie is a child, Amma lets him dress up in her clothes, but is forced to stop after the family sees him in the bride-bride sari. Like Arjie, she often silently disagrees with many of the cultural norms that determine life in Sri Lanka: although she forces young Arjie to play with the other boys, for instance, her inability to justify herself reveals "how little she actually believe[s] in the justness of her actions." Similarly, Amma's relationship with **Daryl Uncle** shows Arjie that, unlike many other Sri Lankans, she does not see ethnicity as a defining trait, although she eventually comes to agree with the **Tamil Tigers** that **Tamils** might need a separate state to overcome violence from the **Sinhalese**. Her zealous effort to investigate Daryl Uncle's death reveals her commitment to justice, but her willingness to give it up shows that she considers her family's safety primary. In this vein, she is also the first to suggest the family move to Canada.

During the riots, which (unlike **Appa**) she predicted, Amma comforts not only her children but also **Chithra Aunty** (even though the Chelvaratnams' own house was the one burned down).

Appa

Arjie's distant, authoritative, and successful father ("Appa" is the Tamil word for "father"). Although he is a brother to **Mala Aunty, Kanthi Aunty, Radha Aunty** (among others), Appa seldom appears in the first half of the book; in the third chapter, he quits his job at the bank to buy a hotel that proves very lucrative and skyrockets the family into Sri Lanka's upper class. He plays a more prominent role in the last three chapters; in "Small Choices," Appa takes in **Jegan Parameswaran** because he made a pact with Jegan's father in his school days, but ends up torn—at first, between his affinity for Jegan (who reminds Appa of his father) and his fear of Jegan's political associations, and later, between his promise to Jegan and the safety of his family (which is threatened by the community's harsh response to Jegan after his arrest). Throughout the book, he worries intensely about Arjie's masculinity and sexuality. He sends Arjie to the Queen Victoria Academy in the fifth chapter so that he will "become a man," but is deeply disappointed when Arjie befriends the equally "funny" **Shehan**. At the end of the book, he stays in Sri Lanka to wrap up his business, while the rest of the family leaves for Canada.

Radha Aunty

Appa's younger sister, who comes back to Sri Lanka when **Arjie** is seven. She is engaged to Rajan Nagendra, whom she met during her four years studying in America. However, she is nothing like the fair-skinned, elegant, formal aunty Arjie was expecting; instead, she is rebellious, freethinking, a poor pianist, and "as dark as a labourer." But she also lets Arjie dress up in her clothes and wear her makeup, which turns them into best friends. They join a local production of **The King and I** together, and during their rehearsals they meet Anil Jayasinghe, who starts hitting on Radha and eventually wins her attention. After **Ammachi** threatens Anil's family, loudly voices her opposition to Radha seeing a **Sinhalese** boy, and decides to send Radha to **Jaffna** to get her away from Anil, she starts to fall for him. However, **Aunty Doris**'s warnings about forbidden love make her question her feelings, and then she gets attacked by a Sinhalese mob on her way home. A family friend saves her, but half of Radha's face is badly bruised, and she grows solemn and pessimistic in the following days. She finds herself unable to keep seeing Anil and decides to marry Rajan.

Jegan Parameswaran

The son of one of **Appa**'s old childhood friends, Jegan helps resettle **Tamil** refugees in **Jaffna** while working for the **Gandhiyam Movement** and briefly joins the **Tamil Tigers** before moving to stay with **Arjie**'s family in **Colombo**. After his father's death, Jegan's mother asks Appa to care for Jegan by invoking an old pact Appa made with Jegan's father in school: they promised to "always protect each other and each others' familys [sic]." Jegan quickly grows close to Appa (who employs him and thinks he resembles his father) and Arjie (who finds him attractive and understanding). But Jegan's freethinking soon becomes a liability for the family; the **Sinhalese** employees at Appa's work and hotel grow suspicious of Jegan, and eventually the police arrest him on false charges, but after his release everyone thinks of him as associated with the Tamil Tigers and Appa begins receiving threats. After a Sinhalese gang nearly attacks the family and someone writes "Death to all Tamil pariahs" on the outside wall of Jegan's room at the hotel, causing all the guests to check out, Appa realizes that his business can only remain successful if he fires Jegan. Arjie is dismayed to watch this happen, and Jegan is understandably dismissive and bitter when he moves out of the family's house, never to be seen again. His fate, like **Daryl**'s, shows how some of the conflict's worst injustices were inflicted upon those with the purest motives.

Daryl Uncle

A **burgher** journalist who grew up in Sri Lanka with **Amma** but has been living in Australia for more than a decade. In the chapter "See No Evil, Hear No Evil," Daryl Uncle visits in order to investigate the government's abuses of power under the **Prevention of Terrorism Act**. While **Arjie**'s whole family ridicules him for reading **Little Women**, Daryl mentions his own affinity for the book and buys him the sequels, which brings them closer together. However, the rest of the family—especially Neliya Aunty—openly resents Daryl and his close relationship with Amma. During a trip with Daryl and Amma to the mountains in central Sri Lanka, Arjie begins to feel the same way, especially as he realizes that Daryl and Amma's relationship used to be romantic long ago, before he left Sri Lanka; they could never marry because he was white and she was **Tamil**. After this trip, Daryl goes to **Jaffna** to research his story, but he never returns; his body washes up on the shore of a fishing village, and Amma is confident that the government is to blame. Daryl's death shows the danger in pursuing justice and forces Arjie to think about how to balance his desire to confront power with the need to stay safe.

Black Tie

The cruel, traditionalist principal of Victoria Academy. Universally feared by the students, Black Tie is often seen wearing an old-school British colonial outfit, overlooking Victoria Academy from the balcony next to his office. When a lock of **Shehan**'s hair falls out of place, Black Tie gives Shehan a rudimentary haircut and punishes him endlessly along with the other students he deems the "future ills and burdens of Sri Lanka." A proponent of keeping the school multiethnic, Black Tie faces a challenge from **Mr. Lokubandara**, who wants to take his job. To help keep his power, Black Tie organizes a ceremony for a prominent politician and enlists **Arjie** to recite two of his favourite poems at this ceremony. When Arjie messes up the poems' words, Black Tie canes both him and Shehan, and he eventually forces them to kneel outside on the balcony for hours for the same reason. Arjie eventually decides to purposefully botch the poems he is to recite during the ceremony in order to ensure that Black Tie loses his job and Shehan is no longer senselessly punished with the "ills and burdens."

Shehan Soyza

Another student at Victoria Academy and **Arjie**'s first real love interest. Initially, Shehan helps protect Arjie from **Salgado**'s bullying; they exchange smiles and Arjie immediately feels attracted to Shehan's charisma, confidence, and long hair. But this long hair gets Shehan into trouble with **Black Tie**, who names him as one of the "ills and burdens" and punishes him extensively for little apparent reason. Through their punishments in Black Tie's office, Arjie and Shehan bond, and eventually they begin to meet outside of school. Once, when their plot to get released from Black Tie's punishments succeeds, Arjie and Shehan suddenly kiss; when **Diggy** tells Arjie that Shehan has a reputation for having sex with other boys, Arjie is both intrigued and confused. Eventually, Arjie and Shehan do have sex, but Arjie feels intensely guilty and blames Shehan. Over time, they reconcile and become regular lovers, and Arjie sabotages Black Tie's award ceremony to put a stop to the "ills and burdens" group. Near the end of the book, they are still close and spend much of their time together, but they grow distant as their experiences during the 1983 riots differ and, finally, as Arjie plans to immigrate to Canada.

Ammachi

Arjie's overbearing, opinionated, cruel, racist grandmother, who punishes Arjie excessively for fighting with **Her Fatness** and tries to break up her daughter **Radha Aunty**'s budding romance with the **Sinhalese Anil** by sending her to **Jaffna** and trying to convince her to quit the play **The King and I**. During the family's monthly "spend-the-days" at her and Appachi's house, Ammachi always insists the kids give her an uncomfortably tight hug and then retires for the rest of the day. After her father was killed by a Sinhalese mob during the 1958 ethnic riots, Ammachi refused to associate with Sinhalese people and staunchly supported the **Tamil Tigers**' fight for an independent **Tamil** state. Alongside **Appachi**, she is also murdered by such a mob in 1983, just before Arjie's family leaves for Canada.

Aunty Doris

An old **burgher** woman who directs the production of **The King and I** that **Arjie** and Rahda Aunty join. During Radha's conflict over whether to marry Anil or **Rajan**, Doris encourages to think her decision through (instead of simply leaving Anil all at once, like **Ammachi** wants) but warns about her own experience. Decades before, Doris went against her English family's wishes by marrying a **Tamil** man; in retaliation, her family left Sri Lanka and never contacted her again. Now that her husband has died, Aunty Doris wonders whether her marriage was even worth it; her experience demonstrates that, sometimes, it is foolish to give into the power of love and, in the process, undervalue family.

Anil Jayasinghe

A likable, friendly **Sinhalese** boy who acts in **The King and I** with Radha Aunty and **Arjie.** He starts out by shamelessly hitting on Radha, joking about pollinating flowers and offering her rides home, which annoys her to no end. But eventually she starts to enjoy Anil's company; the problem is that both of their parents are fiercely opposed to the idea of letting their child even associate with someone outside their ethnic group. After **Ammachi** voices her opposition to Radha's apparent relationship with Anil, she actually starts to fall in love with him. Anil proposes Radha marry him instead of **Rajan**, but after a Sinhalese mob attacks her train from **Jaffna** to **Colombo**, Radha cannot bring herself to marry Anil and ends up marrying Rajan, as she had originally planned.

Sena Uncle

Chithra Aunty's husband and a family friend of **Amma** and **Appa;** all four go out together for formal dinners, shows, and parties in **Colombo** when Appa buys the Paradise Beach Resort. During the riots, Sena and Chithra (who are **Sinhalese**) shelter **Arjie**'s family, although Sena frequently becomes the bearer of bad news. Initially, he gets stuck after a mob steals the petrol from his van to set a **Tamil** family and their car on fire. After the family makes it to Sena and Chithra's house, Sena gets a threatening phone call—which is followed by the arrival of another mob—and ends up having to hide Arjie's family away again, this time in his mother's house. Later, he reports to the family that **Ammachi** and **Appachi,** too, have been burned alive in their car.

Chithra Aunty

Sena Uncle's wife and **Amma**'s best friend, who goes out with her frequently both when **Appa** is in Sri Lanka and while he is on vacation in Europe, and who often accompanies the family to the Paradise Beach Resort that they own. She and Sena Uncle shelter **Arjie**'s family during the 1983 riots, and Arjie finds it particularly ironic when she shows up to the **Pereras'** house (where the family is hiding out) and breaks down in tears because Arjie's family's house has burned down.

Mr. Lokubandara

The **Sinhalese** vice principal of Victoria Academy, who is allegedly poised to take the principal position from **Black Tie** due to his extensive political connections. Mr. Lokubandara's docile and mild-mannered personality belies his explicit preference for Sinhala students like **Salgado** and desire to make the school officially Buddhist (the religion of most Sinhalas, but almost no **Tamils**). However, **Arjie** ultimately decides to support Mr. Lokundabara's attempts to take over the school by botching his poetry recital at Black Tie's awards ceremony.

Tanuja/Her Fatness

Tanuja, **Kanthi Aunty** and **Cyril Uncle**'s young daughter, gets nicknamed "Her Fatness" by the rest of her cousins. Self-serving, spoiled, and unpopular, she manipulates the family into letting her play the prestigious role of bride at the girls' monthly "bride-bride" game. After trying to impress the other girls with her dolls and gregarious behaviour as the groom, she insults **Arjie** for being a "pansy," "faggot," and "sissy" before complaining to her mother Kanthi, who marches Arjie out in front of all the aunties and uncles to answer for his effeminacy. When Her Fatness and Arjie fight again over the sari and the role of bride, she cries out in front of **Ammachi**, who blames and punishes Arjie.

Mahagodagé Somaratne

A servant boy who works in Daryl Uncle's house. When Arjie and

Amma stop by during their search for the missing Daryl, they encounter his room in shambles, and Somaratne disappears soon thereafter, leading the police to ultimately accuse him of stealing Daryl's possessions. Arjie and Amma then go to Somaratne's village in an attempt to locate Daryl and meet Somaratne's mother, who informs them that Somaratne returned with his arm paralyzed and has since hidden away. The villagers start throwing bottles at Amma and Arjie on their way out, who realize how disconnected they are from the realities and struggles of Sri Lanka's rural underclass.

Diggy

Arjie's boisterous, athletic older brother, whose conventional masculinity contrasts with Arjie's effeminacy. The family encourages Arjie to follow in Diggy's shoes, for instance by playing cricket with the boys during the family's "spend-the-days" and by going to the Queen Victoria Academy. Diggy grows jealous of Arjie's close friendship with **Jegan** and encourages him to stay away from **Shehan** at school.

Appachi

Arjie's grandfather on his father's side, a quiet and steadfast old man who seldom interacts with his grandchildren. During the riots at the end of the book in 1983, he and **Ammachi** have their house burned down and, on a completely separate occasion, are murdered by a **Sinhalese** mob that sets their car on fire with them still inside.

Janaki

Ammachi and **Appachi**'s overworked **Sinhalese** servant, who is responsible for cooking for everyone and looking after the children during the family's monthly spend-the-days. While she is generally too stressed out to play with the children, Janaki takes pity on **Arjie** when Ammachi starts making him perform housework, and so she lets him read her Sinhala love comics, which spark his mental image of the perfect wedding.

Meena

One of **Arjie**'s cousins, a girl who plays with the boys' group (much as he plays with the girls). She and Arjie's brother **Diggy** struggle for power among the boys, and they both try to pawn Arjie off onto the other cricket team when **Amma** forces him to play with the boys.

Anil's Father

A bigoted **Sinhalese** man who threatens Radha Aunty and **Arjie** for being **Tamil**, suggesting that the Sinhalese are on the verge of kicking the Tamils out of Sri Lanka. He is furious about his son **Anil**'s relationship with Radha and promises never to let his son "marry some non-Sinhalese" or someone not "from a good family."

Neliya Auntie

Amma's old, traditionally minded sister, who moves in with **Arjie**'s family around the time that **Appa** buys the Paradise Beach Resort. When **Daryl** starts visiting the family, Neliya is visibly uncomfortable with his presence because she knows about his past relationship with Amma. However, she consistently supports her sister and the family, helping around the house and caring for Arjie during the riots.

3.4.3 Chapter 1—Pigs can't fly

The family keep one Sunday a month for a spend-the-day when the adults are privileged to free themselves "from their progeny" throughout the day. Arjuna, his brother Varuna, and his sister Sonali are driven to their grandparents' for the spend-the-day of that month. The ancient setting of the house with its long and dark corridor, its ancestral photographs on the walls, and its high ceiling inculcate fear in the hero Arjuna. Ammachchi and Appachchi (Grandma and Grandpa) enthroned in their large, reclining chairs represent an alien generation, aggravating the fear in Arjuna and Ammachchi's kisses reach his face with physical pain. Both the adults and the children benefit from the spend-the-day arrangement. The children take leave of the parents "without even a pretence of sorrow" to be free from "parental control," "ever watchful eyes," and "tale-bearing tongues of the house servants." Yet they are in the care of Ammachchi and the housemaid Janaki. Ammachchi is like earth-goddess in fairytales and any disturbance of her peace would invite a catastrophic earthquake.

The children have their own strategies of preventing conflict—"territoriality and leadership." Under territoriality the premises are divided into two as the boys' area and the girls' area. In the boys' area there are two leaders, Meena and Varuna alias Diggy. In the girls' area there is one leader, and that is Arjuna. The boys always played cricket but the girls played more creative games like "cooking-cooking," "Thumbelina," "Cinderella," or "bride-bride." Arjuna is popular among all the girls and his leadership is rewarded with the role of bride in "bride-bride." The girls loved the game and Arjuna in his *saree* is considered "an icon, a graceful, benevolent, perfect being upon whom the adoring eyes of the world rested."

The popular bride-bride game ends in a disheartening manner. Auntie Kanthy comes back from abroad with her husband Uncle Cyril and their daughter Thanuja. The children call Thanuja "Her Fatness" because of her obesity. No sooner they have settled down in Colombo, Thanuja joins the girls in their games. Thanuja accepts the role of the bridegroom in the game "bride-bride" on two consecutive spend-the-days and on the third spend-the-day everything changes. All adults gather there and stay for lunch as it is Ammachchi's birthday. As his mother is supposed to wear a sari, Arjuna's family usually get late to leave home. Arjuna enjoys watching his mother dressing herself. Here it is clear that he is led by his libidinal feelings. Auntie Kanthy seems to be a cynical woman. Carried away by Thanuja's lies, she questions Arjuna, the leader of the girls' games, as to why her daughter is not taken for games. The boy escapes from her, as grandmother gets holds of him to kiss. Auntie Kanthy seems to capitalise on the sympathy the others hold for her for having a tough time when she was abroad. Meanwhile Thanuja attempts to attract the other girls' favour with her exotic foreign dolls. However, she fails to prevent the others from their involvement in the bride-bride. All girls laugh at Thanuja dressed as the bridegroom. Thanuja in her groom role violates the rules and conditions of the game by assuming a dictatorial mood.

When the others try to quieten her she demands the role of the bride. She challenges Arjuna's enactment of the bride role being a boy. Failing to win over the other girls, she calls Arjuna names "Pansy", "faggot", and "sissy". The other girls call her in a chorus, "Go away you fatty boom boom." She breaks away from them and runs to her mother leaving her clothes.

Auntie Kanthy comes to the porch, threatens the girls for calling her daughter fatty, gets hold of Arjuna in a tight grip, and pulls him along the corridor into the drawing room where all the adults have gathered. All the adults laugh at him calling him funny. Embarrassed by the disgrace, Arjuna's parents remain upset. When the parents are at home, the father blames the mother for allowing Arjuna in her room while she gets dressed. Usually, Arjuna with his keen eyes feasts on the mother's figure in her underskirt and blouse. He enjoys the perfume smell of her jewellery. The technique she uses in wearing her *saree* fascinates him. "You should have been a film star," he remarks while admiring her beauty. But after he gets caught in a *saree,* his mother does not allow him in her room while dressing herself. Since he hears the word "funny" being uttered by a number of adults, he has been wondering what it means. The mother keeps aloof of him. He feels it.

The mother, on the next spend-the-day, orders Varuna that Arjuna should be included in his cricket team. When the two boys protest against this, the mother declares, "If the child turns out wrong, it's the mother they always blame not the father." The mother does not show any sympathy for their pleading. Arjuna imagines how Thanuja will take his place, and plans to escape from cricket and manoeuvre the game of bride-bride. He stealthily takes the *saree* with him in his sister's bag. While in the car, when Varuna asks the mother, why Arjuna cannot play with the girls, she replies, "The sky is high; and pigs can't fly." When the mother leaves the children at the grandparents', Varuna tries to take Arjuna into his cricket team. But the others reject him. Everybody calls him, "Girlie Boy." Arjuna wants to use it to his own advantage. In deciding the batting order, the players have to select one out of a column of hyphens drawn against a column of numbers that are covered at the moment of selection and that represent the positions that players would occupy by luck. Arjuna acquires number one position in the batting order, but he is not given it. He protests against Murugesu taking over his position. The boys try to negotiate with him but he persists in his protest. Then he is chased out for his stubbornness.

Ultimately, he goes to join the girls. There Thanuja has already taken control. She shouts at him, "Go away!.. Boys are not allowed here..." Finally, he offers to play "the groom" in the bride-bride and manages to join them. But he cannot join them in the cooking. Being creative, he uses his office-employed groom position to have fun and one by one the girls leave the cooking and start operating at his commands as the officer. Unable to tolerate this, again Thanuja wants him out. Then he threatens her not to give the *saree* for bride-bride. Thanuja who has already picked it up from Sonali's bag challenges that he does not have it. She allows him to search for it but laughs at his failure. Finally, she runs away with the *saree* and he tries to grab it from her by pulling her by the hair. The *saree* gets torn and the children retaliate this by tearing her blouse. Even the dominant Janaki feels helpless at the sight of her howling. Ammachchi comes to the scene with the sternest look on her face. She seems not considerate about his explanations but wants to punish him. So he shouts at the old woman, "I hate you old fatty." He runs away and ends up on the beach. He finds no refuge there but goes back to the grandparents', expecting a severe thrashing. He glances at the torn *saree* again, and ponders on his deprivation of entering the girls' world. He feels that he does not belong either to the boys or to the girls. Arjuna's life changes drastically after this.

3.4.4 Chapter 2—Auntie Radha

Auntie Radha is the youngest sister of Arjuna's father. Auntie Radha and Rajan meet in America and get impressed by each other. Later on Rajan informs his parents and gets them to make a proposal for Auntie Radha. The old Mr Nagendra, Rajan's father, is a contemporary of the grandfather and everybody in the family is happy about it. The young man is known as an engineer working for an American company, neither an alcoholic nor a womaniser, hailing from a family of healthy people. Arjuna is thrilled by the idea of attending a real church wedding in the family with a real bride. He visualises the *saree*, the confetti, the cakes, the *pala haram*, and the jasmine garlands that would go for the wedding. Influenced by romance and marriage in Sinhala films and Janaki's love comics, he tries to figure out how Auntie Radha looks and imagines her to be like the famous film star Auntie Malani Fonseka, plump with rounded hips, fair complexioned, khol rimmed eyes, wearing her straight hair into an elaborate coiffure on top of her head, in a Manipuri *saree* with a gold border. Arjuna eavesdrops when the adults are talking about Auntie Radha.

He is now not allowed to move with the other children since he has fought with Thanuja, and is to do some work in the house ordered by Ammachchi. Now and then he receives a knock on his head for his silly mistakes. Janaki who has taken pity on him allows him to be in her room and read through her Sinhala love comics. He finds a book on two lovers – Manilal and Sakuntala and imagines the story of Rajan Nagendra and Auntie Radha. Day by day, his enthusiasm about the on-coming wedding in the family keeps growing. He waits for Auntie Radha to come from America. Only a week after her arrival at home, Arjuna gets an opportunity to visit her. He notices Auntie Radha playing the piano at home, but disagrees about it within himself, expecting her to have an exciting romantic relationship with Rajan, shopping, going out with him, cooking and cleaning the house for him. Arjuna's imagination of Auntie Radha is different from the real. She is pitch dark brown and does not look like a film star of Malini Fonseka's calibre. Her hair is frizzy; she is thin; she does not wear a *saree*, but a top, strange trousers, and odd shoes. She appears totally different from his imagination.

As usual Ammachchi gives Arjuna his day's assignment. This time he has to dust all the brass ornaments in the drawing room. Arjuna is conscious of Auntie Radha's mistakes in playing the piano, but does not laugh at her as she is friendly towards him. She kisses him and starts playing a romantic tune. While dusting the brass items, he feels cheated by Auntie Radha. What he expected in her is not there. When Ammachchi shouts at Arjuna with a punitive correctionism, Auntie Radha openly criticises her, "You treat him like a servant boy." Later she speaks to him politely and enquires about his not playing with the others. She differs from the other adults in the Chelvanayagam family as she does not have their cynicism. She invites him into her room and allows him to play there. He starts examining the cosmetics on her dressing table. Auntie Radha decorates his face by rouging the cheeks, putting a *pottu* on his forehead, colouring his eye-brows etc. etc. She enjoys doing it and shares the pleasure of it with Janaki, but the latter warns her against it. She does not mind it though, and allows him to play with her knickknack the whole afternoon. He develops a boldness to talk to Auntie Radha about her on-coming wedding. Auntie Radha is amused by his knowledge about Rajan Nagendra. He makes suggestions for the wedding such as wearing a long veil, deploying ten bridesmaids to hold it, and having seven page boys and seven flower girls to accompany her. He offers to be a page boy but does not want Thanuja to be a flower girl. He even suggests costumes for the entire bridal party. Because of her indulgence, Arjuna considers Auntie Radha to be his most favourite aunt. In the meantime Thanuja comes in her costume for bride-bride and tries to run Arjuna down, expecting to find envy in his eyes. But Arjuna returns a glance of contempt and shows off his fingers so that she could eye his nails coloured with cutes. When she sees the coloured nails, her face becomes clouded with jealousy.

Auntie Radha gets a role in the theatrical production of "The King and I." As the director Auntie Doris, a family friend, is looking for child actors to play the children of the King of Siam, the mother offers Arjuna a chance. Arjuna likes theatre because of make-up. He asks the mother whether the King marries the English Governess at the end of the story, and the mother says, "No".

Arjuna imagines that every meeting between a man and a woman ends in marriage. The rehearsals take place at St Theresa's convent, and Auntie Radha and Arjuna go there together. Auntie Doris the director of the play calls on them. She remarks Arjuna with such tender features should be a girl. Auntie Radha joins a group of people including Anil who are discussing some song. Auntie Radha wins over everybody with her rhetoric over a joke connected with her and Anil as a rose and a bee respectively. "I would rather wither and drop off my stem than be pollinated by a bee like you." She cheers up everybody including her opponent Anil who has already developed an interest in her. The other girls comments on it annoy Auntie Radha. After the rehearsal, Auntie Radha and Arjuna happen to enjoy a lift home by Anil in his car. They get down at the road top by Anil in his car.

Ammachchi is surprised by their quick return home. Auntie Radha shares a secret with Arjuna, telling that they got a quick bus home. Ammachchi is too mature to fool. In no time she catches Auntie Radha with the truth through a banana seller at the road top, she finds out all about Anil Jayasinghe and expresses her concern over his being a Sinhalese.

Arjuna wonders why it causes so much consternation in the family as they live, study, work, and associate with the Sinhalese people. He later gets to know that someone in the family had been killed by a Sinhalese. Auntie Radha seems to be very broadminded about the subject and argues that history is no reason to hate all the Sinhalese people. She is against racism. Arjuna learns from the father about the Sinhala-Tamil rift for the first time, while getting the word "racist" clarified by him. The father elaborates on the riots caused between the Sinhalese and the Tamils on making Sinhala the national language of Sri Lanka in 1959. Arjuna learns about the Tamil Tigers in Jaffna after this description. Ammachchi, an uneducated middle-class Tamil, sympathises with the Tamil Tigers, but the father, an educated middle-class Tamil, disapproves of their activities. He brings up the children in exposure to Sinhala. The children are educated in a Sinhlala-medium school to make them adaptable to the national requirement. The Sinhala-Tamil rift in the school became more and more significant in the light of his knowledge obtained from the father.

Ammachchi is a real schemer. She visits the Jayasinghe's and stops Anil giving lifts to Auntie Radha. Having known this, Auntie Radha becomes upset, and, that afternoon, her plan is to meet Anil and apologise him for what happened. She visits him with Arjuna and meets him along with his father. His father considers the remarks made by her mother an insult, and declares that his wish for his son Anil is a Sinhalese wife. His father loses his temper but the tension subsides when his mother comes in. Anil remains polite to her throughout the meeting. He reveals his knowledge of her engagement to Rajan, but she expresses her uncertainty about it.

Arjuna's learning process speeds up in exposure to these conflicts. He considers Anil with his boyish features too young to be a lover. At the next rehearsal Auntie Radha tries her best to avoid Anil, but, under various circumstances, they happen to meet. However, Auntie Radha declines all his offers. The other boys tease Anil for being specially concerned about Auntie Radha. They laugh at Anil congratulatingly. Auntie Radha is overtly angry, but could not help laughing. Anil speaks to Auntie Radha out of curiosity, but Auntie Radha responds curtly. Finally, Anil manages to foot the bill at the Green Cabin. He proposes marriage to Auntie Radha and says that he can get his father's consent if she likes it.

When they arrive home that evening, Auntie Mala has already come there. She and her husband had seen Auntie Radha and Anil at the Green Cabin, and have come to discuss the matter with Auntie Radha. A medical doctor, Auntie Mala wants everybody to calm down. However, there is great dispute at the dining table. Ammachchi slaps Auntie Radha on the face. Auntie Kanthy casts cynical remarks about her. Auntie Radha leaves the dining room in tears, while Ammachchi tells about sending her to Jaffna. When Auntie Mala comments on the slapping, Ammachchi tries to assert that she is right as a mother. Auntie Mala talks to Auntie Radha privately in her room. Arjuna manages to walk out on the pretext of going to urinate, and eavesdrops the conversation between Auntie Mala and Auntie Radha. Auntie Radha divulges that she loves Anil. She even says that, like the other Sinhala-Tamil couples, they can live in harmony. Auntie Mala talks about the determination of the Tamil Tigers, but Auntie Radha abhors separatism the Tamil Tigers work with. Auntie Mala cannot deny Auntie Radha' position.

Ammachchi's plan to keep Auntie Radha away from Anil receives a set-back. Auntie Doris stands in her way. Finally, they come to a compromise. Appachchi drives her to the convent and Auntie Doris lets her off for a few weeks so that Amachchi could send her to Jaffna. At the next rehearsal, Anil is not there as it is for the King of Siam's Wives and Children. Auntie Doris tells Auntie Radha about the demerits of mixed marriages, taking her own marriage as an example. She explains how she was ostracised by her father, which left her at a great disadvantage. She missed the funerals of both her parents, and when she found free access to her sister, it was too late as they had git used to her absence. Since her husband Paaskaran died, she has been alone. Auntie Doris tells all that as a warning in keeping with the compromise she has made for Ammachchi.

Arjuna thinks about Auntie Radha's situation and calculates how her destiny will be, if she marries Anil. Already Arjuna believes that Aunty Radha is his only friend and is very concerned about the person she should marry. Auntie Radha meets Anil outside the rehearsals despite the turmoil in the family. Arjuna remains Auntie Radha's most faithful ally and, together with him she meets Anil at the zoo. Auntie Radha becomes very close to Arjuna for protecting her secrets. In the mean time Auntie Radha discloses her secret to Janaki and confides to her that she would marry Anil soon after her return from Jaffna. After Auntie Radha leaves for Jaffna, Arjuna goes for the rehearsals all alone. Each time he bumps onto Anil, he finds his company very comfortable compared to that of the adults he meets at home.

Troubles break out in Jaffna. Some Tamils set the market on fire. A wave of violence arises throughout the region. Auntie Radha is due to return to Colombo the following day by the Night Mail. That day Arjuna goes for the rehearsals and, after the session has been over, waits for his mother. As his mother does not come, Anil drives him home. The sight of a fleet of cars parked in front of the grandparents' house and a group of people gathered inside causes fear in Arjuna. They are worried as the Night Mail coming from Jaffna had been attacked by the Snhalese people in Anuradhapura in retaliation to what the Tamils had done in Jaffna. Anil lets Arjuna out of his car and joins his family. Despite the others' indifference, Arjuna's mother behaves politely towards Anil. He learns from her that Auntie Radha is safe and checks whether he could see her on her arrival in Colombo. Arjuna's mother is sympathetic with him but Auntie Kanthy is adamant that he should not be sympathised with at all, "Don't start that poor man nonsense."

Arjuna is confused about communal violence which had started two days before. While everybody is taking lunch, Auntie Radha comes home with Mr Rasaiah, the face swollen and the head bandaged, blood-stained and covered with a scarf. Though Ammachchi tries to sooth her, Auntie Radha protests against it, clinging on to Mr Rasaiah's arm. In her room, Auntie Mala examines Auntie Radha's wound and states that she does not need stitches. Arjuna silently commiserates with Auntie Radha. Mr Rasaiah's account on violent on the train sounds unreal to Arjuna, but he is compelled to believe and wonders how cruel people can be. Concerned about Auntie Radha, Anil comes to visit her, but Auntie Kanthy and Ammachchi virtually chase him. Auntie Radha comes to live for some time at Arjuna's with Ammachchi and Appachchi. The rehearsals begin. Anil meets Auntie Radha. She turns different after the communal attack on her. Radha disappears from the rehearsals and is sitting in a classroom, crying. Anil comes to see her. Arjuna is sent away. After they have discussed the situation, they agree not to meet any more.

Radha resigns from the play. A few days later Rajan Nagendran comes from America, and Radha is presented to him by her parents. Arjuna observes that, though Radha is not happy, she resembles the Radha he used to imagine at heart. The Nagendrans and the Chelvanayagams meet. A pastor is invited to bless the rings they would exchange with each other. Listening to Janaki pound something with the mall and pestle, he imagines the possibilities created by marriage for the individuals concerned. The "mall and pestle" action suggests the kind of pounding implied in sex. Arjuna finds a lacuna in the situation. He goes to his bride-bride venue and watches the deteriorated alter. He himself does not know what is missing on the occasion of the engagement. So the reader is meant to imagine that what he has seen in the archetypical lovers in films has not taken place between Auntie Radha and Rajan.

3.4.5 Chapter 3—Say No Evil; Hear No Evil

A sudden change occurs in the lifestyle of the Chelvanayagams. Arjuna's parents start associating closely with Uncle Sena and Auntie Chithra. The entire family frequent the Oberoi Supper Club. They start buying fancy foods such as blue berry jam, kippers, and canned apricot at Cornell's Supermarket, where they start doing the shopping. The two families once go in their cars to the down south of Sri Lanka and stop at a hotel which is still under construction. Only there Arjuna gets to know that the father had quitted his banking job and entered the hotel industry with Uncle Sena. The Paradise Beach Resort looks elegant. The gatekeeper and the manager Mr Samarakoon are very respectful to the family. The stretch of beach seen from the hotel appears to be the most beautiful one Arjuna has ever seen in his life. He gets thrilled by the information that the hotel is partly his family's.

The father is about to go to Europe to take a holiday as well as to promote the hotel. He advises the kids to order five items to be brought from Europe. Arjuna has been fascinated by the contents in Auntie Nelya's collection of "Little Women." Auntie Nelya gives him what she has of them as she is not married and does not have a family of her own. The father remarks that "Little Women" was for girls, but Arjuna wants the sequels to "Little Women" to be brought from Europe.

After the father's departure the mother continues the lifestyle they had started together. She starts associating with the elite of Colombo, including the Ministers and the former Prime Minister Mrs Bandaranayake ripped of her civic rights. Then, as if to contradict her optimism, Uncle Daryl enters her life. Arjuna takes him for a European white man but gets astonished with his perfect Sinhala. He was a member of the next door family of Auntie Nelya. So Auntie Nelya recognises him as one of the oldest and dearest friends the family had. Daryl who has now returned from Australia after 15 years is a Burgher. When the mother meets Uncle Daryl she gets so excited that Arjuna notices that there should have been a romantic relationship between the two of them.

Uncle Daryl visits the mother the following day too. But that day Arjuna is in bed down with fever. He finds Uncle Daryl to be a friendly person, as he brings him some sequels to "Little Women" from an old bookshop.

Daryl has come to Sri Lanka to investigate what is happening in terms of state terrorism. From the conversation, Arjuna learns that the mother is against Tamil Tigers and considers them terrorists but Uncle Daryl holds a different view. A European woman journalist had told him about the Prevention of Terrorism Act in Sri Lanka which has led to state terrorism. Arjuna learns that Daryl is a sympathiser of the Tamil Tigers. Auntie Nelya and the mother talk about Uncle Daryl. The mother brushes off Auntie Nelya's apprehension about Uncle Daryl's visits. The mother says that there is nothing strange about it. A free economy with the freedom of the press is the mother's wish.

Arjuna recovers in the mean time. Daryl comes one day and give him the copies of Little Women, Little Men, and Joy Boys. Arjuna is thrilled to have them. He notices that the mother going out in her smartest clothes and feels that something is going on between the mother and Uncle Daryl. Auntie Nelya is often angry with the mother for this; Sonali becomes quiet as if to hide something; and Varuna loses his temper. Finally, Varuna and Sonali both behave rudely towards Uncle Daryl.

After some time the mother takes Arjuna to the country on a short holiday. Uncle Daryl meets them both at the bungalow they reside. First Arjuna feels worried about it but becomes cheerful, remembering his generosity. They get close to each other and Arjuna finds Uncle Daryl more impressive than the father in his figure and deportment.

Uncle Daryl visits them everyday in this bungalow in the hills. As Arjuna is no problem, the mother feels more and more loving and kind towards Uncle Daryl. The final day in the hills, mother and Uncle Daryl have an argument over his plans to go to Jaffna. Mother tries to dissuade him from going as it is too dangerous, but Uncle Daryl is adamant that he should. Arjuna feels like an unwitting accomplice in the Mother-Uncle Daryl affair. While they live alone in the hills away from the family, he fears if a divorce transpires between the mother and the father.

Unlce Daryl leaves for Jaffna. Arjuna and mother come home to Colombo. They are received by the rest of the family at the Railway station. Back home they get back to their normal work.

When the school starts after a few months, Ajuna finds it difficult to cope with the "rigid timetables, cantankerous teachers, and irritating boy." On his final day at school, mother comes to collect him with Uncle Daryl. They seem to have been in a fight.

Mother drives Uncle Daryl home. He tries to touch her but she objects, as he is going to Jaffna again the following day. When they arrive home Aunt Nelya is to ask Arjuna about what happened but he escapes from her. After Uncle Daryl's departure for Jaffna, mother starts again going with Aunt Chithra out to parties, fashion shows, and dances but not with her early enthusiasm.

On the radio it is announced that Jaffna has been in heavy troubles. A policeman has been killed and a group of policemen have rampaged through a village. The TULF office and an MP's house have been burnt down. When mother comes home Arjuna tells her all that and asks about Uncle Daryl. Mother is really upset. The following day on their way back from school Arjuna and mother go to Uncle Daryl's place. They find a mess in his room. The news of the day sounds very bad. The Jaffna Library has been burnt down with 95,000 books. When they have come home they speak with Aunt Nelya about Uncle Daryl. But Aunt Nelya's advice is not to get the police involved in the search. However, mother goes to the police station and makes a complaint. Then a senior police officer speaks to her and takes the matter to the officer inside. After some time mother is summoned to the ASP's room. He takes down mother's complaint and arranges a team of police constables to go to the place where Uncle Daryl lives. The police officers search the house. The servant boy tries to run away but he is caught by a policeman. Despite mother's declaration that the boy is innocent, he is taken into police custody and is taken to the police station.

The ASP very tactfully elicits from mother all the necessary information about Uncle Daryl. He has gone to Jaffna on behalf of a newspaper to investigate police torture of Jaffna Tamils. The ASP tells mother that the police generally do not torture people though some individual policemen take the law into their hand.

That evening father calls from Europe. Mother speaks with him as if nothing unusual has happened. The following day on a call from the ASP mother and Arjuna go to the police station again. The ASP tells mother about his acquaintance with father as a result of playing badminton together. He introduces the boy as a thief and tells that he has robbed some valuables from the room. He later cheekily says, "My regards to your husband. I'm sure he'll be fascinated by all that's happened in his absence." The implication is horrible. The police investigation has probed into mother's secret relationship with Uncle Daryl.

That evening mother receives a telephone call to the effect that Uncle Daryl's body has been found. Mother and Aunt Nelya are summoned by the police to the shore to identify Uncle Daryl's body found by some fishermen. On their return home, mother speaks about the hypocrisy of the police; "Of course, they have witnesses who saw him go swimming."

She musters up her courage to protest against Uncle Daryl's killing. Aunt Nelya tells that it would be futile after he has died. Mother, while suffering from a headache, regrets her failure to stop him from going to Jaffna. She really wants to do something against state terrorism that has raised its ugly head but does not know what to do. She laments. Arjuna compares the situation with that in which Beth dies in *Little Women.*

Mother goes with Arjuna to see QC Appadurei regarding Uncle Daryl's death or murder. The old man revives some ancient memories about mother and Uncle Daryl. Grandafather sends mother to Kerala with QC Appadurei for a three-month holiday to change her. She relates to the QC everything about Daryl save her private meetings and asks for his advice as a civil rights lawyer. The QC's advice is, "Let it rest, child." He justifies his position with the fact that any pursuance of it would invite troubles not only to her personally but to the entire family. Mother leaves the QC. He reveals that all their telephone conversations can be tapped by the police. His advice is related to the three wise monkeys who maintained the stand, "See no evil; hear no evil; and speak no evil."

On their way home they go to Uncle Daryl's home and find an old woman in lieu of the boy. The boy Somaratne has gone back to his village. Mother obtains the information and returns home. She realises what the QC said. A click is heard when mother phones Aunt Mala. Arjuna phones a friend and again the click is heard. So they realise that they cannot escape. They are spied.

That evening mother tells she is going to Somaratne the following morning. Arjuna offers to join her. Despite it is Varuna's birthday, mother has already decided it. After a long drive they arrive at Somaratne's. The boy's mother and a few other women start shouting at mother. They refuse to show them Somaratne. Finally, after receiving many insults, they return to the car. They learn from the shouting that Somaratne's brother had been killed during the 1971 insurrection and this time Somaratne has come with a paralysed arm. When they started returning the villagers hurled stones at them. They ran towards the car. A stone hits Arjuna and he is badly hurt in the back.

In the car Arjuna shouts at mother for taking such a risk as they have been nearly killed in that village. They drive back to Colombo. When they arrive home it is late. Aunt Nelya gives mother a visiting card from a man from Daryl's paper "Sunday Morning Star." She warns her not to get involved in this matter as it is too dangerous. The following day the man from the press comes to see mother. He enquires from her about her relationship with Uncle Daryl and about her ideas about his death. She gives very curt responses and the man goes away. She cannot help behaving indifferently towards a colleague of her lover Daryl Brohier.

Arjuna is relieved that mother is cautious. He imagines how they would return to the old life after father has returned home. Father phones mother from England to organise a party to celebrate his return home and his birthday together. The due day the house is visited by about 75 people. Mother looks happy though she has been tired and sad inside. The old lamps in the garden make the people and the surroundings seem insubstantial.

3.4.6 Chapter 4—Small Choices

Arjuna's father receives a letter from his old friend Buddy Parameswaran's wife. The letter is accompanied by a piece of yellowed paper in which Arjuna's father had agreed to protect his family under any circumstance by signing in blood. The letter is a request for a job for his son Jagan who is already working as an accountant for a pro-LTTE campaign called Gandhian Movement. Ascertained to himself that if he were a Tiger he would be straight away out, Arjuna's father makes up his mind to see Jagan. One evening Jagan visits. Arjuna's father remains stunned to see him as he looks just like his father Buddy Parameswaran. He readily offers to help Jagan. When Jagan uses the apostrophe "Sir" to call Arjuna's father, the latter tells him to replace it by "Uncle." When Arjuna's mother enquires from him about Gandhian Movement, Jagan replies that there is no policy-wise connection between the Gandhians and the Tigers. His father discourages his mother's inquiries as he has already decided that Jagan could work for him. Arjuna remains infatuated by Jagan's hefty personality. He observes the latter's arms, neck, and thighs. Arjuna connects his observations with his puberty. As a teenager he has already undergone some physical changes including his voice. He wants to be a physically attractive and graceful man.

Arjuna's father invites Jagan to stay for dinner. In the mean time he apologises his inability to have attended the funeral of Jagan's father. Later he tells Arjuna's mother that he is planning to give Jagan the store room to stay. Arjuna's mother agrees to this suggestion. Arjuna is very happy that Jagan has come to live with them. The following day Arjuna visits Jagan in his own room in the house that his mother and Aunty Nelya had taken a lot of trouble to clean and arrange. The room is cosy. Soon Jagan and Arjuna's father become inseparables. They go to work together. By listening to conversations between them Arjuna learns that his father has had a similar childhood as his. Once he learns that he has had a romantic relationship with an English girl working in his university in England. He did not marry her. After coming back to Sri Lanka he came to his senses. The low class is the low class either in England or in Sri Lanka.

Arjuna's father talks with Jagan about Arjuna's tendency to play with dollies and read books. He expresses his pleasure over the growing relationship between Arjuna and Jagan as he believes that it would lead to a healthy development of the boy. Jagan sounds sympathetic with the idea and tells that there is nothing wrong with Arjuna. Arjuna feels grateful to Jagan for defending him.

The Government of Sri Lanka is about to hold a referendum to extend its term by another six years without an election. The ballot paper designed for this has two signs—the lamp for proposition and the pot for opposition. The voter who does not want an election crosses the square next to the lamp and the one who wants an election, the square next to the pot. Greedy for power, the Government promotes the lamp by putting up posters everywhere. A man is found putting up a poster on the parapet wall of the Chelvanayagams. The entire household including Jagan come out to see him doing it. Arjuna's father tells the man that it is illegal to put up posters on private walls. The man does not regard his protest. Jagan intervenes in the situation on behalf of the Chelvanayagams. He assaults the man and tears the poster. The man threatens, "It is government property." Everybody is panicked by the man's threatening. Arjuna's father regrets that Jagan has had an unnecessary fight with the man, but his mother justifies what Jagan did.

As Jagan is an efficient person, he gets promoted to a supervisory rank. Arjuna's father and Uncle Sena agree that if Jagan does the supervision, they can concentrate on the next hotel project in Trincomalee. The entire family visit their hotel three hours to the south from Colombo. There are many tourists on the beach. Jagan notices the tourists exploiting the poor children on the beach around the hotel and makes a remark about it. Jagan's father explains that the tourists come to Sri Lanka not only for the beaches but also for fun with other natural resources. The implication is sex.

The following day afternoon there is a dispute between Jagan and the hotel manager. Jagan wants to correct a worker and the hotel manager suggests to him that he conveys the matter to the manager and the manager will take action. Jagan considers this funny and complains it to Arjuna's father, but Arjuna's father justifies the manager's position about it. He explains further to Jagan that the hotel is a Sinhala-Tamil joint business and these things happen in a diplomatic way, as the Tamils are vulnerable in a Sinhlala-dominant area. He draws an example, that, during the racial troubles, the hotel was protected because of its Sinhala partnership. Banduratne Mudalali the biggest hotelier in the area is a racist and killed many Tamil families and burned them. So Jagan is advised to follow the set procedure and make a good living by working in collaboration with the others. The bottom line is that to be diplomatic is important as otherwise there may be many sensitive issues.

Jagan tells Arjuna about Sinhala violence upon Tamils. The Tamils are tortured to death by the Sinhala military and police. One friend of his was tortured and he left for Canada. Jagan has had a brief stint with the Tigers. But he has now left them. The Tamils live second-class citizens in Sri Lanka under threats from the Sinhalese. Jagan finds Arjuna identical with his friend who left for Canada. He tells about the Tiger camps in India and his friend in the Gandhian Movement.

Back in Colombo Arjuna joins Jagan in jogging in the evenings. His brother Varuna is jealous about this but Jagan is internally happy. Varuna is also a bit arrogant towards Jagan. Jagan accosts a Tamil minister at the Sports Ministry grounds. He has been a schoolmate of Jagan's but does not want to have any rapport with him. His expensive car has been parked outside the grounds. After this meeting Jagan does not want to go to the police grounds in the future.

One day the police call in search of Jagan. The entire family is in turmoil because of this. When Jagan has come home he is told about it. Arjuna's father inquires from Jagan whether he has had any connection with the Tigers and Jagan replies that he used to have but not any more. Then he suggests that Jagan goes to the police well-dressed and speaks to a senior police officer in favour of Jagan. Arjuna's father accompanies Jagan to the police station, and Jagan is kept at the police station for questioning under the Prvention of Terrorism Act. Arjuna's father comes home alone. This depresses everybody at home including Arjuna.

Arjuna's father reveals that Jagan has been searched because he has been found talking to two Tamil men at the Sports Ministry grounds. They are Tigers and they have planned to kill a Tamil minister who has been considered a traitor by the LTTE. It is on a tip given by the minister that Jagan has been taken into custody.

The charges are false but it is a Tamil minister who made the complaint. Arjuna's father comes home the following day. In the papers it appears that Jagan Parameswaran alleged to have assassinated a minister has been found with a hotelier. The entire story with personal names appears in the papers. Following this, Arjuna's family receives many filthy calls from unknown people.

The hotel is in a mess as Uncle Sena and the staff get many filthy calls. There is a note on Arjuna's father's desk accusing him of being a Tiger. The family suspect that it must be the work of a staff member. That evening Jagan comes home on being released by the police. Jagan remains reticent about his interrogation. Arjuna's father suggests that Jagan takes a holiday for some time, despite Jagan's denial. His idea is to keep Jagan out of the scene for some time as the newspaper releases have created a mess in the hotel. All Tamil and Muslim members of the hotel staff express their disbelief about Jagan's allegations but the manager Mr Samarakoon and the receptionist Mr Wickremasinghe keep silent. However, Jagan goes to work the following day but feels very uncomfortable.

Jagan experiences insubordination from a peon who makes a mistake in delivering a parcel. All people take the peon's side including Arjuna's father. When Arjuna's mother comments on the injustice caused to Jagan, his father reveals the danger of taking Jagan's side. There is a notion that speaking Tamil in public is dangerous and Tamil helping a Tamil in whatever matter is dangerous however reasonable it is. Arjuna's mother seems to have started considering that the Tigers and their separate state have some meaning in a situation where the Tamils are suppressed by the Sinhalese. His father considers she is mad to think so.

A week later, inspection time comes around. Mr Samarakoon is assigned to supervise Jagan. This time Aunty Chitra, Uncle Sena, Arjuna's father, and his mother, all are going, as their presence will help Jagan. Everybody is vigilant about the treatment Jagan receives from the others. It is decisive for Jagan. The front staff warmly greet Jagan. Inside the hotel it is all comfortable. In the afternoon, Arjuna, his mother, his brother, his sister, Aunty Chitra, and Jagan go out to visit a rock on the beach. They walk along.

Some people are found laughing and singing at an open van. They calm down when the group get close to them, but while they are returning they shout, "Ado Tiger." Jagan gets excited. A little later a bottle falls at him. Following this, the entire group run to the hotel. At the hotel Mr Samarakoon explains that they are the sons of Banduratne Mudalali.

Arjuna's father and Uncle Sena get the security tightened for that night. After the gathering has dispersed Arjuna's father and his mother talk about going to Canada. His father is adamant that he is not going there and expresses his displeasure over the treatment the coloured people receive in America and other countries in the hands of the white people there.

That night after dinner there is unrest in the hotel. Someone has written across a window in Sinhala, "Death to all Tamil pariahs." This worries everybody in the hotel. Foreign guests in the hotel are too very excited and do all remain gathered around Jegan. Uncle Sena tries his best to calm down them but the guests are very anxious. They keep on questioning what the words mean. Leaving the situation to Mr Samarakoon and Ms De Silva, Arjuna's father and Uncle Sena leave the hotel with their families. They find Jegan's suitcase open and his clothes all torn. This seems to have been done by a member of the hotel staff. The writing across the window and the messing of Jegan's room have a connection. Uncle Sena claims that calling the police has no use as that will harass the innocent and leave the culprits free. In a while Ms De Silva complains that all the guests are checking out as they have received an interpretation of the writing across the window as that the hotel will be bombed that night. Uncle Sena and Aunty Chitra try to salvage the situation. The head house keeper expresses fear to remove the writing across the window. Then Arjuna's mother does it with Arjuna and Sonali. Arjuna's mother cleans Jegan's window and tells him to be active. But Jegan's does not know what to do.

The following day Arjuna's father keeps drinking while the rest of the family join Chitra for a swim. They walk to the beach and Uncle Sena and Arjuna's father discuss how to remove Jegan. They plan to send him to the Middle East. Jegan is upset about the whole thing. Arjuna is worried about his father's failure to keep his promise to Jegan's father. Arjuna notices Jegan putting the luggage on to the roof rack of the car. He learns that Jegan does not want to go to the Middle East. It is presumable that he wants to join the LTTE instead. Arjuna starts hating Jegan.

The following day the family find Jegan has left the house. When Arjuna arrives home with his brother and sister after school, his mother is found removing the furniture that had lied in Jegan's room back into their early place.

The referendum takes place after Jegan has left. The ruling party MPs get the ballot boxes stuffed with papers marked in favour of their wish. The average voter is intimidated and is not allowed to cast his/her vote. Finally, the results are announced on TV and accordingly, the ruling party is supposed to stay in power for another six years without an election.

3.4.7 Chapter 5—The Best School of All

Arjuna's father decides to transfer him from St Gabriel to Victoria Academy which is attended by Varuna. St Gabriel is run by Catholic priests whereas Victoria Academy by a principal appointed by the Ministry of Education. The punishments imposed on the boys at Victoria Academy are more severe than those at St Gabriel. But the management of Victoria is interfered by politics.

Abeysinghe, the principal, is in a battle with Lokubandara, the vice-principal, whose brother is a Minister. Therefore, Abeysinghe may have to step down from his post and give way to Lokubandara. Abeysinghe is a strict disciplinarian who believes in corporal punishment. He punishes the boys severely even for minor offences.

Arjuna cannot object to his father's decision and is supposed to start at Victoria from January the following year. Father's sole idea is to change Arjuna from being "funny" or "girlish." He trusts that Victoria will mould him as a man. Arjuna already finds the boys at Victoria with their "loud confidence" threatening. So he is anticipating a challenging school life in Victoria the following year.

After the Christmas holidays, Arjuna has to go to the new school. He is very unhappy about it. However, he goes to Victoria with his brother. His brother shows Arjuna the principal Black Tie. He looks old fashioned in his fully white kit and black tie and the sola topee. Then they come to the class that Arjuna is supposed to join 9C. One boy Salgado tries to direct Arjuna and Varuna both to the Tamil Class 9F but Varuna tells him that Arjuna is due to join 9C. Again Salgado tries to send Arjuna to the Tamil class and Zoysa comes to his rescue, saying, "Salgado, you are the guy who wants Tamils to learn Sinhala." They somehow calm down when the teacher comes in.

Arjuna takes an interest in Zoysa and looks at him too often. During Mathematics he uses Zoysa's protractor and sends him a note of thanks for it. But Zoysa with his long hair does not regard it important. Arjuna is in a dilemma about whether to send a note like that was right or wrong. Arjuna's observation of him gives more clues to Zoysa's character.

During PE Zoysa goes out on the pretext of using the toilet and comes back after the interval. His immaculately white ironed clothes have been crumpled when he returns. Once Arjuna goes to the toilet he finds Salgado and a few others harassing Chelliah. Later he gets to know that Cheliah is the leader of the Tamil section and Salgado and he are sworn enemies. He says that Lokubandara backs Salgado's racism. Lokubandara is considered "a snake in the grass."

The next day the PE period is taken by a prefect. After a short while one Mr Sundaralingam takes the class. He gets the class to read some lines from 'The Best School of All' by Sir Henry Newbolt. The prefect predicts that he is going to rope Arjuna into a theatrical production. Later that morning Arjuna gets summons from Black Tie through Angel of Death. The prefect nicknamed him so because he always brings bad news.

When he goes to Black Tie's office he finds Mr Sundaralingam seated next to him. Arjuna is given two poems – 'The Best School of All' and 'Vitae Lampada' – and is asked to learn them and come prepared to give a perfect recital of them the following day. In fact his plan is to get him to recite them at the next prize giving. After the school is over that day, Zoysa catches Arjuna and asks him about the meeting with Black Tie. He describes what happened and Zoysa is surprised by the distinction.

Varuna meets them together, and after Zoysa has gone Varuna warns him against associating with Zoysa and reveals his sexual connections with the head prefect. Arjuna charges Varuna in return for inventing a story to insult someone whom he likes. He does not believe Varuna at all.

Although Arjuna does not like the poems he manages to commit them to his memory. He finds both poems misinterpreting the reality. The following day Arjuna goes to the principal's office. He gets Zoysa to check his recitation, trying to recite them from memory. He fails due to being frightened by Black Tie. So he receives a terrible caning. The principal behaves like a brute in the whole scenario. With a cane in his presence, he wants the child to recite two poems. So under harassment he fails to give a proper rendition of the poems. Then, finally, he gets severely punished. His interpretation is that if does not do it at the moment the student will ruin his future.

After the school has been over, Arjuna comes to his classroom with Zoysa and collects his books to go home. His anger over the humiliation and pain was so much that he tares the sheets with the poems into pieces. Zoysa tries to stop him but it proves useless. Then he tells that the sheets are needed for the following day meeting with Black Tie. They decide to go to the British Council and get the two poems photocopied. Arjuna and Zoysa become good friends on this matter. They leave each other physically but Arjuna is highly preoccupied with Zoysa the whole night. The dream he has of Zoysa ends with a wetness on his saron.

The following day Arjuna goes ready to recite the poems but in the sight of the cane he forgets everything. He receives a severe caning from Black Tie for this. This time a severe type of caning is served on Zoysa too. Arjuna sees Mr Sundaralingam over this. When he relates everything to Mr Sundaralingam the latter explains that he has to put up with this as Black Tie belongs to a different generation of people. An orphan raised by the former principal Mr Lawson now behaves like that because of various shortcomings he has had as an orphan during his education. "Our principal is a strict man but he is not cruel." Sundaralingam says to Arjuna.

Through Mr Sundaralingam's intervention both Arjuna and Zoysa get released by the principal. In acknowledgement of this comfort, Zoysa kisses Arjuna in his mouth and it has a shocking effect on Arjuna. They plan to meet at Zoysa's place at five-thirty that afternoon. Zoysa recreates that experience in his mind and wants to have it in real (in all its detail and sensation) again. They meet in the evening at Zoysa's but nothing happens.

When Arjuna comes home in the evening and reveals to his family that he went to visit a friend in the Cinnamon Gardens, they become happy and encourage him to invite his friend to lunch. Varuna warns Arjuna against this connection but in vain.

On Saturday that week Arjuna invites Zoysa to his place. They join Sonali and her friends in a game of hide and seek. Arjuna and Zoysa hide in the garage and there they have their first homosexual intercourse. After the act Arjuna has a repulsive feeling. They have been rather too long in the garage. When they join the rest of the family, the others are curious as to what they had been doing so long. Arjuna comes to realise that Varuna is right when he recalls the experience. Even Arjuna's father does not approve of Zoysa. Arjuna feels therefore that he has betrayed his family by getting involved with Zoysa. Thus, his weekend ends in disillusionment with him.

That night he dreams of Zoysa again. He refers to head prefect. This time the sexual act appears to him in concrete. He becomes conscious that he likes the act with Zoysa but he has the repulsive feeling about the wet salivary sperms dripping along his legs.

The following day when Arjuna is at school he notices Zoysa to be a different person. His emotions have become more conspicuous than before. He does not vanish from the class during the interval. Salgado also notices this. That day the vice principal comes to the class and snatches him by the ear for not reporting to his office. Arjuna feels sorry for Zoysa. He is concerned about Zoysa's welfare. Arjuna regrets the way in which he treated Zoysa after realising that Zoysa neither debased nor degraded him but offered his love to him in the garage.

He feels grateful to Zoysa for his being kind to him during his detention on the balcony and wants to befriend him again. Then when Zoysa returns to the classroom after school he speaks to him trying to repair his friendship. But the response from Zoysa does not sound very conducive.

After he comes home Arjuna waits for a call from Zoysa but finally decides to go and meet him on his own. He arrives at Zoysa's and finds him in a miserable state. He talks to him for reconciliation. Zoysa implies that he has already forgiven Arjuna. Finally, he declares his real worry. He cannot stand constant punishment but that is what he is faced with at school.

Arjuna starts wondering about the power structure in society. The principal and father being adults are the ones who create rules for the others to follow as they are endowed with authority, and he and Zoysa have to follow them. Whether they are right or wrong or fair or unfair, Arjuna could not stand the pattern in which order and discipline are maintained in society. He starts wondering whether people like him or Zoysa will ever have a chance of being powerful.

The following day Zoysa comes to school with a new idea. His mother is in England and is planning to join her with his father's blessings. Arjuna does not have any idea about it at all, and therefore he is a bit sad. After the second period Arjuna goes to the principal's office and recites the poems very fluently. The principal is satisfied and wants Arjuna to retain them in memory as they represent some values which are already in the process of disappearance.

Arjuna is supposed to recite the poems at the prize giving as the principal has decided to write his speech based on these poems. But Arjuna wants to fail Black Tie as that would release Zoysa from his daily punishment, and because any shortcomings at the prize giving would lead to Black Tie's defeat at his battle with Lokubandara.

For the prize giving all parents including Arjuna's come to the school. They have already taken their seats in the auditorium. The ceremony starts with the playing of the national anthem. Soon after the national anthem, Arjuna's recitation takes place. Arjuna receives all necessary moral support from the teachers including Mr Sundaralingam. The principal and his wife are seated in the front row along with the Minister. So Arjuna deliberately confuses his recital of the poems. He does so, in order to work out the expulsion of the principal.

After the recitation, except for Mr Sundaralingam, the teachers recoil from Arjuna, as if he is carrying a contagious disease. Mr Sundaralingam consoles him, "Never mind, Chelvanayagam, you did your best." The principal starts his speech soon after Arjuna's recitation. First he charges Arjuna as an example of the deterioration the nation is heading for. People start laughing their heads off, but thanks to the microphone he continues his speech. With an enormous difficulty he ends his speech, and invites the Minister to address the gathering. When the prize giving starts Arjuna goes out of the auditorium and meets Zoysa. Alone with Zoysa in a classroom, he divulges that he deliberately messed up the recitation mainly for the sake of Zoysa. "I did it for you... I could not bear to see you suffer any more..." After some homosexual fun, they leave the classroom and enter the auditorium to attend the school anthem. Arjuna finds him getting away from his mother and holding Zoysa as part and parcel of his life. He meets Zoysa again and again and learns how their bodies respond to each other in homosexual embrace.

3.4.8 Chapter 6—Riot Journal: An Epilogue

The final section of *Funny Boy* consists of a number of Arjie's journal entries from July and August of 1983. The first entry begins on July 25 at 6 AM. Arjie writes that the phone rang in the early hours of the morning and Appa informed the family that "there was trouble in Colombo. All the Tamil houses near the Kanaththa Cemetery had been burnt." The family is dumbstruck and Amma wonders why; Appa explains that it is in retaliation for a Tamil Tigers attack against some soldiers, whose funeral took place the previous night. But Appa says not to worry, and that the reports are probably being blown out of proportion. Arjie feels that writing is the only thing he can do. Neliya Aunty and Amma have breakfast as normal in an "attempt to provide some normalcy," but this only shows Arjie "how frighteningly different" today is.

At 9:30 AM on the same day, Arjie writes that Sena Uncle and Chithra Aunty visited the site of the riots and confirmed that the Tamils' houses really were burned down, and the violence is spreading. The adults finish their conversation in Appa's study, and the children hear Amma sounding concerned inside. When they come out, the adults announce that the family will stay with Chithra and Sena for some time. Amma promises it is "just a precaution" but the children do not believe her; Amma has even sent Anula away. They each bring a backpack with clothes and one important personal item. Most of the family is okay, but "Ammachi and Appachi's area is particularly bad" and they might have to hide in neighbors' houses. The radio transmissions do not mention violence, and even announce that there is no curfew.

At 11 AM, Arjie learns what the adults were talking about in secret: he overheard the adults in the garden explain that the government is supporting the riots, which is why there is no curfew, police attempts to stop the violence, or information on the radio. In fact, "the mobs [got] electoral lists" from the government and used them to find Tamil families—which means Arjie's family has to leave their house, or they will remain at risk.

At 12:30 PM, still on July 25, Arjie writes that he is "frightened" because the family's phones are not working and Sena Uncle has not come to pick them up.

At 1 PM, Arjie writes that "the government has now declared curfew," which is a relief "because this means that the government is not behind the rioting." Because of the curfew, however, Sena Uncle cannot come get the family. Appa and Arjie think "the situation will soon be under control," but Amma still wants to go to Chithra's house.

At 3 PM, Arjie explains that the riots have actually worsened since the curfew, and describes what happened to Sena Uncle: A man stops at the family's front gate and Appa cautiously goes outside to meet him. The man, an employee of Appa's, tells him that "thugs stole all the petrol from" Sena Uncle's van. In fact, the man rushed out of work when he learned of the riots—which he passed on his way, and where he saw the police doing nothing. Appa's colleague came across people pouring the oil from Sena Uncle's van on a car with a family inside, and then a man asking around for a match. Appa's colleague left as fast as possible and came to inform Arjie's family, who now cannot stop thinking about the family in the car but try to go on with their days as normal.

At 6:45 PM, still on July 25, Arjie writes that Amma and Appa told the children how to escape the house in case the mob shows up at their doorstep. They will climb a ladder and hide with their neighbors, the Pereras, who have already taken their valuables and birth certificates. The whole family is "certain that the mob will come," only unsure *when*.

At 11:30 PM, Arjie writes that he cannot stand waiting for the mob to show up, and almost wants them to come now and "put [the family] out of this misery." Everyone went to bed with day clothes on and nobody has fallen asleep. The adults will wake the children up during the night if the mob comes.

At 12:30 PM on July 26, Arjie writes that "it seems unbelievable" that so much has passed since his last journal entry 13 hours before, and that "our lives have completely changed." Neliya Aunty woke him up in the middle of the night, and they quietly made their way to the dining room as the mob's chants approached the house. The family made their way to the backyard and, one by one, climbed the ladder up the wall and jumped into the Pereras' yard. Appa and Diggy hid the ladder, and then the family hid in the Pereras' storeroom, which has a small window high on the wall.

The same journal entry continues. The mob has stopped yelling, but Arjie and his family hear their front door shatter and their house get ransacked. And then they see smoke out of the small window and realize that the mob is burning their house down. The room gets intensely bright for a while, and then dark again, and the mob has left; all the family can hear are the beams of their house falling down. After the commotion, Perera Uncle opens the storeroom door. Appa wants to check out the house immediately, but Amma insists he wait until the morning. The family goes out for tea with the Pereras.

In the morning, the family goes to survey their burned-down house, which is unrecognizable except for the gate out front and generally seems much smaller. They go inside and look at their old possessions, now completely destroyed, but Arjie feels "not a trace of remorse, not a touch of sorrow for the loss and destruction around [him]," because his "heart refuses to understand" that his house is gone. Finally, Chithra Aunty and Sena Uncle stop by in their van—Chithra Aunty cries and, ironically enough, Amma comforts her. Neighbors stop by and pay their respects. The family's women collect their few surviving possessions; the men do not. As they head off with Sena Uncle and Chithra Aunty, the neighbors bring them provisions.

At 3 PM, still on July 26, the family learns that Ammachi and Appachi have also had their house burned down—their whole street, full of burned houses, "looks as if someone has dropped a bomb on it." Ammachi and Appachi go to stay with Kanthi Aunty. Arjie remembers passing spend-the-days there in his childhood and cries.

At 6 PM the same day, Arjie writes that "something awful has happened." Someone anonymously called Sena Uncle and said they knew he was sheltering Tamils, and that that night they would all be killed and his house burned. Amma and Appa want to go to a refugee camp, but Sena Uncle insists they stay, so they make another escape plan: they can go through a hidden door to Sena Uncle's mother's neighboring house and hide in her library. Arjie is "tired of these escape plans" and "just want[s] it all to end."

At 11 PM, Arjie explains that they had another "scare" two hours before. After dinner, a group of men came to the door and the family had to hide in Sena Uncle's mother's library for an hour until they left. The men claimed to only have been "collecting funds for a sport meet," but Arjie thinks "it is obvious that something odd is going on." Sena Uncle thinks the men are only after money, but Appa and Amma still want to go to the refugee camp.

On the next day, July 27, at 6 PM, Arjie writes that the brief break in the curfew—for the purpose of buying groceries—was useless, because so many grocery stores were Tamil-owned and thus burned down. Many people visit Arjie, but "only bring dismal and depressing news." The only person Arjie is happy to see is Shehan, whom he "wanted more than anything else to hold" but could not because of his family's presence; Amma tells Diggy not to follow them out into the garden, where Shehan tells Arjie he visited the house only to find it burned down. Shehan changes the subject and they make plans to see a movie, but then Arjie realizes something: "Shehan was Sinhalese and I was not."

The same entry continues. An uncle from Canada, Lakshman, calls to explain that there are protests in Canada, India, and England over the riots, and that the family can get refugee status and go to Canada. The family is hopeful, and Appa says that they should "watch the situation for a little longer and then decide." But Arjie hears him later quietly telling Amma to apply for the children's passports.

The next evening, on July 28, at 8 PM, Arjie writes that the family has learned that Appa's hotel was attacked and almost burned down, although the guests had been moved out. The president gave an address which "expressed no sympathy for what we Tamils have suffered, nor [...] condemn[ed] the actions of the thugs." In the garden, Appa tells Amma that "it is very clear that we no longer belong in this country." In retrospect, Appa says, he should have known that this would happen. He asks Amma how she, on the other hand, clearly knew that this violence was coming. They decide that they will plan for Canada after the violence ends. Arjie is "glad," as he "long[s] to be out of this country" because it is not safe for him and no longer his home.

On July 29, at 10 AM, Arjie writes that the visitors continue—this time, it is Ammachi and Appachi, who are just talking about losing their own house. Arjie is "irritated and lethargic," but not "sad and nostalgic," about losing his house. He misses only his things and his private space, and especially Shehan. Amma has started crying in the bathroom about losing the house.

At 1 PM on the same day, Arjie writes that the rioters have returned, yelling that the Tamil Tigers are now in Colombo—a story that the radio denies. Ammachi and Appachi left for Kanthi's house, but did not arrive, and everyone is worried and praying. There is a curfew again.

Four days later, on August 2nd, Arjie writes that "so many things have happened." Sena Uncle came back shortly after the previous journal entry and reported that a mob burned Ammachi and Appachi's car, with them inside. Amma broke down crying; Appa insisted on going to the scene of the crime to investigate what happened to his parents. The rest did not let him; Sena Uncle went back, instead, to "look out for [...] stray dogs and cats." The family was silent; Amma said they should "inform the rest of the family."

In the same entry, Arjie's narration jumps to the day before, three days after Ammachi and Appachi were killed, and the day of their funeral. Radha Aunty came from America, and the way she held her head reminded Arjie of Ammachi. The funeral seemed "unreal," and out of shock and disbelief, nobody cried; Arjie feels that the world is forever changed.

Almost a month later, on August 25, Arjie writes that he has gotten his passport and now "finally realize[s] that we are really leaving Sri Lanka" and heading to Canada in two days. He remembers fantasizing about foreign lands as a child with Diggy and Sonali, but recognizes "that great difficulties lie ahead." Appa is staying in Sri Lanka for some time to "settle many things." They will go to stay with their Lakshman Uncle, whom they barely know. And they can barely bring any money. Arjie sees a beggar at a traffic light and "wonder[s] if this would be our plight in Canada."

On August 27, Arjie writes that he has visited Shehan for the last time and "can still smell his particular odor on my body, which always lingers after we make love," and which this time he does not want to wash off, lest he "lose this final memento." Their lovemaking was "passionless, uncoordinated, and tentative," emotionally withdrawn because they were both afraid of getting hurt.

On his ride home from Shehan's house to Sena Uncle's, Arjie realized that he had forgotten something, and went to visit the remnants of his family's old burned-down house, which "looked even more bare, even more desolate than before." He was astonished to see that "everything that was not burnt had been stolen," from doors and furniture to rain pipes. Arjie began to cry loudly, out of anger, until he exhausted himself. He turned around and realized that even the flowers in the garden were stolen, probably for pooja (prayers) by people hoping "to increase their chances of a better life in the next birth." As it began to rain torrentially, Arjie left the gate open and biked back to Sena Uncle's house. From the top of a hill, he looks back to the house, which he sees momentarily before "the rain fell faster and thicker, obscuring it."

Although this chapter is listed as an epilogue, it is actually an integral part of the novel, essential for understanding Sri Lanka's history and Arjie's retrospective narrative voice in light of the other chapters. However, as a series of journal entries, this chapter is also narratively distinct, because it is the only one that Arjie narrates during the action, in the present tense. This contributes to his sense of urgency but also forces readers to fill in the gaps between entries. It also helps account for Arjie's decision to narrate his past: he notes here that, when overcome by fear and anxiety, he naturally gravitated toward writing to find solace. Readers may already know that July 1983 was when the Sri Lankan Civil War began; regardless, Arjie immediately realizes that the family's longstanding fears of violence in Colombo have finally come true, and they know this could have profound consequences for their future.

After learning about Amma's personal flaws, moral conflicts, emotional history, and judgment errors throughout the book, Arjie easily sees through her attempts at feigning normalcy. Given his knowledge of the unpredictability of violence and memory of visiting Somaratne's village, Arjie can no longer trust that Amma will protect him—he is now old enough to know better and recognize that nothing can guarantee the family's safety. While their fear stems from others' possibility of treating them as homogeneous representatives of an ethnic group rather than complex human individuals, their faith in neighbors suggests that their interpersonal relationships with those around them can serve as a humanizing force to counterbalance against the reductionism of nationalist violence.

As the police's sinister persecution of Daryl Uncle and Jegan foreshadowed, now Sri Lanka is caught in conflict not only between certain Sinhalese and certain Tamils, but between the government and the Tamil population. The government uses the Tamil Tigers as an excuse to try and ethnically cleanse its own population, and this makes the family's situation all the more frightening: now defined as the enemy, they cannot turn to the government that is supposed to protect them against violence.

Waiting appears to be the most grating part of the riots, because it forces Arjie to process his own fears and recognize his ultimate vulnerability to violence. Sena Uncle's delay suggests that something may have gone wrong.

Arjie and his family's momentary relief demonstrates how accustomed they are to living through threats of violence; in the past, any escalation has been small-scale and momentary, and (besides the trouble reaching Colombo) there is no obvious indication that this time should or will be any different.

In fact, Arjie sees that the government is far more sinister than he thought, and that the curfew is likely the opposite of what it looked like: a way of ensuring that Tamils will be at home and therefore vulnerable to mob attacks. Appa's employee's report—which clearly implied that the mob was going to burn alive the Tamil family in the car—is frightening not only because of the extreme violence but also because of the senselessness and sheer anonymity of this violence, which testifies to the utter inhumanity of killers incapable of seeing their victims as human.

The very fact that the Chelvaratnams rely on their Sinhalese neighbors to shield them against a Sinhalese mob exposes the patent absurdity of the race riots, which turn individuals into the pawns of political movements and personal rage on the basis of ethnicity.

As the anticipation of violence hangs over its head, the family's habitual attempts to keep up even the most rudimentary appearances of normalcy—by going to bed when they expect to be attacked by an angry mob—no longer serves any function.

Unfortunately, the family was correct to predict the mob's imminent arrival and prudent to develop an escape plan. Although they were prepared for it, writing the day afterward, Arjie seems shocked that they could face such a direct threat in such an unpredictable context. Like the punishments doled out by

Ammachi and Black Tie, the beating Radha Aunty suffers, and Daryl and Jegan's surprise arrivals in Colombo, what proves to be the most consequential moment in the lives of Arjie's family members has no real connection, ethical or causal, to their own behaviour. They are being punished and made to suffer, but not for any distinct reason, and to Arjie the utter meaninglessness of their suffering is perhaps the most disturbing part of their fate.

The burning of the Chelvaratnams' house is particularly distressing because it serves as a message that they are no longer welcome in their own country, and that their identity is being forcibly uprooted by political conflicts. Although he already knows what he would see if he went outside, Appa's impulse to go look at the ruined house when the mob may still be nearby reflects his desire to salvage what he can of their physical possessions as well as their place in Sri Lankan society. Again, faced with circumstances that promise to drastically upend their futures, the Chelvaratnams do what little they can—have tea with the Pereras—to live normally in the meantime.

Burned to a shell of its former self, the house loses all the defining characteristics that would have previously made it identifiably Arjie's. Its loss is more bleak than heartbreaking, and the men and women differ over whether to try and salvage what they can to bring continuity into their new lives, or to leave everything behind and start anew. Because she is slightly further removed from the events, Chithra is able to process her emotions in a way the Chelvaratnams remain too traumatized—and perhaps too afraid—to do.

The apocalyptic imagery of the bomb suggests a kind of finality to the Tamils' experience in Colombo, a sign that life can and will never be the same again. The destruction of Ammachi and Appachi's house is significant not only because it shows the family continues to suffer even more seriously than before, but also because the house was so significant to Arjie's childhood, as a place of both freedom and gender socialization.

Arjie's family gets no chance to rest and process what has happened; the phone threat forces them back onto the defensive, and they appear poised to relive the horror of their previous night. Again, the threat to their lives is completely anonymous, unpredictable, and unconnected to anything that the family has itself done to deserve punishment.

Although they cannot know the intentions of the group of men who "visit" Sena Uncle, the family continues to expect violence and ends up reliving their previous night. Uncertainty—about whether these men are innocent or bloodthirsty, whether the phone threat was real or random, and whether they remain targets—becomes the Sinhalese and the government's most powerful tool against the Tamils.

The futility of the curfew shows that different ethnic communities in Sri Lanka are economically interdependent, and therefore exposes the socially self-destructive nature of the anti-Tamil riots. Now that he is forced to share Sena's home, Arjie encounters yet another burden that gets in the way of his processing his grief and spending quality time with Shehan: his lack of privacy. Arjie's recognition that "Shehan was Sinhalese and I was not" reflects Shehan's desire for normalcy—to see a movie—which is something Arjie knows he cannot easily return to, even though his family has been feigning normalcy since the beginning of the riots. Arjie also realizes for the first time that, no matter how little the Tamil-Sinhalese divide means to him, the simple fact that it matters so much to so many others means it creates a gap between the experiences of Tamil and Sinhalese Sri Lankans, further driving the groups apart in a vicious cycle.

Now, immigration looks far more attractive than it did last time; the international community's outrage underlines the moral horror of the government's stance but also suggests that the family has a brighter future to look forward to outside of Sri Lanka. Appa clearly fears leaving behind his country and business, but he also recognizes that the family can no longer continue fighting for a place in a country that has resolutely decided not to accept them.

As things begin to fall apart on a national scale, Arjie's family loses both faith that the government will try to quell the protests and their main economic reason for staying in Sri Lanka (their hotel). For perhaps the first time in the book, Appa acknowledges Amma's superior wisdom—perhaps because his thinking was so clouded by his desire for his business to work out, and because of her experience with Daryl Uncle. After insisting for years that only the Tamils or Sinhalese can belong in Sri Lanka, nationalist forces on both sides have turned this false choice into a reality.

Inundated with his experiences and his grandparents' stories of violence and loss, Arjie finds it difficult to continue feeling the constant stream of negative emotions that his situation warrants; in fact, the things he misses are not only symbols of the normalcy he can never recover, but also the very things that would allow him to emotionally process his pain: time and space alone, plus the chance to converse with the only person around whom he can truly be vulnerable.

The radio—and, by extension, the government—officially denies the rioters' tall tales, but it is clear that the government has both little genuine interest in saving Tamils and little power over the rioters it has unleashed.

The epilogue's final and most horrible act of violence brings the book full circle: back to Ammachi and Appachi, in whose care Arjie has his fondest memories of Sri Lanka. Like after the house burned down, Appa seems unable to accept the fact of his parents' deaths unless he sees it with his own eyes. Knowing how Appa would react but also that the bodies must be guarded from animals, Sena Uncle again steps up to help the family when it is too dangerous or painful for them to go out themselves.

Again, the funeral is so far outside the realm of Arjie's normal experience that he seems unable to emotionally process it at the time, especially since the threat of violence continues. Ammachi and Appachi's violent end helps explain the sense of nostalgia Arjie (as narrator) feels about his childhood with them, and Radha Aunty's arrival gestures to the long-term trauma she suffered after her attack, raising the question of how Arjie will adapt to his experiences in the long term.

Although he has had some time to process the trauma of losing his house and his grandparents, now Arjie is again thrown into a whirlwind, forced to pack up and reenvision his life in order to move into yet another uncertain future. When he contemplates Canada, he wonders about the possibility of a pluralist democracy: whether people like his family will be accepted in North America or will simply be treated yet again as outsiders to be controlled.

Like Radha's relationship with Anil and Amma's with Daryl Uncle, Arjie and Shehan are driven apart by political circumstances out of their control. When they have to break up, both of them clearly recognize what they are losing, but neither is devastated to see the other go; by maintaining an emotional distance, they sacrifice the chance to express their feelings a final time in addition to saving themselves from hurt. And yet, in retrospect, Arjie neither yearns for Shehan nor laments leaving him, but rather sees their relationship as an important growing experience. In this sense, throughout the book Arjie progresses from idealizing the romantic love of "bride-bride" and Sinhala love comics to recognizing that, although loss inevitably follows most love, it can still be a positive experience, worth enduring even if it does not itself endure.

In the closing passage of Funny Boy, Arjie confronts the house that represents his traumatic uprooting for the last time. The house's desolation stands for how his own life has been reduced to nothing; everything that has mattered to him has now become insignificant in the wake of the riots. His crying appears cathartic and suggests that he is finally beginning to process the trauma and suffering of his experiences on an emotional level. Arjie's musings about the stolen flowers point to the "next birth" he is about to undergo, when he moves halfway across the world to start over in an unknown place. In this vein, it is noteworthy that Selvadurai does not follow Arjie to Canada (and has also clarified that he has no plans to write a sequel). Instead, he leaves the boy's future open at the end of the novel, offering the reader a sense of Arjie's wonder, confusion, and anxiety; the reader knows what Arjie's future may hold just as well as he does, and he leaves Sri Lanka on the cusp of adulthood's radical uncertainty, carrying with him only the moral fortitude he has developed through his difficult childhood and adolescence.

3.5 THEMES IN *FUNNY BOY* BY SHYAM SELVADURAI

3.5.1 Masculinity and Queerness

Set from the late 1960s to the early 1980s in Sri Lanka, *Funny Boy* follows the childhood and adolescence of Arjie Chelvaratnam as his nation hurdles toward civil war. At the same time as he watches Sri Lanka's Sinhalese majority gradually turn against his minority **Tamil** community, Arjie comes to terms with the consequences of being gay in a patriarchal culture and family. From his earliest days, Arjie fails to meet his family's expectations of a boy; he prefers staging weddings with his girl cousins, acting in plays, and reading love comics and **Little Women** to playing cricket with his male cousins or **rugger** with the boys at school. When his parents start openly worrying about his "funny" sexuality and Arjie realizes that he is indeed gay, they all react with deep embarrassment and shame. Ultimately, Arjie' does not manage to find acceptance for his sexuality or even come out to his family during the novel; instead, his great accomplishment is simply learning to accept himself, reject shame, and disavow his family's demand that he follow in other men's footsteps.

Arjie grows up in a family and society structured by rigid gender roles and a distinct concept of masculinity that he does not, and never will, fit into. At the family's monthly gatherings, which they call "spend-the-days," Arjie and his numerous cousins have complete freedom to play and invariably split up by gender: the boys play cricket, and the girls act out weddings—along with Arjie, who is always the bride. When Arjie's cousin Tanuja (also known as "Her Fatness") tries to take over his role, she calls him a "pansy," "faggot," and "sissy." Although she is no older than ten, she already has a deeply ingrained sense of what masculinity—the "proper" way of being male—requires. In order to cultivate his masculinity, Arjie's dad (whom he calls **Appa**, the Tamil word for "father") sends him to his brother **Diggy**'s school, Victoria Academy, in the novel's penultimate chapter. As Diggy puts it, Appa "doesn't want [Arjie] turning out funny," but instead thinks he can "force [Arjie] to become a man" by surrounding him with Victoria's rambunctious, aggressive, athletic students. Indeed, Appa's continual fear that Arjie will become "funny" and his commitment to masculinizing his son suggest that he sees masculinity, femininity, and sexuality as changeable, rather than innate, which means that being properly masculine is in one's control and reflective of one's value as a human being.

Arjie's deviation from traditional masculinity leads his family to continuously shame him, and he quickly internalizes this shame and begins to think of himself as inherently flawed. Largely because they do not know what to make of him and fear that his failure to be conventionally masculine reflects their failure as a family, the Chelvaratnams repeatedly call Arjie "funny"—a word that both betrays the family's anxiety about admitting the possibility of having a gay son and shows that their homophobia is based on an unjustified, instinctual revulsion, tied to the cultural norm of heterosexual marriage and families. While he is too young to even understand his family's conviction that he is the wrong kind of boy, Arjie understands that he is being punished for simply being himself and following his desires, things over which he has no control. Although Arjie's sexuality mostly falls out of view during the middle part of the book, when he goes to Victoria Academy, he befriends and falls in love with a boy named **Shehan**, about whom his brother Diggy repeatedly warns him. After Arjie and Shehan first have sex, Arjie immediately sees that Appa disapproves of Shehan and thus lashes out at him, although internally, Arjie actually blames himself for committing a "dreadful act" and feels he has betrayed his family. Over time, Arjie has absorbed his family and culture's sense of shame surrounding queerness, and like many young people overcome with such shame about sex, he is unable to fully appreciate or embrace his first love.

Ultimately, however, Arjie does manage to overcome his shame, and this shows the groundlessness and arbitrariness of the conventional gender roles his family tried to squeeze him into. Even in the first chapter, when Amma forces Arjie to play with the boys rather than the girls, she reveals that she does not completely believe in the restrictive notion of masculinity she is enforcing: she says that Arjie must go with the boys "because the sky is so high and pigs can't fly," as though gender separation is just an inherent and necessary feature of the world. When Arjie challenges her, Amma's frantic reaction proves to him "how little she actually believed in the justness of her actions." She has done what she was pressured to do, not what she believes. Eventually, Arjie learns to form his own beliefs about gender and love; he learns to see "powerful and hidden possibilities" in his friendship with Shehan, to recognize that the same behaviour his family shames him for also allows him to uncover his true self and pursue his true desires without self-censorship. After berating Shehan, Arjie soon realizes that what they share is love, not deviance: he sees that Shehan "had not debased me or degraded me, but rather offered me his love," and so he decides to take this at face value instead of continuing to fight against his genuine desires.

In simply deciding that his own feelings are more important than the roles he is asked to fit into, Arjie overcomes his family's restrictive assumptions and accepts himself. Although Arjie does not come out to his family or win their acceptance—which is another, longer battle—he does realize that society's scripts for what men should do, how they should carry themselves, and who they should love really just reflect everyone else's fear of difference. While others see gender roles as inevitable, like the fact that "the sky is so high and pigs can't fly," Arjie proves to himself that an alternative is possible and learns to reject shame in favour of self-acceptance.

3.5.2 Forbidden Love and Family

While *Funny Boy*'s most important love story is undeniably about **Arjie** discovering his sexuality and meeting **Shehan**, the vast majority of the book follows other relationships, in all of which people fall in love across, despite, and even because of the social boundaries that separate them. Like Arjie's sexuality, these forbidden relationships draw familial ire; and yet, whereas Arjie learns to accept his sexuality despite his family's criticism, the book's forbidden relationships seem to end, for the greater good, because of a similar family pressure. While *Funny Boy* shows how class, race, ethnicity, and culture are never absolute barriers to desire, it also makes a case for prioritizing family—to whom one is already committed—over particular love interests.

Beyond Arjie's own love story, *Funny Boy* is full of relationships that cross social barriers and prove that differences of class, race, ethnicity, and culture can seldom stamp out the feelings of love—and, in many cases, are precisely what attract people to one another. One example of such a relationship is **Radha Aunty**'s relationship with **Anil, a Sinhala** boy who acts alongside her in a production of **The King and I.** Although she initially finds him annoying, Radha grows attracted to Anil because she realizes that he loves her despite belonging to an opposed ethnic group. In fact, *The King and I* also foreshadows the failure of Radha and Anil's interethnic relationship: in the play, an English governess and her employer, the King of Siam, fall in love but can never be together because, as **Amma** explains, interracial love was not (and in many places is still not) conventionally accepted. Amma's ambivalence about interracial love becomes even more clear when Arjie learns about her previous relationship with **Daryl Uncle**, a white **burgher** who grew up in Sri Lanka but has lived elsewhere for at least 15 years. And beyond Arjie's relationship with Shehan, his early affinity for romantic Sinhala comic books and insistence on playing the bride during his mock weddings with his girl cousins demonstrate how his romantic desires consistently land outside the sphere of social acceptability. Whether ethnic, cultural, racial, or class-based, social barriers cannot quash the feelings of love.

And yet all these characters face immense pressure for loving someone outside their social group; they are ultimately forced to choose between romance and family. Both Radha Aunty's mother (**Ammachi**) and **Anil's father** are horrified that their children are dating across ethnic lines. And Daryl's return to Sri Lanka, while Appa is in Europe for business, sows division in Arjie's family. **Neliya Aunty, Diggy,** and **Sonali** grow distant and resentful as Amma and Daryl grow close; Arjie is horribly ill the whole time, and when he recovers, Amma brings him to a bungalow in the hills, where Daryl soon shows up. As Daryl explains that burghers and native Sri Lankans were effectively barred from dating one another in the past because of social prejudice (obviously referring to his history with Amma), Arjie, too, begins to resent him for getting between Amma and the rest of the family. As though to prove Daryl's point about the social pressures against interracial marriage, **Aunty Doris,** the school theatre director who is also a burgher, warns Radha about marrying Anil by divulging the fact that her own family rejected her—by moving back to England without even informing her or leaving contact information—when she married a **Tamil** man. Radha, Anil, Amma, and Daryl—plus, eventually, Arjie and Shehan—end up in moral dilemmas: while they know their families are wrong to reject their love, they still have to pick between the sure thing that is family and the enchanting uncertainty that is romance.

Ultimately, while the novel openly criticizes the social divisions and norms that make intergroup marriages taboo, it also suggests that people are correct to choose family over their transgressive relationships. When Radha gets violently attacked by a Sinhala mob on a train, she finally caves in to her mother's pressure, quits the play, and marries **Rajan**, the Tamil man to whom she was already engaged. After this, Arjie explains that he has lost the ability to think "that if two people loved each other everything was possible," a view that might strike a young reader as cynical, but is full of wisdom: love is powerful but can always be rediscovered, and sometimes prudence requires sacrificing it and waiting. Amma loves and loses Daryl twice: once in her youth, and then again when he dies while covering the Tamil-Sinhala riots in the northern city of **Jaffna**. While his death is a tragedy, Daryl Uncle likely would have broken up Arjie's family had he stayed with Amma. (When she visits the civil rights lawyer Q.C. Uncle, he encourages her to do something similar: to give up her passionate desire to avenge Daryl's death in order to save her family from the government's wrath.) Aunty Doris, of all people, is the one to deliver the book's message about hasty love: after her husband's death, Doris explains, she began to wonder whether it was really worth it to marry the person she loved and lose her family, since she presumably could have had a successful marriage with someone else down the line. In *Funny Boy*, romance is fleeting and limitless, while family is enduring and finite; it is always possible to find another love but never possible to find new parents and siblings.

Although *Funny Boy* shows how the social constraints around love will never stop people from falling in love and sees a deep tragedy in relationships cut off by family and cultural pressures, it also shows how, in many cases, the tragedy of losing love might be preferable to the tragedy of losing one's community or family. Despite this preference for family ties, *Funny Boy* also pushes for constructing a world in which people are not forced to choose between love and community, in which difference makes relationships more vibrant instead of more difficult.

3.5.3 Nationalism, Ethnic Conflict, and Violence

Behind **Arjie's** coming of age, *Funny Boy* also traces the lead-up to the Sri Lankan Civil War, a growing tension between Sri Lanka's **Sinhala** majority and sizable Tamil minority that eventually erupts into violent conflict and becomes the book's driving force, uprooting Arjie and his family forever. And yet Selvadurai presents this ethnic conflict from the perspective of a boy who scarcely cares about ethnicity. In doing so, he sheds light on the fundamental illogic of the quest to secure a country for a single group of people, and a single group of people for one's country, in addition to showing the horrifying impact of the random violence that seems to inevitably emerge from such ethno-nationalist politics. By emphasizing personal relationships that transcend the ethnic divide, Selvadurai suggests that pluralism is the only route to political coexistence.

During Arjie's childhood and adolescence, the reader watches Sinhala and Tamil Sri Lankans grow increasingly mistrustful of and violent toward one another. Arjie's first encounter with this tension is hearing about **Ammachi's** hatred toward the Sinhalese, a response to her own father's murder by a racist Sinhalese mob in 1958. At this point, not only does the young Arjie fail to understand Ammachi's racism, but he does not even know what the word "racist" means. When **Daryl Uncle** returns to Sri Lanka after 15 years, he is there to document the violent conflict between Tamils and Sinhalese in the northern region around **Jaffna**. His mysterious death, declared an accident by the police likely responsible for it, shows that the Sri Lankan government actively backed the Sinhalese and drove the nation toward war. In the following chapter, a young man named **Jegan**, the son of **Appa's** old friend, comes to live with Arjie's family. A former Tamil Tiger, Jegan's presence makes **Appa's** Sinhalese employees suspicious; after the police falsely but publicly accuse Jegan of plotting an assassination and then quietly release him, thugs deface Appa's hotel with threats and Appa feels he has no choice but to fire Jegan. Although he disapproves of violence, Jegan is treated as a threat and a pariah, which reflects Sri Lankans' severe ethnic paranoia in the lead-up to the war. The book's Epilogue most saliently captures the toll of Sri Lanka's ethnic violence, as Arjie and his family have to flee their house (which is then burned down), **Appachi** and Ammachi are murdered, Appa's hotel is burned down, and numerous Tamils lose their homes and businesses, not to mention their lives.

The conflict between Sri Lanka's Tamils and Sinhalese is fundamentally a conflict over belonging: it is about who gets to own the nation, whom the government should serve, and whether different groups can coexist at all. Over the book's course, Arjie's family increasingly feels that they are being defined out of the national identity and made foreigners in their own homeland. The novel explains that the earliest waves of Tamil rebellion and violence followed the government's attempts to make Sinhala the nation's only official language. The Tamil Tigers demanded their own state because they felt Tamils were being made sub-citizens, while being Sri Lankan increasingly came to mean being Sinhalese. Yet ethnicity never means anything to Arjie, who is no more attached to Tamil than Sinhalese identity; he shows how it is not at all inevitable for ethnic identities to take on political weight. He takes Sinhala-medium classes and surrounds himself with Sinhala friends; in fact, he does not even speak Tamil. Despite this, when Jegan comes to **Colombo**, the family realizes that, as Tamils, they are under constant threat from the government, which can declare them extremists and targeted them whenever it wishes. And near the book's end, Arjie and **Shehan** grow distant, despite being one another's primary source of emotional support; Shehan cannot understand Arjie's sense of constant persecution, and Arjie can't fathom how Shehan feels normal enough to propose they go see a movie. While they never turn against each other, their rift shows how the experiential and empathetic gap between a majority group and an oppressed minority group can easily foster misunderstanding.

The book also shows numerous close relationships between Tamils and Sinhalese that prove mutual understanding is possible and disprove the government and Tamil Tigers' shared assumption that successful nations should be drawn on ethnic lines. During the riots, Sinhalese neighbors and friends save Arjie's family: the **Pereras** shelter them from the mob that burns down their house, and **Chithra Aunty** and Sena Uncle lodge them afterwards. In other words, the Chelvaratnams manage to survive because of Sinhalese people who put personal relationships and human connections before the bare fact of ethnic difference. Similarly, in the last chapter, Arjie chooses to side with the pro-Sinhalese Mr. Lokubandara over the school's racially indifferent principal, **Black Tie**, in order to save Shehan from Black Tie's cruel punishments. In a Sri Lanka apparently unable to see past ethnicity, Arjie stubbornly insists on doing so, and in his last reflections on immigration he expresses hope that Canada might be able to accept him in a way his own home country cannot. However, he also sees it possible that Canada will be just as racist as Sri Lanka, and that his family could be reduced to begging. While he can envision a better kind of nation, then, Arjie does not necessarily expect it to be possible.

In *Funny Boy*, Selvadurai shows both how real people are far more complex than ethnicity and also how they are nevertheless reduced to it by political forces. In doing so, he points to the insolubility of ethnic conflict over national identity: people will never be as one-dimensional or cut-and-dry as nationalists and racists want them to be, and so nationalism and racism, beyond perpetrating horrible violence, cannot achieve the kinds of societies they want to begin with. It is only because some Sinhalese and Tamils do not care about being Sinhalese or Tamil, in other words, that the efforts to create a fully Sinhalese or Tamil nation will inevitably fail.

3.5.4 Justice, Power, and Moral Awakening

As it follows **Arjie's** coming of age, *Funny Boy* also becomes a tale of moral development: Arjie encounters and grapples with blatant injustices that challenge his initial faith in human goodness. Yet, rather than giving up on the idea of a just world and resigning himself to the self-interested worldviews of those around him—including, at times, his own family—Arjie continues to pursue the just world he recognizes as impossible. Nevertheless, in responding to the abuses of power around him, he learns that pressure and manipulation—the very tools of injustice—are often the only way to convince the powerful to give the powerless their due.

Arjie learns early and clearly the world is not just, and in fact that the same adults who claim to be the bearers of morality often fail to choose good over evil. When Arjie and his younger cousin Tanuja (whom he calls "Her Fatness") fight over the **sari** they use in their game of bride-bride, **Ammachi** immediately blames Arjie and ignores the rest of the children's attempts to fully explain the situation. Because **Kanthi Aunty** had already shamed Arjie for his femininity, Ammachi decides the fight is his fault and makes him do housework instead of playing with the cousins on the family's subsequent Sunday gatherings. Similarly, in the chapter "The Best School of All," Victoria Academy's draconian principal, **Black Tie**, arbitrarily and cruelly punishes students he calls the "future ills and burdens of Sri Lanka" for offenses like wearing long hair or winking, even as he ignores violent bullying by students like **Salgado**. And **Daryl Uncle's** death shows how such abuses of power play out on a larger scale. The Sri Lankan government targets Daryl for documenting its human rights violations against **Tamils**, and then refuses to investigate his mysterious death—for which **Amma** is convinced it is responsible.

And Arjie sees another dimension of injustice—his own family's complicity in it—when he learns that his father's hotel is supporting the prostitution of underage boys and, later, goes with Amma to the village of Daryl's servant boy, **Somaratne**, only to be violently kicked out because the village's impoverished inhabitants are so used to being exploited by wealthy city people like Arjie's family.

While witnessing, experiencing, and learning about his complicity in profound injustices could have easily led Arjie to give up on his faith in good and evil altogether, instead it actually inspires him to pursue the kind of justice he thinks the world deserves. Daryl and **Jegan**, who dedicate their careers to exposing the Sri Lankan government's abuses of power and helping beleaguered Tamils, respectively, inspire Arjie to try and live with a sense of moral purpose rather than simply following the path of least resistance. And he continues to feel inspired by them even after they suffer horribly for taking moral stands. Due to his respect for both Daryl and Jegan, Arjie takes a prominent role in his family's attempts to save each of them: he insists on helping his mother search for Daryl (including by visiting Somaratne's village) and tries to support Jegan while Appa grapples with the consequences of firing him. In both cases, though, despite his sense of what is right and effort to pursue it, Arjie does not yet have the means to make a difference. His first serious opportunity to stop an abuse of power comes when Black Tie labels Arjie's friend and lover, **Shehan**, as one of the so-called "ills and burdens." When Black Tie makes Arjie recite poems, he punishes Arjie and Shehan together whenever Arjie messes up; even though Arjie is ostensibly one of Black Tie's favourites and Shehan one of the "ills and burdens," their struggle becomes one and the same, and ultimately Arjie ends up deliberately messing up the poems in order to sabotage Black Tie's important ceremony and ensure that the more docile vice principal, **Mr. Lokubandara**, takes over Black Tie's job. In doing so, Arjie willfully disobeys authority for the first time in order to end Shehan's unjust and unequal punishment.

In fact, by the end of the book, Arjie learns that he must fight those who abuse their power with their own tools: ruthlessness and manipulation. Because they do not care about morality, the perpetrators of injustice do not respond to moral appeals; instead, they must be pressured to correct their ways or be forced out of power. Arjie first learns this in childhood, after Her Fatness ousts him from the game of bride-bride and the adults force him to play cricket with the boys. When reasoning with the adults and cousins fails, Arjie hatches a plot: he hides the bride's **sari**, he so seriously disrupts the boys' group that they kick him out of their cricket game, and when Her Fatness agrees to make him the groom in exchange for the sari, he uses his sense of humor to steal his cousins' attention and ruin her moment, as if to remind her that she is not the game's legitimate bride. But Arjie truly proves his willingness to fight dirty for the right cause when he deliberately botches his poetry recital at Victoria Academy, which makes Black Tie's speech based on the poems look nonsensical. The audience breaks out in laughter when Black Tie furiously insults Arjie before dutifully reading the contradictory speech that he had prepared. At the end of the chapter, Black Tie is poised to lose the presidency and stop unfairly punishing Shehan for simply having had long hair on one day months before.

As a tale of moral development, then, *Funny Boy* is peculiar for showing not only how Arjie gains a moral compass, but also how he realizes that far too much of the adult world seriously lacks one. The systematic injustices Arjie sees in Sri Lanka come from unchecked power, and so he learns to respond to these injustices on the only terms that they know: by doing everything in his power to hold the unaccountable accountable.

3.6 SYMBOLS IN *FUNNY BOY* BY SHYAM SELVADURAI

3.6.1 The Bride-Bride Sari

During his childhood "spend-the-days" at **Ammachi** and **Appachi**'s house, young **Arjie** plays the game "bride-bride" with his girl cousins, which consists of staging a fantasy wedding. During these weddings, he invariably gets the position of honor: that of the bride herself. When he puts on the rudimentary sari (a traditional draped cloth garment) he made out of a bedsheet, Arjie feels like a film hero and declares that he is "ascend[ing] into another, more brilliant, more beautiful self." Many years before he even realizes that he is attracted to men, this sari illuminates and stands for the changing and conflicted relationship between Arjie's gender expression, social norms, and the promise of romantic love.

Beyond clearly representing his break from gender norms and affinity for things considered conventionally feminine—which soon gets him in trouble—the sari also shows how Arjie, as a boy who does not fit in, only gets to pursue his real desires (here, the desire to be beautiful and fall in love) in the register of fantasy. Indeed, when **Kanthi Aunty** finds him in the sari, she marches him out in front of all the other adults, who fall silent in horror at Arjie's effeminate outfit. In this sense, the sari comes to represent Arjie's shame before his family, and his family's shame before the world; it crystalizes what is wrong and "funny" about Arjie in everyone else's eyes (except the children's). Even his most innocent desire—to play with the girls—becomes seen as a deviation from the "correct" way of being and threat to his family's honor. When he withholds the sari in order to try and win his role back from his vicious cousin Tanuja ("Her Fatness"), Arjie and Tanuja end up literally fighting over an emblem of womanhood, which Arjie tries but fails to hide (like his feminine disposition and his own sexuality later in the book) and ultimately gets punished even more harshly for seeking out. His conflict during bride-bride is both a prediction and a microcosm of the struggles he will face as gay teenager in his conservative **Tamil** family and Sri Lankan community.

Ultimately, the sari both exposes and ridicules the unchallenged norm of heterosexual love. By donning the sari, Arjie gets to fulfill his nascent desire to love a man, but only in fantasy, by roleplaying a heterosexual marriage; the children have no concept of a marriage except as a bride marrying a groom, and so when Arjie dons the sari, one of the girl children—namely, Arjie's sister, **Sonali**—ends up with the unwanted role of groom. In this sense, while it reveals the strong norms of gender, tradition, and heterosexuality that ultimately constrain Arjie's self-realization throughout the book, the sari also circumscribes an inverted realm of play in which femininity is power and masculinity is irrelevant.

3.6.2 Arjie's Burned-Down House

During the epilogue chapter of *Funny Boy*, as ethnic riots break out in 1983, a **Sinhalese** mob shows up at **Arjie**'s house in the middle of the night and set fire to the house, which comes to represent. Luckily, his family has a plan and escapes in time, taking shelter in the storeroom of their neighbors, the **Pereras**. The next morning, they go outside and see that their house is completely unrecognizable. With nearly everything destroyed, it feels small and alien, nothing like the familiar space at the centre of their past lives. Beyond marking an abrupt break between the past and the future, this moment shows Arjie's family the severe dangers they face as **Tamils** in Sri Lanka: with their home, their country also becomes a forever foreign and unlivable place in the blink of an eye.

This points to the ambivalent nostalgia that characterizes Arjie's narrative voice throughout the novel: living in Canada after the narrative's events, he writes to remember the place (Sri Lanka, his home, and his sense of belonging in both) from which he was abruptly uprooted and to which he cannot return. In the book's closing lines, on the day he is supposed to leave for Canada, Arjie visits his home once more and realizes that "everything that was not burnt had been stolen," from pipes to furniture to flowers in the garden (presumably to be used in prayers "to increase [devotees'] chances of a better life in the next birth," which clearly also serves as a metaphor for Arjie's hope for a better life in Canada). The house now has a new layer of meaning: in addition to standing for the past that Arjie is now enthusiastically and resolutely putting behind him, it also points to the way his life was robbed of significance by the self-interest and shortsightedness of those who involved Sri Lanka in the war.

3.7 CRITIQUE ON *FUNNY BOY* BY SHYAM SELVADURAI

3.7.1 The Nine Instances of Funny and Their Insistence

Set in postcolonial Sri Lanka, Shyam Selvadurai's *Funny Boy* (1994) tells the story of a young Tamil's (Arjie Chelvaratnam's) realization of his same-sex desire while studying at a school in Colombo modelled on English public schools and teaching colonial literary texts which promote British values. Arjie's affair with a Sinhalese boy becomes a critique both of his own ethnicity and of the nationalism that has driven rioters to destroy Tamil property, later breaking out into civil war. Such large-scale violence represents a re-enactment of the sexual and patriarchal intolerance within his Tamil family. The violence is heaped upon the narrator as a "funny boy." Colonial forces haunt the former colony to construct ideologies of sexuality and gender, defining heteronormativity within colonial discourse. In this paper, I examine the word "funny" as it is used throughout the novel by exploring the ways language dominates textual discourses which are rendered funny, and comparing its usage in the family's domestic life with that in the public realm. Through an examination of another ambiguous word, "tendencies," in the novel's intertextual references and allusions to British canonical literature, this paper explores how the novel's critical "funniness" negotiates such seemingly stabilizing but violent and castrating forces as imperialism and nationalism. The novel poses challenges to the British colonialism which framed modern Sri Lanka. I attempt to show how *Funny Boy*, as a postcolonial text, resists the essentializing discourses implied in the country's national and sexual ideologies. Queen Victoria Academy, the school where Arjie studies before leaving Sri Lanka, can be seen as the nexus of these potent tendencies: the nationalist versus the separationist, the postcolonial versus the colonial, and the heteronormative versus the "funny." Funny Boy, told in six "stories" according to the subtitle of the book, recounts Arjie's life before his family's relocation to Canada following the 1983 riots that presented a direct physical threat to the lives of the Tamil minority. The novel opens in 1972, when Arjie is seven. The final chapter, "Riot Journal: An Epilogue," includes diary entries recording the historical communal riots in Sri Lanka. The Tamil/Sinhalese struggle appears as an ongoing cycle of events, culminating in the 1983 riots which end not only Arjie's memoir but also his relationship with his Sinhalese boyfriend Shehan. Triggered by a Tamil protest against the government's policy to officially recognize Sinhala as the national language of Sri Lanka, mass killings of Tamils were carried out by "some Sinhalese people" (Funny Boy 59) in 1958, in which Arjie's great-grandfather died (59), followed by the pogroms of 1971, 1977, 1981, and the outbreak of civil war in 1983 (Funny Boy 144, 156, 170, 279-305). Arjie's personal story about desire and sexuality is interwoven with politics and ethnicity in years of turmoil.

The word "funny" does not only imply otherness and the comical, but also carries political connotations. Following Edward Said's influential thesis in Orientalism, the colonized is feminized by the colonizer: "The Oriental was linked thus to elements in

Western society (delinquents, the insane, women, the poor) having in common an identity best described as lamentably alien" (207). Colonial discourse categorizes the native, the Other, as "funny," but in the novel it is not colonial discourse that describes the narrator as "funny," but postcolonial (or, in the historical context of Funny Boy, neocolonial) discourse, which perpetuates the language of colonialism. The culture that Arjie reacts to is dominated by patriarchal power. The novel shows how queer sexuality critiques the national identity-building of modern Sri Lanka. But since nationalism is partly induced by the Sinhalese forces, as opposed to the Tamil minority seeking autonomy, that critique comes from a double marginalization: from a position which is "homosexual," not heterosexual, and Tamil, not Sinhalese (Hawley 124). Colonial history under the British, the Sinhalese/Tamil split in postcolonial Sri Lanka, and the clash between two major religions (Buddhist/Hindu) threaten to shatter the nation by creating the civil war that appears in full force at the end of the novel. There have been attempts to read the text as a "gay novel," or even as one about "coming out," but homosexuality understood as subjectivity, I argue, only imposes another form of violence by giving closure to the text. Instead of forging a single identity for the nation and the individual, the concept of funniness subverts the idea of a unified personal and national identity.

The word "funny" appears nine times in the novel, including in the book title. The first instance occurs when the family discovers Arjie's cross-dressing during "bride-bride," a children's imitation game of playing the wedding couple; Cyril Uncle cries out "jovially" to Appa, Arjie's father, "looks like you have a funny one here" (Funny Boy 14). "Funny" here, as in all other instances in the book, is ambiguous in meaning. It is the description of the tone of Cyril's comment as "jovial" that illuminates the meaning of "funny," steering the signification of the word to the first definition given by the OED: "affording fun, mirth-producing, comical, facetious." Arjie nonetheless does not know what his uncle means. It is not necessarily the crossdressing that interests Arjie, because in his innocent mind what he desires is "to wear makeup and costumes and dance around" (52) like the child actor in the play The Pied Piper of Hamelin, probably a dramatization of Robert Browning's poem.

We may start with a disclaimer about Arjie's "homosexuality":

calling him homosexual is problematic, not only because the term comes from a Western, Christian, medical discourse which is hostile to same-sex acts, but also because labelling an adolescent "homosexual" essentializes homosexuality. The term is never used in Funny Boy, but the idea is described and implied in the words "funny" and "tendencies." Perera takes Arjie's transformation into a "funny boy" while at school as confirmation that his "latent homosexual tendencies" emerged in childhood ("Some Responses" 258), assuming the sexual connotation of the word "funny." Lesk asserts that Arjie's "sexual identity ... earns him the ascription 'funny'" (35), without questioning its plural meanings. He notes that the Sri Lankan equivalent for homosexual is "ponnaya," and that Arjie "strangely, never uses the word" (Lesk 44). Although Lesk argues that "Arjie does not have the language to access what his desires might mean" (44), there is unfortunately no further exploration of what the word "funny" means. Interestingly, "ponnaya" is indeed used in Selvadurai's 2005 novel *Swimming in the Monsoon Sea,* but the English word "homosexual" is never mentioned. Unlike Arjie, who seems to be more affirmative about his sexuality in Funny Boy, Amrith de Alwis, the protagonist of Swimming in the Monsoon Sea, struggles to face his same-sex desire. Despite being alone in front of his mother's tombstone, Amrith cannot bring himself to articulate the word "ponnaya," but only "I am ... different" (Swimming 267; ellipsis in original). It is necessary to start with what Lesk leaves out, examining what the word "funny" could imply.

That evening, Cyril's diction is repeated in the second instance of the use of the word by Appa, who warns his wife Amma, "If he turns out funny like that Rankotwera boy, if he turns out to be the laughing stock of Colombo, it'll be your fault," and "You always spoil him and encourage all his nonsense" (14). Through the off-stage "Rankotwera boy," the Chelvaratnams communicates with each other. Everything in the word "funny" depends on its euphemistic force, which is powerful and determining because of its lack of definition. The differences between Cyril's usage of the word ("a funny one") and Appa's ("turns out funny") are suggestive. Cyril's exclamation implies that Arjie is already "funny," whereas Appa sees a potentiality in Arjie's behaviour—"if he turns out funny." The first is accompanied by Cyril's laughter, so Arjie's funniness is already being laughed at, but

Appa's statement is a warning against Arjie becoming a "laughingstock," which is not "funny" at all. The two instances of "funny" are different in their usage.

Arjie realizes that the meaning is not in the spoken word, but in the paralinguistics of the affect people show when speaking. Minoli Salgado asserts the significance of the ambiguity of the word "funny," arguing that Arjie is not called "gay" or "homosexual" because "funny" implies the "instability of his subject-positioning" ("Writing Sri Lanka" 11). But such a potentially dangerous position is directed toward something laughable.

The oxymoronic nature of the word is noticed by Arjie. After the Cyril Uncle incident, Amma prohibits Arjie from seeing her change clothes, attempting to transform him into a "normal" male. Arjie realizes that the meaning is not in the spoken word, but in the paralinguistics of the affect people show when speaking. Minoli Salgado asserts the significance of the ambiguity of the word "funny," arguing that Arjie is not called "gay" or "homosexual" because "funny" implies the "instability of his subject-positioning" ("Writing Sri Lanka" 11). But such a potentially dangerous position is directed toward something laughable.

Laughter serves the function of protecting the laughing subject, giving them a sense of superiority over those who are being laughed at, as illustrated in the case of Cyril's laugh. Laughter creates a hierarchy over the "abnormal," as implied by Thomas Hobbes' definition: laughter is a "sudden glory," implying a feeling of superiority, which "is the passion which maketh those Grimaces called Laughter" (6.125; emphasis in original). Laughter "is caused either by some sudden act of their own, that pleaseth them" or "by the apprehension of some deformed thing in another, by comparison whereof they suddenly applaud themselves" (6.125). For Hobbes, those who laugh at others feel superior because laughter constructs normality by marginalizing "deform[ity]." People who laugh are "conscious of the fewest abilities in themselves; who are forced to keep themselves in their own favour, by observing the imperfections of other men. And therefore much laughter at the defects of others, is a sign of pusillanimity" (6.125). Pusillanimity here, the opposite of Aristotelian megalopsuchia (magnanimity), means mediocrity, meanness, and a lack of generosity. The act of laughing at what is constructed by the pusillanimous as "funny," and desiring to fix funniness, are both reactions to a crisis of identity, instanced in the case where the colonizer laughs at the colonized (Billig 51). When the colonizers find someone or something "funny," the non-specificity and the implied pusillanimity are caused by what Freud calls "Verleugnung" (disavowal or denial) ("Fetishism" 353). Its mechanism is similar to his formulation of fetishism (355-56), which is paraphrased best in Octave Mannoni's title "Je sais bien, mais quand-même" ("I Know Well, but All the Same"). The fetishist disavows or disregards what is seen in reality, saying what is there when it is not, or turning what is absent into presence. Verleugnung is stronger than "Verdrängung" (repression) because it denies an external reality ("Fetishism" 353). Nietzsche argues that the lack of spontaneity promoted by Christian culture in modernity yields what he calls ressentiment, an affect of rancor, bitterness, and envy (472-75, 480-82). While pusillanimity is bound up with ressentiment, Hobbes would say ressentiment is veiled within laughter which involves the disavowal of the laughing person's lack of spontaneous being. Colonialism produces pusillanimity, which translates into ressentiment, showing itself in heteronormativity. The fourth use of "funny" in the novel appears in chapter 2, "Radha Aunty," when Radha, a Tamil woman engaged to a man of the same ethnicity, is allegedly having an affair with Anil, who is Sinhalese.

"Funny" is contrasted by Radha with her "serious" love toward Anil, who does not fit into Arjie's childish idea of a lover because he was "not serious enough" (66). But even so, Anil is not regarded as "funny." Radha's response to her mother's question plays upon the binary opposition of serious/funny. Radha deliberately exploits the double meaning of the word "funny" in Ammachi's rhetorical question, managing to announce her anti-traditional attitude towards the cross-ethnic relationship. Radha's ability to exploit language's ambiguity allows her to temporarily resist that dominating power.

When Arjie's other aunty asks Radha if she is in love with "this boy" Anil, Radha replies, "No ... I don't know," and "The funny thing is I never thought of him like that [as a lover] until Amma started to make a fuss. It was only after she went to speak to his parents that I began to see him differently" (76; ellipsis in original). This fifth "funny" connotes a sense of irony in cause and effect. Radha's first reaction is negation, and the indicator for being in love is that apart from her fiancé, she is "thinking of Anil as well" (76). Life's strangeness arrests Radha, confronting her with the oddity of relationships: love is activated by a third party and denial of love itself.

Hobbes describes people laughing at deformity, but such an attempt to affirm normality is outdone by life's strangeness. This appears in the next passage (the sixth example of the word "funny"), where Aunty Doris warns Radha not "to make the same mistake" as she did: "Life is a funny thing, you know. It goes on, whatever decisions you make. Ultimately you have children or don't have children and then you grow old. Whether you married the person you loved or not seems to become less important as time passes" (79). It is life that could be called the "funny boy": heterogeneous, or "curious, queer, odd, strange," (the early eighteenth-century meaning of "funny," as indicated by OED). Life, as Doris's third sentence suggests, robs situations from signifying any single meaning.

The seventh instance appears in "The Best School of All" (ch. 5), when Arjie asks his brother Diggy why he must be sent to the ex-British colonial school, Queen Victoria Academy. Diggy says that Appa "doesn't want you turning out funny or anything like that" (205). Arjie feels "a flush rise into [his] face," and he refuses to meet Diggy's accusing gaze when the latter asks, "You're not, are you?" (205). Arjie's flush is a sign of shame and desire. It suggests shame, as though he is being looked at by an imagined internalized authority, creating desire, signaled in a flush, or in Norman Brown's words, as "a mild erection of the entire head" (194). For Michel Foucault, normative desire and disgust are produced discursively. The function of confession is to produce a split subject: the more a subject confesses, the more developed and more vulnerable his subjectivity becomes (62). The word exists in discourse with the power to define and marginalize, as Foucault suggests that language always does, but its power is its imprecision, that it is not clear whether someone is funny or not.

The eighth use of the word "funny" appears when Black Tie cuts Shehan Soyza's hair as a punishment in Queen Victoria Academy. "Funny" here functions like the reply which Radha makes, as the opposite of "serious": Arjie does not like being called "fresh meat," which has sexual implications, nor that Shehan has had his hair cut. It is not clear what Arjie protests against more,

Shehan's hair or being called fresh meat. The joke may be on him as vulnerable (fresh meat) or on Shehan, who thinks "it" funny. "Funny" may be read beyond Shehan's sense, meaning that Arjie's response shows his "funniness"—his affection toward Shehan, which makes "funny" positive. Sharanya Jayawickrama maintains, "The word 'funny' that is initially used derogatively to refer to Arjie's identity is reclaimed by the end of the novel when he himself initiates laughter that proves redemptive of his position" (133). It seems to recognize otherness, or marginality. So, Shehan's claim "it's extremely funny" indicates that he accepts the marginal place they share, but such an acceptance can only be achieved by maintaining equivocality. Being disingenuous becomes a form of politics, enabling a plurality of meanings.

Lastly, the word "funny" appears in the title Funny Boy: A Novel in Six Stories. "Pig Can't Fly," the first chapter, was first published as a short story in The Toronto South Asian Review, and was also collected in the "gay stories" anthology Meanwhile, in Another Part of the Forest. The title Funny Boy simultaneously unifies by giving a sense of identity (however ambiguous and plural the word is) to the protagonist, and fragments the chapters of which the novel is composed, because the subtitle suggests that the six stories may be read as separable and independent works. Their protagonists, while all called Arjie, are not necessarily one person; or if they are one person, the assumed homogeneity of personhood over different stages is challenged. The separating tendency in funniness is already installed in the novel's title.

"Funniness" betrays Arjie when the ambiguous nature of the word is denied and its signification fixed, expelling not only him, but also those who are "funny": anyone who is not regarded as "proper" within the dominant ideology is banished simply by labelling them "funny." Such violent expulsion accumulates not as a direct force, but within repeated forward and backward steps. In this "Novel in Six Stories," each chapter begins with what Freud calls "the return of the repressed" ("Repression" 154), and ends with a compromise, or a further repression. This structure can be illustrated through the fourth "story," "Small Choices," which gives an example of repression in the father, both sexual and political. The chapter opens with the unveiling of a childhood friendship followed by a series of events which reveal Appa's potential sexual funniness; it ends with political oppression, intolerance to a Tamil, and ethnic "funniness," which Appa refuses to admit. Arjie's suffering and the family's exile are actually both caused by the repeated repression of some version of funniness. At the beginning of the chapter, Appa reads aloud an unexpected letter from the widow of a childhood friend:

Dear Mr. Chelvaratnam, I am writing to request a favour in memory of my late husband. My son, Jegan, is a qualified accountant. He's twenty-five years old and has spent the last year as a relief worker for the Gandhiyam movement, but, due to recent problems, I removed him from the organization. He is currently unemployed. Would you be able to find him a post in your business? I am sure his skills will be useful to you. Yours truly, Grace Parameswaran.

P.S. I found the attached document among my husband's belongings, and I am sending it to you as a souvenir of your friendship with him. (151-52)

The letter implies a repression, starting with the old "yellowing piece of paper" (152), followed by the appearance of Jegan, the son of "Buddy Parameswaran," and then with him being sent away. The parallel between Buddy and Mr. Chelvaratnam (Appa)'s relationship, as separated close childhood friends, with that of Arjie and Shehan opens up the possibility that Arjie's undefined funniness may be derived from the father, suggesting that the entry into patriarchy depends on the repression of something homosocial or homoerotic, of tendencies which cannot be acknowledged. When Arjie's father first discovers Arjie in bridal dress, everyone laughs except Appa, who "pretended he had not heard [the laughter] and, with an inclination of his head, indicated to Amma to get rid of me" (14). The father's reaction may suggest his repression. He cannot laugh at his son, not just because he dislikes the crossdressing, but also perhaps because it reminds him of his own "funniness," his own "tendencies." Whereas the text suggests that Arjie's life is a repetition of Appa's, reoccurrences of words such as "funny" and "tendencies" in the novel can be understood as what Lacan calls l'instance in "L'instance de la lettre dans l'inconscient" ["The Instance of the Letter in the Unconscious"]. For Lacan, l'instance means both the instance and insistence. "Funny" belongs to such literality of language, which "insists" through the specific language of repeated generations. The tendency (or "insistence") of the word "funny" is to accrue non-specific but marginalized meanings, and to "insist" in the unconscious, tending to create a history that the conscious self is unaware of.

Arjie's "critical funniness" includes the carnivalization (turning upside-down) of the colonial order, and the exposing of Newbolt's ideology and his double role as an educator promoting British literary superiority and an advocate of imperial wars. Arjie's laughter is not pusillanimity, but a spontaneous critique of colonial discourse, with its normalizing tendencies which may be dependent on a secret and disavowed homosexuality. Read that way, Arjie and Shehan's same-sex acts could be performative, a never completed "coming out" process unveiling the double standard towards homosexuality that British colonialism implemented because same-sex acts remain officially illegal in contemporary Sri Lanka. According to Homi Bhabha, hybridity "erases any essentialist claims for the inherent authenticity or purity of [dominating] cultures" (58), and its power is desired in postcolonial cultures and subcultures. Arjie's creation of himself as a "funny boy" by making fun of the recitation requires him to concede to the Sinhalese nationalist discourse that destabilizes him in terms of national identity. Katherine Bell defends Arjie's jumbling up Newbolt's poems during the prize-giving ceremony as a crucial act of resistance and revolt instead of merely an unwitting self-sabotaging revenge against his own ethnic alliance because "even if it [the poetry recitation] takes place on a singular level, [it] is intrinsically engaged with public life" (273). This is because "when Arjie refuses to be a temporal and emotive signifier and publically bows out of the literary encounter to which he had been subjected, he leaves generative space for dialogue" (272). Enlisting Julia Kristeva's Intimate Revolt (2002), Bell argues that Arjie's action could be classified as a revolt, which, "instead of imposing new values, questions and displaces the past by bringing to light its conflictuality" (272). She asserts, "Funny Boy should not be seen as a failure of traditional Bildung philosophy but, rather, an opening for and insistence upon a more pluralist ethos" (273). Such an opening is not merely done through Arjie's actions, but also, more subtly and more powerfully, by the insistence of the text, which is installed by Arjie's very act of writing his own memoir. Critical funniness operates on two levels. First, creating funniness within the novel with Arjie as the central figure, his six stories allow spontaneous laughter criticizing discourses which promote fixed subjectivity, including sexuality, nationalism, and imperialism. Second, through conscious or unconscious literary allusions to the English canon, the textual tendencies of the memoir, a postcolonial text written in yet another former British colony, Canada, complicate and criticize dominating and oppressive cultures by making them "funny." Arjie's unfortunate stories are told in a text with funny tendencies, offering resistance and challenges to discourses promoting homogeneous subjectivity. Though Arjie may be expelled from Sri Lanka, his narrative's radical funniness nonetheless insists on returning through the sexual/textual tendencies, mocking the notion of any single subject position, be it national, ethnic, sexual, or gendered.

Unit IV
Graphic Novel

Historically literature has been known to be admirable if it included enough detail to paint a mental image for the reader, and graphic text just expands on that model. Graphic texts are not a new concept to study of literature. Most of the people have a mental bank of images that subconsciously translates from a form of text. When one views a word, he does not view the stark letters of the word but an image of what that word means. Before symbols of letters were created to represent sound and words, man used images to express a narrative. The earlier people communicated through images instead of language, and even the words we read are created from a systematic order of character or images. We view the world as groups of images and our mind labels these images with words that we have stored in our mental databanks. Our mind creates an organized stream of words to be able to express what we see. The mind takes the jumble and makes it linear. The use of graphic novel aids in the reconstruction of the holistic world that the writer of a text skillfully conveys while expanding beyond what cannot be placed in the linear timeline of verbal language. Here we see how language and image are an interlocking concept; we cannot have one without the other. Therefore, this concept of combining image and text is a logical concept to look at when discussing literacy and literary issues.

Comics – first ignored by academia, yet eventually embraced as 'graphic novels' illustrates that hierarchies in the arts are never fixed. Graphic novel is an art as well as literary form that deals with the arrangement of pictures or images and words to narrate a story or dramatize an idea. In Understanding Comics Scott

McCloud defines comics as juxtaposed pictorial and other images in deliberate sequence, intended to convey information and /or produce an aesthetic response in the viewer.

The credit for popularizing the graphic narrative in India must go in a huge measure to the Penguin Group which had brought out a series featuring Feluda, the detective-hero created by Satyajit Ray. Although the Feluda collection has been called a "comic book" series, it is more than a mere collection of comic strips. It is a set of self-contained detective stories by Satyajit Ray, rendered in English by Subhadra Sengupta and illustrated by Tapas Guha. Both in production and style of illustration, the books do seem to be modeled on the Tintin series, as Ray was profoundly influenced by them, although the ambience of the stories is faithfully Indian. Feluda had first made his appearance in 1965 in the Bengali children's magazine *Sandesh* edited and published by Ray's family, all of whom were children's authors. Soon Feluda became quite popular among children in the urban sections of West Bengal. Ray wrote numerous Feluda stories, and with son Sandip Ray, filmed quite a few of them. This has been discussed in detail a little later in this chapter. Penguin had brought out unabridged translations of all his adventures and now Puffin Books has come out with graphic versions of them.

Today the Indian graphic narrative has surely come of age because from suspense and mythology, its scope has expanded in the course of time to fables and folklore, fiction, humour and wit, Sanskrit literature, conflict, social inequities to biographies of historical figures and nationalist leaders as well as autobiographies.

Although most of the graphic narratives dealing with Indian history are based on popular perceptions of history rather than in depth scholarly research, they have succeeded in creating awareness and interest about India's rich historical heritage. Incidents of warfare or struggle are depicted without crudeness or ugliness. Although, most of these works boast of spectacular illustrations, very few, if any, are imitative of Western graphic narratives.

In spite of the threat from animated series in film and television, graphic narratives are slowly but surely going from strength to strength in India. Undoubtedly inspired and influenced by developments in other countries, they have Indianized the

Western influences on them and successfully grown into a truly Indian style of narrativization. The use of mixed media and the blending of genres once more transcend limitations, bringing into the story intense emotional mood, abstract ideas, and possibilities of interpretation.

Unlike their more traditional text-only counterparts, contemporary Indian graphic novels tend toward diverse voices and stories, and these narratives are also slowly escaping the stereotype that they are picture books with no value to literacy instruction. Their new status opens avenues for more educators to realize that these texts can be taught using nearly the same approaches as any other book, fiction or otherwise. They can be used in nearly every subject and are particularly valuable as counter-texts in social studies and language classrooms. Setting, pacing, and story structure are largely the same, but the units used to tell the story differ.

Besides Sarnath Banerjee, Parismita Singh and Samhita Arni there are quite a few others who have painstakingly created a niche for themselves in this form of narration. Some of them being Orijit Sen, considered by many as another pioneer of sequential art in India, Samit Basu, Salil Chaturvedi, Vishwajyoti Ghosh, Sarbajit Sen, Nikhil Chaudhary, Ambarish Satwik, Sanjay Ghosh, Amitabh Kumar, Priya Kuriyan, Madhav Nair, Anpu Varkey and the list goes on.

In India though sequential art has come of age with regard to the themes covered and the various styles of art incorporated in the narratives, readers are still warming up to the idea that graphic narratives can be created specifically for an adult readership, just like their hallowed prose counterparts. Artists and writers have long bemoaned the lack of interest shown by publishers, the preconceived notions and all of the cultural snobbery which they've had to put up with. Of course, this isn't something which is limited to this country alone, which is the reason why path breaking graphic narrative anthologies have had to be self-published in many cases. Hence, it is heartening to see the initiative which led to the publication of the Pao Collective—a group of five immensely talented artists "more or less based in Delhi" (Singh 2012: 8), comprising of Orijit Sen, Sarnath Banerjee, Amitabh Kumar, Vishwajyoti Ghosh and Parismita Singh coming together to create this anthology of graphic narratives. This first-ever Pao anthology has brilliant narratives from all of the above, as well as several other writers and artists.

In India this form of storytelling has thus come of age as the practitioners of this form have unapologetically chosen it over the traditional story telling methods to unravel the unsaid. Voices from the peripherals, from the oppressed, from the ones about to break free and the ones who are responsible for the changes, all seem to find power and true representation in this narrative medium.

4.1 DURGABAI VYAM AND SUBHASH VYAM, *BHIMAYANA: EXPERIENCES OF UNTOUCHABILITY*

4.1.1 *Bhimayana: Experiences of Untouchability*

Bhimayana: Incidents in the Life of Bhimrao Ramji Ambedkar is a graphic biography of Bhimrao Ramji Ambedkar published in 2011 by Navayana, a publishing house that focuses on the issue of caste from an anti-caste perspective. In this ground-breaking work, Pardhan-Gond artists Durgabai Vyam and Subhash Vyam interweave past events with current occurrences, infusing vibrant life into the graphic idiom through their awe-inspiring art. My attempt in this essay is to examine the artistic choices that went into the making of this graphic novel, and to weigh their political significance against the majority of the literature available to us in modern India.

Bhimayana unfolds in the context of a conversation at a bus stop, apparently between a Dalit woman and a caste Hindu man. The man complains about his dead-end job and blames his situation on job quotas for Backward and Scheduled Castes. This serves as a catalyst for the woman to begin narrating what is essentially the plot of the novel – various instances from the life of Ambedkar and their parallels in the modern scenario.

The novel is divided into four small chapters or 'books'. Book 1, Water, highlights the pervasive presence of caste in Ambedkar's daily life. A young Bhim could not drink from the same tap as his upper-caste classmates; furthermore, on a trip with his family, not a single person along the way gave him water for fear of being polluted. This would turn out to be the most unforgettable lesson about untouchability that he would learn. Throughout the chapter, we see excerpts from various modern news articles that show how untouchability is certainly not just a concern of the past. Book 2, Shelter, is premised around Ambedkar's experiences in Baroda as an adult. He was driven out of a hotel run by a Parsi man for being a non-Parsi, and was further denied accommodation in his Hindu and Christian friends' houses as well. These moments of transparency show us that untouchability was present even outside the Hindu social order. Book 3, Travel, takes place in Chalisgaon, Nasik where Ambedkar was looking into the social boycott by caste Hindus of the Untouchables in Dhulia. On the insistence of the people, Ambedkar agreed to stay the night with them, but the journey to their neighbourhood was a rather unsteady one. The tongawallas (vehicle drivers) refused to drive Ambedkar and so his tonga had to be driven by a complete novice, leading to an accident. This taught Ambedkar that a Hindu tongawalla, menial in the eyes of caste Hindus, can look upon himself as superior to all Untouchables. It is at the end of this chapter that the initial conversation wraps up. The Hindu man admits to having a new-found respect for Ambedkar and sees why he is such an icon for Dalits today, despite still disagreeing with his ideology. Book 4, The Art of Bhimayana, introduces the artists and writers and gives us a sneak peek into the making of the graphic novel. We learn about the creative processes that went into the novel as well as the rationale behind them.

Bhimayana is a political graphic novel published by Navayana, self-proclaimed as India's first and only publishing house to focus on the issue of caste from an anti-caste perspective. Named after Dr. B.R. Ambedkar's socially and morally concerned interpretation of Buddhism, Navayana translates to 'new vehicle'. In relation to this, there seems to be a certain significance of 'Bhimayana' as a title. A semantic analysis of the word indicates to an obvious reference to 'Ramayana'. In the words of Durgabai Vyam, the artist responsible for the novel "While doing the book I once told Anand (the publisher), this is like the Ramayana! He said, 'No, this is Bhimayana'—and that's how we hit upon this title." Bhimayana translates to Bhim's journey, which is an accurate description of the plot within the novel, however, its deeper political significance exists in the parallels it draws with Ramayana. Reworked folk songs have acted as key tools for the Bahujan Samaj Party in spreading Ambedkar's ideology since the 1990s. For instance, in one song, Kaushalya Rani (the eldest wife of King Dashratha in

Ramayana) is replaced by Ambedkar's mother. Ram is a central figure in Hinduism and is revered as 'maryada purushottama' or the perfect man. Replacing his image in popular culture with that of Ambedkar's is a powerful subaltern move which essentially flips the Hindu social order on its head, with an Untouchable man as the ideal.

The graphic novel is a term first coined in English in 1964, thus being a very young form of artistic expression. Pardhan-Gond artists Durgabai Vyam and Subhash Vyam added their own twist to the art form, by not confining their characters to boxes, creating 'space for all to breathe'. With customary tribal patronage dwindling over the past century, tribal art has become a dying medium, and in this context, the decision to employ tribal artists to illustrate the story of an Untouchable leader becomes all the more significant.

Several artistic choices throughout the novel are quite obviously politically charged. The speech bubbles that contain dialogue are of two types. One is in the shape of a bird, and it contains the dialogues of 'characters whose speech is soft, the lovable characters, the victims of caste'. The second type takes the shape of a scorpion's tale, holding the dialogues of 'characters who love caste, whose words carry a sting and contain poison'. This polarisation of characters is a clear representation of the authors' perspective, which is unabashedly anti-caste. It depicts Ambedkar as the well-meaning protagonist and caste Hindus as the evil antagonists. A third bubble is that of the thought bubble, pictured to be stemming from the mind's eye to 'contain words that cannot be heard but can be perceived'. This appears to be a subtle reference to the Third eye in Buddhism, which is the inner eye or eye of wisdom. The artists incredibly infuse deep meaning into features that can be overlooked as simple aesthetic tools.

Bhimayana is generous with its symbolism. The ecology of Pardhan Gond art is such that even when dealing with urban subjects, we see freefalling animals, birds, and trees. A thirsty young Ambedkar is visualised as a fish and happiness is depicted not through smiling faces but a dancing peacock. The artists introduce poignancy into situations and characters through drawings where words would otherwise be lacking. The novel features the image of pointing fingers throughout the narrative. One may interpret the pointing fingers as being aimed in a discriminatory fashion towards the Untouchables. A more pronounced observation, however, may be supplemented by the fact that most statues of Ambedkar erected in his honour depict him pointing forward. This could be a metaphor for progress, a collective movement towards a better, equalitarian future. Another example of universal equality in the novel is shown in the drawing of people; each person irrespective of caste, class, or gender, is drawn in black and white with similar strokes and textures. It subtly encourages the readers to view every character as fundamentally alike. A more pervasive, though perhaps understated symbolic value is injected in the colour blue. It is featured prominently in the novel, whether as bright blue water, or a more muted blue in the clothes of Ambedkar. This bolsters the use of the popular Ambedkarite greeting 'neel salam' or blue salute, which embodies Ambedkarite ideals.

The writing in Bhimayana is lucid and accessible. The historic tale of Ambedkar is seamlessly interwoven with modern examples. The text borrows heavily from contemporary news articles, a tactic which triumphs in giving the reader a solid foundation in the reality of caste. The matter is structured to retain the interest of the reader, and when combined with the artwork, we are presented with a piece of literature that is unapologetically deliberate in its narrative.

Bhimayana is a departure from the norm that successfully punctures the mainstream narrative and aims spotlights at issues that escape widespread coverage. The novel is remarkable for the authors' immersion of the story within a folk-art tradition and their crafting of a politically-engaged account that remains open to a diversity of audiences. If it is possible to draw from this book a child's description of good versus evil, this is because the simplest narratives are the most politically expedient.

The book is dedicated to Jangarh Singh Shyam, a pioneer in contemporary Pardhan Gond art. He is credited by Udayan Vajpeyi to be the creator of a new school of art called Jangarh Kalam.

He encouraged and guided Durgabai and Subhash Vyam, along with many other members of the Pardhan Gond community, to become artists. He was also Subhash Vyam's brother-in-law.

In the foreword, art critic John Berger, most famous for his 1972 essay "Ways of Seeing", commends the refreshing form of story-telling that the book uses. Of it, he says, 'No more proscenium arch. No more rectangular framing or unilinear time. No more profiled individuals. Instead, a conference of corporeal experiences across generations, full of pain and empathy, and nurtured by a complicity and endurance that can outlive the Market'. He believes that such texts will make readers more vested in the story and its message.

The graphic account begins with a frame story of an unnamed character complaining about the 'these damn job quotas for Backward and Scheduled Castes!' who is immediately challenged by another character leading to a conversation about the history of caste atrocities in India. He is advised to read about Ambedkar to understand what happened at Khairlanji.

The book then moves on to the narrative of Ambedkar's life in Books I, II and III.

4.1.2 Book I –Water

'Water' sets the scene in 1901, on an ordinary day in Ambedkar's life as a 10-year-old Mahar schoolboy. He is humiliated at the hands of the Brahmin teacher and the peon who, paranoid about the possibility of contamination, refuse him water. Young Bhim goes back home where he asks his aunt why he cannot drink from the tap like other boys, despite being cleaner than upper-caste students. The text also juxtaposes Ambedkar's own lack of access to water at school with his father's work in Goregaon, which entails 'helping build a water tank for famine-stricken people who would die if it weren't for his work'.

Young Bhim along with his siblings is invited to stay with his father in Masur. They get off the train to find that no one has come to receive them and seek the station master's help. As soon as they reveal that they are Mahars, the stationmaster turns hostile. He finds them a cart-ride on the condition that they pay double. Eventually they find their father's house. It turns out that his secretary had forgotten to inform him of their arrival.

The narrative voice moves back to the frame story here, and the unnamed storyteller concludes that Ambedkar said it was because of the secretary's mistake that he had learnt 'the most unforgettable lesson about untouchability'. The section ends with an account of Ambedkar's Mahad satyagraha against lack of access to water from the Chavadar Tank.

4.1.3: Book II–Shelter

This section is set in 1917, after Ambedkar returns from Columbia University to work for the Maharaja of Baroda who had sponsored his education. It starts with him boarding a train to Baroda and engaging in a conversation with a Brahmin. Soon Ambedkar realizes that his status as an untouchable, although forgotten by him during his stay abroad, is still an enormous issue in India.

In Baroda, he is subsequently denied entry into a Hindu hotel due to his caste status. Unable to find proper accommodation, he shifts into a decrepit Parsi inn but is thrown out after a few days. As he attempts to find shelter, his friends evade helping him citing problems at home, forcing him to wait in the Kamathi Baug public garden and subsequently, leave for Bombay.

The section ends with the narrative voice of the frame story re-emerging and highlighting caste based discrimination practiced by 'liberal' city dwellers. An article from The Hindu titled "Dalit Siblings Thrashed by Landlord" is also put forward to illustrate the difficulties faced by dalits while trying to find shelter in urban areas as well.

4.1.4 Book III–Travel

This section is set in Aurangabad, 1934, wherein Ambedkar travels to Daulatabad with a group of political workers of Mahar and other untouchable castes. Ambedkar reminisces about his experience during his trip to Bombay in 1929, when the untouchables of Chalisgaon sent their nephew to drive Ambedkar to their house on a Tonga because all the Tonga-drivers refused to give Ambedkar, a Mahar, a ride. The driver was unskilled and they meet with an accident, but receive prompt medical aid. Ambedkar then confronts the harsh truth that in a graded Indian society, a highly educated and renowned dalit will continue to be oppressed and deprived of dignity. The section mentions cases of dalits being denied medical care by hospitals. The narrative then shifts to the present, where Ambedkar and his colleagues are prevented from drinking from the water-tank at the Daulatabad fort by a mob of Muslims.

The section ends with the characters from the frame story discussing Ambedkar's contribution to social equality and justice in India as both an agitator and an architect of the Constitution. The polemic of Gandhi versus Ambedkar towards the end brings to the reader's attention that, unlike Gandhi, Ambedkar's was a far more universal struggle against injustice perpetrated by home-grown casteist oppressors.

4.1.4 Book IV–The Art of Bhimayana

This section focuses on the makers of Bhimayana through the same image-text language that has been used throughout the previous sections. This chapter is narrated through the voices of Durgabai Vyam and Subhash Vyam. They describe their own background, community, and the importance of Ambedkar in their own lives.

This is followed by an afterword by S. Anand, which explores the process of making Bhimayana and the sources that were used to write the story. In the process, he points out the role of Pardhan Gond bards as the tradition-bearers of their communities in central India, arguing for their continued relevance through the cross-mediation of their performance narratives. He points out the communal nature of the Vyams' creative process and describes the importance of recognizing traditional crafts-persons as artists in their own right. The title, Anand suggests, is a pun on Ramayana, the Hindu epic tale of Lord Rama.

Anand concludes by describing the collaborative process and how he and the Vyams constantly renegotiated the story itself, incorporating new characters and a greater presence of nature, as well as taking some small liberties with the stories' source material for the sake of the larger narrative. This section concludes with a focus on the need to address caste and its continued presence as discrimination in India.

4.2 ARTWORK

Nature imagery is present throughout the book—fortresses are fierce beasts; trains are snakes; the road is a peacock's long neck; the handle of a water pump turns into an elephant's trunk. The first section of the book, which deals with the right to water, is full of water-based imagery—when the young Ambedkar is thirsty, his torso turns into a fish; and when he urges a crowd to stand up for their rights, the speakers morph into showers sprinkling water onto the audience. A section on shelter has the recurring imagery of the banyan tree and its many twisted roots. Even the speech bubbles have significance—harsh or prejudiced words are given a tail like a scorpion's to evoke their sting. Gentle words are encased in bubbles shaped like birds, and unspoken thoughts are given an icon to denote the mind's eye.

The pages are not formally structured and digna patterns divide the story into loose frames for a khulla (open) visual imagery. Metaphors of carnivores and herbivores are used for Brahmins and dalits respectively. The speech-bubbles carry clues about narrative sympathy—the speech bubble issuing from young Bhim is in the shape of a bird, while the speech-bubble issuing from the peon is in the shape of a scorpion. This technique is used throughout the book. Anthropomorphism is also used as the train and the tap are portrayed to be live beings.

4.3 SYMBOLISM IN *BHIMAYANA: EXPERIENCES OF UNTOUCHABILITY*

Bhimayana chooses the iconic dialectical approach of storytelling through a conversational style. This has been used by Plato in his *'Republic'* and Gandhi in *'Hind Swaraj'*. This is no coincidence. Neither is it a choice for the purpose of making the story most accessible. It is a symbolic statement regarding the historical significance of the story of Bhim's life.

The narrative ploy of representing the woman as the Dalit who informs the nonchalant upper caste man is equally radical. As Sirish Rao and Gita Wolf write in the introduction to Bhajju Shyam's *'The London Jungle Book'* (2005), Good Art does not represent, it signifies. When Ambedkar is thirsty, he becomes a fish. When Ambedkar is contemplative in Kamathi Baug, he becomes the garden.

When Ambedkar returns to Baroda after completing his studies in Columbia, his life takes a full circle. The naive Ambedkar is under the impression that he has risen above his social status and Caste identity but the Brahmin copassenger on the train to Baroda is quick to make him conscious of it. The cyclical nature of identity based oppression is depicted through the circuitous path of the slithering train.

The book uses different bubbles to represent different thought processes. A person whose thought process is casteist speaks from a snake-like bubble. All victims of caste-based discrimination speak from bird-like bubbles. A third kind of bubble is the thought bubble that has eyes of its own and represents things that remain unspoken. In the end, the upper caste man finds himself speaking the language of the oppressed after having received a lesson in his caste privilege from the Dalit woman. When he says "Jai Bhim!" to her before boarding the bus, his speech bubble transforms from a snake to a bird for the first and only time in the book.

But the most symbolic metaphor in the book remains the use of hands in it. Hands of all kinds can be found in it. The hand that refuses to touch and hence leaves behind an echo of casteism is recurring element. Whenever a character makes a casteist remark, s/he is shown having a progressing trail of hands that point at the oppressed. Similarly, the Mahars leave a trail of their footsteps wherever they go. The hands of solidarity, the touch of the hand amongst Dalits, the strength of the fist and the profound message entailed in a raised hand with a finger pointing upwards while the other hand carries the book serve varying purposes in the overarching narrative of Bhimayana.

4.4 CRITIQUE ON *BHIMAYANA: EXPERIENCES OF UNTOUCHABILITY*

4.4.1 Inequality and Adversity in Content and Form: The Indian Graphic Novel *Bhimayana*

The Indian graphic novel *Bhimayana: experiences of untouchability* were published in 2012 by a New Delhi-based company called Navayana. The book charts the life of Bhimrao Ramji Ambedkar (1891 – 1956) who campaigned for equal rights and an end to social discrimination in particular towards 'untouchables' or 'casteless people' in India. He was the principal architect of the Indian Constitution. The graphic novel blends biography, Indian legislation, letters penned by Gandhi and primary source material in the form of newspaper clippings of the post-millennial period; the clippings sadly underscoring how important issues of untouchabilty remain in today's India. Untouchability in contemporary India, like earlier eras, ostracises groups of people by depriving them of their legal mandate and excluding them from social customs and cultures. Ambedkar, one of India's 'foremost revolutionaries' (Bhimayana 2012 – back cover) grew up as an untouchable and faced discrimination throughout his life; this graphic novel explores such instances as he is refused water, accommodation and his right to education.

My most recent work [1] is interested in visuality and 'new ways of seeing' in post-millennial India and for me Bhimayana (2012) is part of a larger body of work which invokes new ways of seeing in New India. These new ways of seeing correspond to post-millennial trends in visual cultures and creativity which in turn, often depict India in challenging and inauspicious ways. Much of life in New India today involves new forms of cultural consumption and much of that cultural consumption has to do with 'seeing'. Lutgendorf (2006) tells us that '..."seeing" was (and continues to be) understood as a tangible encounter in which sight reaches out to "touch" objects and "take" them back into the seer' (2006: 231). It has been argued that the role of visuality in Indian culture is defining, given the concepts of darshan and drishti which are usually translated as ideas of 'seeing' or 'gazing' and are at the heart of Hindu modes of visuality (see Ramaswamy, 2003: xxv). Freitag (2003) argues that the visual realm is a critical component in South Asian modernity because: '[A]cts of seeing become acts of knowing as viewers/consumers impute new meanings to familiar images. Such agency enables a civil society to grapple with change through indigenous sociologies of knowledge so that it can be naturalised and accommodated.' (2003: 366) Lutgendorf (2006) reminds us of the power of darshan/darœan when he writes that 'darœan is a "gaze" that is returned' (2006: 233, original emphasis) and in his work, he has translated darœan as both 'visual dialog' and 'visual intercourse' (2006: 233) in order to emphasise the idea of communication between the gazer and the gazed upon.

Post-millennial India's immense socio-cultural change has to date involved learning new ways of 'seeing', which in turn have been linked with consumption and markets (Asendorf, 1993: 47). Media, advertising, domestic book cover design, television and satellite are all sites of the new ways India is involved in 'seeing'. The importance of the pictorial within Indian cultures that Pinto (2004: 28) writes of is evidently as significant today as in older Indias; the use of pictorial communications, in particular in advertisements, warnings, social activism, and matters of public health are all commonplace elements of Indian public life. Appadurai and Breckenridge (1998) write of this interaction between people and their ocular experiences saying: 'The interweaving of ocular experiences, which also subsumes the substantive transfer of meanings, scripts, and symbols from one site to another (in surprising ways), is a critical feature of public culture in contemporary India.' (1998: 12)

This idea of new ways of looking, seeing and consumerism certainly speaks to the post-millennial body of graphic fiction within the literary scene in English as this 'new' form of literary expression which evidently involves 'seeing' is becoming ever more popular. In her review of Ghosh's graphic novel Delhi Calm (2010) Nandini Chandra (2010) writes: 'Graphic novels typically characterised as cool and edgy, have emerged as niche pop culture in the youth market.' (2010: 12) This youth market that Chandra speaks of has been particularly evident in activity such as the Comic Con which took place in India for the first time in 2011, or the launch events around newly established comic/graphic novel publishers in urban centres around the country. Such graphic novel publishers are often engaged in narrating challenging and inauspicious India's themes of rape, abuse and terrorism often contest a more 'dignified' history of Indian comic culture. This history is notably the series which celebrated Indian culture through its depictions of India's brave hearts, revolutionaries and Hindu epics. Despite the recent growth in the graphic novel publishing scene, the reception of graphic novels within India remains fractured and uneven. For some, this nascent strand of literary expression is seen as lacking in mastery. For others though, the idea of a visual narrative speaks to much more established notions of Indian storytelling. Pinto (2004) reminds us of the deep connection India has with the pictorial when he writes that '[S]equential art is not a cutting-edge medium; it's been with us since the first patachitras were drawn and then explained in villages.' (2004: 28)

Bhimayana (2012) talks to this idea of a 'deep connection' with the pictorial as its artwork is in the Pardhan Gond style and this type of artwork and painting is referred to as being adivasi or 'tribal' art. The Gond style of artwork can be traced back to Bharat Bhawan, a state-sponsored institution of art and culture (see

Chatterji, 2012: 15). This artwork is therefore relatively recent in its inception and yet is deeply connected to the land through its adivasi (tribal) roots. It was through the institution of Bharat Bhawan that the founder of the Gond art tradition, Jangarh Singh Shyam became established. Jangarh is a Pardhan Gond and his work is strongly influenced by the religious and narrative traditions of the Pardhan Gonds, notably cosmology and the 'mythic universe'. On this artwork Chatterji (2012) writes: 'It was the exposure to new media – brush, paint and paper – that gave the Pardhan-Gonds a new vision. It gave faces to their gods and allowed an iconography to emerge, an iconography that was flexible and unhampered by rigid codification.' (2012: 41)

What is particularly interesting, if not curious about the production of *Bhimayana* (2012) is the choice to use Gond art to visualise and narrate the story of Ambedkar, an untouchable. In one respect, the choice is a precarious one as it might suggest to those new to Gond art that the artists are, like Ambedkar, belonging to an untouchable caste or more worryingly, that all 'tribal' or adivasi peoples are 'untouchable'. In another respect, the choice to tell Ambedkar's story through tribal art makes sense, it carries impact as a unique piece of collaboration and moreover, rides of the back of the Gond art wave of the post-millennial years. Bhimayana (2012) began in 2008 when Navayana's S. Anand first approached two Pardhan Gond artists; Durgabai Vyam and Subhash Vyam. The narrative of Ambedkar – his move from marginal and peripheral socio-cultural positions to empowered and central positions of power and influence – is captured in the artwork of the graphic novel and in turn, this transition echoes the struggle of Gond artists in their move from tribal lifestyles to urban, even international ways of living. Jangarh, the founder of Pardhan Gond art exhibited in cities in India, in Paris at the Pompidou Centre and most latterly Japan. Treated unfairly in Japan whilst on a residency – his paintings fetched a handsome price of which he saw little – with his passport kept by the authorities, Jangarh became depressed. He committed suicide in 2001; he was not even 40 years old.

In an imahe from the graphic novel (a double page spread), Ambedkar is lobbying for the untouchables to take water from a public body of water in a place called Mahad. The colours used here are natural and earth-inspired colours. These colours are taken from clay or matti which is traditionally gathered by the Gond people at different seasons as each season yields a different coloured clay from areas around the Narmada river. At this point the high caste Hindus were preventing the untouchables from having access to the water and the situation was very tense. The artwork on this page also shows the Gond's association of peace with the fish motif. Ambedkar is shown on the right hand-side reaching into a body of water which is kept safe by a fish. No matter how difficult situations became, Ambedkar always looked to resolve the situation peacefully.

Curiously, Navayana's graphic novel *Bhimayana* (2012) does not only speak of the struggles that Ambedkar faced as an untouchable in Indian society, it also narrates the struggle for equality that Gond artists and adivasi artists more generally have faced in recent times. In the afterword of Bhimayana (2012), we are told by one of the artists – Durgabai – that on her arrival at Navayana's office in New Delhi, the landlady of the building would not allow her and her husband in; the landlady could not believe that they were artists and called the couple 'yokels'. Durgabai states in the afterword – visually and narratively – that this incident was abusive and hurtful, and that it reminded the couple of Ambedkar's plight.

Navayana's *Bhimayana* (2012) interrogates new ways of seeing and telling contemporary Indian history. It foregrounds an India of inequality whilst simultaneously celebrating the artwork of the Pardhan Gonds who, like Ambedkar have faced discrimination and maltreatment. This work plays to New India's markets and consumer cultures whilst simultaneously narrating the challenging but maybe more significantly, Bhimayana (2012) allows certain 'acts of seeing' that subsequently translate into 'acts of knowing' as the consumers of Bhimayana (2012) are involved in producing new (more relevant) meanings for the life narratives of one of India's most famous figures: Bhimrao Ramji Ambedkar.

4.1.2 Bhimayana—The Interface of Memory, Orality and Art in the History of India

The Gond art was brought to the forefront by Jangarh Singh Shyam in the mid-nineties who belonged to the Gond tribal community in central India. Their traditional work consisted of maintaining family genealogies, transmitting legends and myths through paintings all which was transmitted to them through the oral culture within the community. The process of internalising of the Ambedkar journeycame easyto Durgabai and SubhasVyam as they heard the stories orally from their daughter. Even though they were made acquainted to the genres of graphic novels by the writer Srividya Natarajan, of Will Eisner, Art Spiegelman, Joe Sacco, Shaun Tan and Osamu Tezuka, the artists counterposed their own ideologies to the visual imagery of the texts. They could relate to the trauma of seclusion and exploitation better than the most. They however did not adhere to the western method of restraining the journey of Ambedkar in panels and gutters, they rather preferred to make it with a lot of open spaces, with air to breath. They felt that their art applied to a system which was 'khulla' and felt that they could not cage an expansive person like Ambedkar in boxes.

The open spaces provides the readers to make cognitive constructs of real and imagined events, creating meaning, interpreting symbols and an ability to predict and create cognitive mind maps, opening their visual fields. Bhimayana is neither a compilation of single-sheet picture nor is straight out linear narrative. The use of the Gond digna is like a double-edged frame containing allusions to grass and grain, running and whirling water, and paling reeds. In the book, digna take the shape of broken circles, fan-like insets, and natural forms like fish and hilltops. Edmunds (2006) suggested that with the sequential art children do not need to decode texts to learn and practice comprehension skills. With an art inspired by the earth and its myriad wonderments, the process of a text book reading becomes easy and approachable.

Bhim is the pint size super hero of the novel, with doe-like eyes who speaks in speech bubbles drawn in the shape of birds. Interestingly the novel has made a demarcation in the form of speech bubbles as a mark of protest, and subtly introduced the boy Bhim in the text. All the characters who are oppressed, differentiated against or denied speak in the form of bird like speech bubbles, whereas the oppressor's speech bubbles are markedly different in the form of a scorpion's sting. The same pattern follows in the story wherein the graphic patois gives reasons to sort out why a stick that beats has eyes similar to a panopticon, or why a water pump seems to want to burst into tears. As Foucault argues in his book *Discipline and Punish* that prison did not become the principal form of punishment just because of the humanitarian concerns of the reformists, but it is about the cultural shifts that led to the predominance of prison via the body and power. The casteist society that denies uniform access to water to young boys from a water pump by the help of sticks is also about a society that enforces its biases through misuse of power and politics of numbers.

The politics of numbers has been following a trajectory which Anand Teltumbde, Dalit activist and author of Khairlanji (2008), while absolutely in favour of the quota system describes it as "a graveyard of dalit aspirations." The numbers of Dalits are dwindling in places where there has to be a show of strength in numbers, the state also plays the role of a panopticon displacing rural Dalits to appropriate lands for mega projects and global investors leaving behind a trail of helplessness and inadequacy. The game of number is always pitched in the same fashion, a few against the majority. Interspersed between the chapters divisions are the current newsarticles in never ending circles about the atrocities heaped on the Dalits even today, which is one of the most striking feature of the graphic novel.

The symbolisms in the Bhimayana is the next important feature of the graphic text. It is divided into three segments primarily, Water, Shelter and Travel. If one looks into the Dalit history, these are the main areas in the day to day living of a dalit, in which he/ she has been a victim to continual harassment and torture. The oral culture of the tribal paintings amply bears out the fact, by the characters and story line of the book. Ambedkar is marked with glasses, perhaps to emphasize his erudition. Muslims have little beards. Brahmins have puny tufts of hair poking out from shaved heads. Characters neither smile nor frown. And eyeliner has been applied artfully to bring about the intentions behind the apparently impassive faces. The contouring of the faces are marked by the gestures borne out by jutting chins, for example the sadness of Bhim's aunt, who waves goodbye to him and his cousins, graduates across her mercurial chin. Furthermore, Ambedkar's speech at the Mahad satyagraha bursts out as fresh blue water through loudspeakers in the shape of spouts. The murder of a Dalit farmer for digging his own well magnifies in the menace of a giant floating hand plough. This harks back to the time when art was used to interpret day to day life, till the time verbosity took over.

4.1.3 The Importance of Bhimayana for Children of India

The irony of a history text book of school is that the major emphasis is on key words and major events mentioned and reiterated by a classroom teaching methodology. The children grow up learning that untouchability, injustices and discrimination have been eradicated by the implementation of fundamental rights and directive principles of the state policy. However with little or no exposure to ground realities, a holistic comprehension of the real scenario is impossible. They grow up to be citizens who are apathetic about cases against atrocities of the depressed classes, with a half-baked sense of justice. The over-dependence on the power of written history as an undeniable, incontestable domain also gives fillip to such a sentiment.

Texts like the Bhimayana bring about a revolutionary change in the thinking processes. The verbal visual texts are remarkable in the narration as they stem from histories from below. India being predominantly an oral society, the tales are unfurled anew at every performance, the telling is different, and it liberates the reader from a rigid storyline and accelerates cognition from various angles of a discourse. The discourse itself becomes fluid in such cases, which gets reflected in the language and the imagery used by the artists. The graphic novel has a huge ramification on the political consciousness of the readers, encourages diverse thinking and makes them question the issues of equality, discrimination, and imbalances in the society. It is explorative, non-judgmental and open to new ideas and forms.

To sum up, it makes Bhimrao Ramji Ambedkar very approachable and relatable, his ideas and causes succinct and justified. The use of animal imagery, earthen colours and traditional fonts give a wholesomeness to a story which has still now remained caged in blurry boxes of the history text books. The interjections by the newspaper clippings reinforces the existence of a parallel system which thrives on casteist power and murky politics, inhumane, nasty and brutish. The exposure through a tribal art and an interesting narrative style would be instrumental in triggering off basic human goodness in the future citizens of India, and make it a better place to live in. This is what the great man Bhimrao Ramji Ambedkar must have dreamt of eventually for his nation.

4.1.4 *Bhimayana*: The Thirst for Khulla

In *Bhimayana: Experience of Untouchability,* a graphic novel by Srividya Natarajan lions and crocodiles, represent the anger of the oppressive Brahmin. Fish and elephants represent the thirst of the Dalits. In figure 1, Ten-year-old Bhim Ambedkar, the famous Dalit revolutionist, stands in front of his teacher with a fish in his stomach asking for a drink of water. The teacher calls him a nuisance because he cannot wait till the bell rings, but when the bell rings the peon, the man at the well gives, all the other students water and the peon goes home. Ambedkar has to leave for home still thirsty. As an untouchable, the South Asian society forbids Ambedkar to make bodily contact with the tap. He might infect the water. The pictures deliver information to the reader the quickest, most effective, way possible. It's this type of image that makes this graphic novel, *Bhimayana: Experience of Untouchablility* by Srividya Natarajan and all political graphic novels, so powerful. In this paper, I will talk about how the graphic novelists use both visual devices and literary devices to tell their stories. This gives the reader an emotional charge other forms do not have. They connect to the story on a personal level.

It is becoming more common for authors to use the graphic novel to tell their stories. Literary and visual artists are beginning to combine their medias to discuss social and political issues and share the cultural experiences seen in the societies in which they live. Authors choose to exercise this form not just because it is fun, creative, and new but because the combination of picture and text gives them something that other forms of writing do not have. They do not just incorporate words; they combine text and images to discuss social and political issues and deliver this information to the reader in the quickest most descriptive way possible. Graphic novels allow authors to provide their readers with a multi-sensory slap in the face. The combination of picture and text forces the reader to come face to face with the social issues these authors are portraying. This visual confrontation is something literary novels, which just feature text, cannot provide.

When people hear the term graphic novel they think of comic

books, but comic books and graphic novels are not the same. Comic books are usually self-interest stories, such as a superhero stories, and typically consist of a serialized, never ending series of books. However, scholars are still using the two terms interchangeably. Graphic novels have characteristics that are much different from comic books. They usually consist of sequential art, "a multilayered narrative; black and with drawings; animal symbolism and anthropomorphization; and biographical elements" (Martin, "Graphic Novels or Novels Graphics", 171). They feature a beginning, middle, and end. This consists of rising action, the climax or turning point, falling action, and the resolution or denouncement. This is something many comic books do not have. Graphic Novels incorporate both literary devices and visual devices to help them tell their story. They generally discuss more serious subject matter and are commonly "described as a 'sophisticated, rich, visionary storytelling'." (Martin, "Graphic Novels or Novels Graphics", 171). While there are many kinds of graphic novels, the most famous address serious often tragic moments in history and engage in social critique. Art Spieglman's *Maus* and Joe Sacco's *Palestine* are two well know examples. Art Spiegelman wrote *Maus* in the graphic novel style to tell the story of his father's experience as a Jew during the holocaust. Palestine is a book about the time Sacco spent in Palestine and deprivation he witnessed while he was there.

With the rise in popularity of this form, authors and artists are starting to expand the boundaries and incorporate their own creative visual styles. Some authors have chosen to feature photography in their books giving an exact image to a scene, while others choose to include abstract art leaving the meaning of the picture hidden and open for interpretation. In 2011, the new graphic novel *Bhimayana: Experience of Untouchability* by Natarajan broke many of these conventions. This book changes the characteristics that are typically associated with the graphic novel. In Bhimayana the artists, Durgabai Vyam and Subhash Vyam eliminate sequential art, which is one of the most common elements in a traditional graphic novel and what most people think tells the story. Srividya, the writer and Durgabai, and Subhash unravel Ambedkar's life story and teachings through a traditional India art form called Pardhan Gond art. The story and pictures flow through the pages. When asked to be the illustrators, artists

Durgabai and Subhash Vyam said, "We'd like to state one thing very clearly at the outset. We shall not force our characters into boxes. It stifles them. We prefer to mount our work in open spaces. Our art is khulla (open) where there's space for all to breathe." (Natarajan, Bhimayana, 102) Durgabai and Subhash draw on digna art as a guideline for how to create structure without boxing in the characters. Pardhan Gond art originates from the digna. "The ecology of Pardhan Gond art is such that even when dealing with urban subjects we see freefalling animals, birds and trees in landscapes without a horizon. The train becomes a snake, the intimidating fort a lion. The happiness of the people of Chalisgaon who receive Bhim Ambedkar is not conveyed through smiling faces but a dancing peacock. An earthmover used by a dalit, who is killed for digging a well, sheds tears as two cows bear witness." (Natarajan, Bhimayana, 102) Gond art does not represent what is actually going on, it applies images to signify emotions and events.

Marjane Satrapi, writer and illustrator of Persepolis, believes that "In graphic novels, the images help tell the story. 'Images are a way of writing,' says Satrapi. 'When you have the talent to be able to write and to draw it seems a shame to choose one. I think it's better to do both.'" (Campbell, "Picture This: Inside the Graphic Novel", 20) Alissa Torres, author of *American Widow,* writes in the graphic novel form because she believes writing about her husband's death during 9/11 was not enough. She needed to be able to show the images that bombarded her every day. "Both Spiegelman and Torres use the graphic novel format to help shape narratives giving them linearality) separate various narrative strands (both begin in medias res) and use flashbacks, and untangle emotions. These traits are characteristic of many other graphic novels as well." (Martin, "*Graphic Novels or Novels Graphics*", 171).

Many authors believe the graphic novel form is a more effective way of discussing the oppression, genocide, and war than just writing a prose novel. They capture the reader's attention and allow them to see what the author wants them to see and pay attention to what they believe is important. The images seen in Joe Sacco's *Palestine* are a perfect example of this. "Graphic novels can emphasize certain aspects of reality that conventional prose sometimes cannot. In *Palestine,* the background drawings—the immediate setting in which Sacco finds himself—convey much information...As Sacco stated at a talk he gave in 2007, the author of conventional prose can occasionally write that 'there is mud everywhere' but cannot do so in every paragraph. Seeing its overwhelming presence throughout the novel's pages, however, can powerfully convey to readers the crumbling infrastructure, economic underdevelopment, and general desperation characterizing life in the West Bank and Gaza." (Juneau, "Narratives in Pencil", 174) You can see this in Figure 2. Through his pictures, Sacco is able to show the reader how bad Palestine really is, forcing the reader to take notice. The text in graphic novels requires the reader to put forth a certain amount of attention, while the images add the sensory aspect and submerge the reader in a visual world.

Bhimayana: Experience of Untouchability is one of the newest graphic novels, first published in January 2011. This book features art by Durgabai Vyam and Subhash Vyam. After Natarajan asked them to be the illustrators for the book, they refused to confine their art into boxes. They believed art should flow and not be restricted to small-boxed spaces. This eliminated the sequential art that is commonly seen in this form and when they made this decision, they created something new. The artists have also added colour to their drawings, which is unusual for this form. They do employ some of the common characteristics within this genre, such as animal symbolism, multilayered narrative, and biographical elements. Most importantly, they added more of India's culture into the novel. Instead of conforming to the usually graphic novel characteristics, the Vyam's made their book stand out from the rest. The Gond artists believe that when you look at a good image it brings good luck, so they decorate their houses and the floors with these images. By utilizing this style to illustrate Bhimayana, the artists surround the book with their cultural beliefs and motifs. This gives the reader some insight into the lives of the people living in India and their values.

Graphic novels feature not only textual modes but also visual modes. Textual modes also called "verbal art" unfolds with time as the reader reads the words on the page, while the visual mode (pictorial art) unfolds "through its use of space" (Kukkonen, "Comics as a Test Case for Transmedial Narratology", 36-37). The audience takes in everything at once with one image. This mode consists of novels and prose, while visual modes would include films, photography, paintings, etc. Graphic novels combine these two modes. Comic theory suggests that one mode does more for the text than the other does, but in actuality, the text needs both to form an accurate, fully comprehensible, story. The pictures concentrate on displaying a wide variety of information in one moment, but can only portray visible actions; the accompanying text shows elements that the pictures cannot portray, such as thoughts and speech. Karin Kukkonen says, "As a multimodal medium, comics make use of all their modes dynamically when unfolding a story to us" (Kukkonen, "Comics as a Test Case for Transmedial Narratology", 35). This is what makes the graphic novel so appealing to the reader. With the combination of the visual and textual modes, the reader connects to the story on a more personal level and the story come to life.

Many people believe that graphic novels are easy to read and are for people who cannot focus on prose novels. This is completely wrong. Graphic novels may be able to hold the attention of those who usually cannot become engrossed in prose novels, but this is probably do to the fact that graphic novels are visual and the images guide the reader through the story as opposed to reading left to right and following the words. Images have the ability to present more information than just words can, and in a smaller space. Graphic novels are actually more complex because they force our brains to move in the space between images and word. In Bhimayana, on page 54, seen in figure 3, there is a picture of the Dalits and the Hindus standing around a pool of water shaped as a fish. It looks as though they are having a tug-o-war with each other over the fish. We know that this fish represents water for the community, but because they are untouchables, the Dalits cannot use this water source. So just from looking at the picture you can see that the Dalits are fighting to obtain access to the water source, with Ambedkar's guidance. Dugabai and Subhash create a figure representing Ambedkar with glasses at the head of the fish. On the opposing page, page 55, there is an entire page backing up this assumption. It is a news article describing the events on March 19, 1927 when the Dalits fought for the right to make contact with the Chavadar Tank. The information the picture gives us in one image takes an entire page of writing. This allows graphic novels to speak to visual learners and auditory learners as well as literate and illiterate.

The graphic novel includes text to narrate the story the novelists are telling by describing the pictures presented and incorporate conversations. Authors do this by using literary devices. The audience reads the rest of the story though the images. The artists apply the image to create feelings, emotions, while delivering information about the story to the reader. The artists do this by exercising different artistic devices, such as colour theory, line theory, and backgrounds. As the reader turns from page to page, they experience visually striking graphics. Scott McCloud, author of *Understanding Comics* is the authority on this subject.

To critics it may seem as though the graphic novel leaves little to the imagination, but different people can interpret all art in a different way. The art in Bhimayana allows this more than other texts in the past. Durgabai and Subhash base their illustrations in Bhimayana on a cultural art form, the digna, rather than the sequential art seen in most graphic novels. Bhimayana features the image of pointing fingers throughout the narrative. For some readers these pointing fingers could be pointing at the people who are participating in the discrimination of Ambedkar, pointing them out and showing them what they are doing, while to another reader the pointing fingers are discriminating fingers pointing at the untouchables. There are things in pictures that some people pick up while other people do not. Many people are not going to notice all the layers of symbolism featured in Bhimayana, such as the peacock featured on page 79, shown in figure 4. Some people may just see it as a peacock, while others will understand it symbolizes the happiness of the Chalisgaon when they meet Ambedkar. (Natarajan, Bhimayana, 102).

Bhimayana employs both colour and black and white. Every image of a person featured in this novel is in black and white. This is because regardless of the caste, race, or profession society should view all people as the same. Every colour, background, shape, and line holds meaning in a graphic novel. These cues allow the reader to draw in information about the subject the authors and artists are trying to discuss. Without these minor differences the reader would not be able to understand the full meaning of the novel.

The effect colour has on a reader is profound. An artist's decision to incorporate colour in his or her graphic novel can be due to many things. Commerce could affect this, or it could be because colour adds or takes away something from the story being. Artists have always seen colour as something powerful and major in fine art. Some artists spent their lives studying colour and believed that it had physical and emotional effects on people. The application of colour in graphic novels and comic books has not had so much luck. In superhero comics, artists used the four-colour scale along with black ink for line work. The colours where flat and colour intensity was restricted to 100%, 50%, and 20%. With colours, artists objectified their subjects and readers became more aware of the subjects physical form than the figures drawn in black and white. Colours are something that graphic novels could start using more effectively. Colours express mood, while tones and modeling could add depth. Colour is a sensation. However, when put with the old shape-sensitive line drawings in comics, these colours seem out of place. Black and white and colour comics can have completely different effects on the reading experience of a comic. In black and white, pictures communicate the subjects behind the art more openly; the meaning of the novel goes beyond the form, and "art approaches language". In comics with flat colours, like superhero comics, the "forms themselves take on more significance". (McCloud, *Understanding Comics,* 192) Graphic novelists can transform their books into a more invigorating environment of sensations (ambiance) with more expressive colours. (McCloud, *Understanding Comics,* 192) Colour does the same thing for images that the application of line and background and text does. It adds to the story as a whole. It gives the reader more information to take in from a picture and portrays emotion, mood, and feelings that would otherwise not be there if it the writers wrote it in a different form.

Durgabai and Subhash Vyam incorporate colour dramatically in their drawings. They draw the people in black and white, while artists highlight much of the background with vibrant colours. This draws the eye towards the background, forcing the reader to focus on what they are displaying in colour in some images. The artists usually draw animals in this type of image. They include these animals to signify the emotions of the human characters, such as peacock in figure 4. Another example of this is on page 66, seen in figure 5. Ambedkar is describing his first week of work. He compares himself to "an ox in the oil-press, walking in circles and going nowhere" (Natarajan, Bhimayana, 66). The illustrators draw Ambedkar and the oxen in black and white, showing their connection to one another, while highlighting the circle they are all walking in and their footprints in colour. In other images, the background is one flat colour with a black and white figure featured in the middle, this frames the figure and the reader focuses on the actions of this figure. The flat colour works as a background for the text; this highlights important news clippings and stories about a caste system still in practice.

Most graphic novels employ black and white drawings as opposed to colour. This could simply be because it cost less money to print in black and white, but it could also be the preference of the author. Bhimayana uses colour because the art stems from the Gond art tradition. Maus would not be the same story if it were published in vibrant colours. The story is about a dark subject, the holocaust, so it is only fitting that it features dark pictures. Artists that choose to draw the images in their books in black and white depend on line theory.

There are many different graphic artists and they all have their own drawing style, each of which fits the novels they are drawing for. The drawings seen in Dick Tracy by Chester Gould, the audience sees the images as grim and deadly because of the bold line, obtuse angles and the heavy black, while Carl Barks' images of Uncle Scrooge reveal the opposite. He depicts a whimsical feeling of childhood and innocence by using gentle curves and open lines. By using different lines and styles, the artists are portraying a feeling they wish to invoke in the reader. The emotion they are creating is imperative when it comes to stories about social issues. Joe Sacco's thick dark lines in Palestine, observed in figure 6, carry a feeling of discomfort for the reader. This discomfort is felt everywhere in Palestine because of the war. The illustrations are the only ways authors can express these feelings to the reader and have the reader keep that feeling throughout the novel. Every line has the potential to hold meaning in a graphic novel, depending on its direction, the shape it forms, or the characteristics of the line. Scholars consider a straight horizontal line passive and timeless, while a perpendicular line is proud and strong, and the slanted line can mean dynamic and changing. A shape with sharp jagged lines is unwelcoming and severe; a rounded curved shape is warm and gentle, while a straight-boxed shape becomes rational and conservative. A scratchy line is savage and deadly, viewers see a blotted, splotchy line as weak and unstable, and a straight line with no gaps represents honest and direct. (McCloud, *Understanding Comics,* 125).

The line work seen in Bhimayana comes from digna patterns. Nearly every line seen in this novel comes from India's Gond art culture. Everything is connected and represented with nature and animals. Durgabai and Subhash apply the Digna patterns to their images to decorate the background and connect the images to one another. The Digna is an art form created by villagers in India to decorate their houses. Digna tribes believe that looking at these images bring luck into their homes and the people who live in them.

The background of an image conveys emotion within a graphic novel. Even if there is little or no way of telling the internal state of the character by looking at the them, a certain background will usually affect the way the reader experiences their state of mind. These feelings will not be associated with the reader, but rather with the character, they are identifying. If artist chooses to use the background, it is usually associated with the characters' inner thoughts, emotions, and not something the viewer can see on his face. (McCloud, *Understanding Comics,* 132) too much McCloud, introduce him as the leading authority and then see if you can include all his quotes but pepper the essay with other authorities. In *Bhimayana,* the artist draw images of animals to convey characters emotions, a lion represents something intimidating, while the dancing peacock is a sign of happiness.

One of the easiest and next most effective ways of conveying emotion is with words. Both cartoonist and comic writers struggle with the ability to create sound in a strictly visual medium. To help overcome this obstacle they employ words, whether it is in a word bubble or written in a narrative box. With text, they incorporate literary devices. To add sound to the word "crash" the artist will typically add some of the line techniques I pointed out earlier. They might, for instance, write it with a jagged line in all caps with an exclamation point and the shape of the letters may be sharp and jagged. Authors bring words into play for thoughts and speech. Words have the ability to describe the invisible and to add feeling to an image that is otherwise completely neutral. The Vyam's include word bubbles in

Bhimayana to represent different things. Durgabai and Subhash employ the word bubbles that are in the shape of birds, seen in figure 7, only for characters that are victims of caste. These characters are soft spoken and loveable. They are "men and women who speak like birds" (Natarajan, Bhimayana, 100). The Vyam's draw the thought bubbles, shown in figure 8, with eyes leading to the bubble and surrounded by a digna pattern. The eyes represent the mind's eye, they carry words "that cannot be heard but can be perceived" (Natarajan, Bhimayana, 100). The bubbles that represent characters who the Hindu religion benefits with the caste system and love it are made up of circles that overlap each other and slowly get bigger leading up to a clouded bubble, observed in figure 9. These are words that "contain poison, whose touch is venomous". (Natarajan, Bhimayana, 101) Nevertheless, words cannot do everything. They "lack the immediate emotional charge of pictures, relying instead on a gradual cumulative effect." (McCloud, Understanding Comics, 135) The application of these images gives meaning that the text lacks. It characterizes the people in the book. These word bubbles and thought bubbles resemble that literary novelist call stream of consciousness. Authors of graphic novels incorporate many of the literary devices seen in literary novels into their novels.

Authors incorporate literary devices in their text to create an interesting and sophisticated story line. They feature the sequencing of events that authors incorporate in their literary novels. This includes rising action, the climax or turning point, falling action, and the resolution or denouncement. Natarajan introduces Bhim Ambedkar in the beginning of her book and tells the story of how badly his peers treated as a child, which directly contributed to his becoming an untouchable revolutionist later in life. The climax is the turning point of the novel; Ambedkar begins the revolution and build up a group of untouchable to help fight those who are oppressing the lower castes. Because of this first demonstration, Ambedkar begins a fight for the lower casts against the upper caste system. The denouncement is not a resolution; the untouchables are still experiencing oppression today. The end of the book points out that the caste system they are fighting against is not a system set up by society, but is justified by their legal system making this graphic novel a story about "India's hidden apartheid". The news clipping and articles that Durgabai and Subhash collected and included in the book show the reader that this system of oppression is still in practice today.

Hindu religion, a primary religion in India, believes untouchables to be diseased or polluted. Higher Castes consider and treat them as the lowest form of life; they are subordinate to animals. They do not allow them to drink public water or bath in public baths. If someone from the upper castes catches them doing this, they usually suffer a beating sometimes resulting in death. The images and text in the book *Bhimayana* tell the story of Ambedkar, an untouchable and a revolutionist. The book takes us through the problems he faced in childhood and still in adulthood, after he graduated from Columbia University and having Sayaji Rao (raja of Baroda State) sponsors his education. Graphic novels are not only stories they incorporate literary and visual devices that allow for a wide variety of artistic expression. This combination connects the reader to the subject on a personal level by making them come face to face with the social and political issues still suffocating the people around us. Many of the graphic novels in the past have stuck to the basic graphic novel structure, while some added photography and other minor changes. Bhimayana changes this structure almost completely. By adding space and colour, this book gives the untouchables something that they never had. The Vyam's give their characters room to breathe, they flow through the pages of this book, and their story is told. By breaking down the traditional form of the graphic novel, the artists have drawn more attention to their book and the subjects within it. The readers of this book do not look at it as a graphic novel; it's a series of drawings that reveal a story. It draws in a more artistic viewer.

Bibliography

Appadurai, A. and Breckenridge, C.A. (1998) 'Public Modernity in India' in C.A. Breckenridge (ed) *Consuming Modernity: Public culture in a South Asian World*, Minneapolis/London: University of Minnesota Press.

Asendorf, C. (1993) *Batteries of Life: On the history of things and the perception in modernity* (Tr. Don Reneau), Berkeley: University of California.

Bargainnier, E.F. (1980). *The Gentle Art of Murder: The Detective Fiction of Agatha Christie*. Ohio: Bowling Green University Popular Press.

Booth, W. 1991 (1961). *The Rhetoric of fiction*. 2nd edition. London: Penguin Books.

British Library. (2020). *The Origins of Children's Literature*. [online] Available at: <https://www.bl.uk/romantics-and-victorians/articles/the-origins-of-childrens-literature> [Accessed 5 May 2020].

Chandra, N. (2010) 'Powerpolis' Biblio September-October http://www.biblio-india.org [Accessed April 2013].

"Characteristics Of Popular Fiction As Literary Genre English Language Essay." UKEssays.com. 11 2018. All Answers Ltd. 04 2020 <https://www.ukessays.com/essays/english-language/characteristics-of-popular-fiction.php?vref=1>.

Chatterji, R. (2012) *Speaking with Pictures: Folk art and the narrative tradition in India*, New Delhi: Routledge India.

Chatman, S. (1993) (1978). *Story and Discourse: Narrative Structure in Fiction and Film*. New York: Cornell University Press.

Christie, A. 2006 (1926). *The Murder of Roger Ackroyd*. London: Harper Collins Publishers.

Christie, A. (2007) (1939). *And Then There Were None*. London: Harper Collins Publishers.

Classic, Popular, And Representative Literature. [online] Available at: <http://coursesite.uhcl.edu/HSH/Whitec/terms/C/classicpopreplit.htm> [Accessed 5 May 2020].

Concentric: Literary and Cultural Studies. 2018. **Sexual/Textual Tendencies In Shyam Selvadurai's Funny Boy*. [online] Available at: <http://www.concentric-literature.url.tw/issues/Contested_Modernity_Place_Space_and_Culture/8.pdf> [Accessed 5 May 2020].

Cripps, Elizabeth A. "Alice and the Reviewers." *Children's Literature* 11 (1983): 32-48.

Cuddon, J.A. (ed.). (1998). *A Dictionary of Literary Terms and Literary Theory*. 4th edition. Oxford: Blackwell Publisher.

Cuddon, J.A. (ed.). 1999 (1977). *The Penguin Dictionary of Literary terms and Literary Theory*, 4th edition. London: Penguin Books.

Dawson Varughese, E. and Lau, L. (2015) *Indian Writing in English and Issues of Representation: Judging More than a Book by its Cover*, Basingstoke: Palgrave Macmillan UK.

Dawson Varughese (2014) 'New ways of seeing in New India': interview with Studio Kokaachi *South Asian Popular Culture* Routledge July 2014; 12(2).

Encyclopedia Britannica. 2020. *Literature—Literature And Its Audience*. [online] Available at: <https://www.britannica.com/art/literature/Literature-and-its-audience#ref51305> [Accessed 5 May 2020].

enotes. (2020). *Twentieth-Century Literary Criticism*. [online] Available at: <https://www.enotes.com/topics/popular-literature> [Accessed 5 May 2020].

enotes. (2020). *The Murder of Roger Ackroyd By Agatha Christie*. [online] Available at: <https://www.enotes.com/topics/murder-roger-ackroyd/critical-essays/critical-context> [Accessed 5 May 2020].

Essays, UK. (November 2018). *Characteristics of Popular Fiction As Literary Genre English Language Essay*. Retrieved from https://www.ukessays.com/essays/english-language/characteristics-of-popular-fiction.php?vref=1

Fitzgibbon, R. (1980). *The Agatha Christie Companion*. Ohio: Bowling Green University Popular Press.

Freitag, S.B. (2003) 'The Realm of the Visual: Agency and modern civil society' in S. Ramaswamy, (ed) *Beyond Appearances?: Visual Practices and Ideologies in Modern India*, New Delhi: SAGE.

Gutkowski, E. 2011. "An Investigation in Pragmatics: Agatha Christie's The Murder of Roger Ackroyd". *Clues: A Journal of Detection*, McFarland & Company. 29: 51-60.

Iser, W. (1993). *Prospecting: from reader response to literary anthropology.* London: Johns Hopkins University Press.

Jeremy Stoll. (2012). "Bhimayana: Experiences of Untouchability: Incidents in the life of Bhimrao Ramji Ambedkar." *Journal of Folklore Research Reviews.*

Lennon, Florence Becker (1971). "Escape Through the Looking-Glass." *Aspects of Alice*. Ed. Robert Phillips. New York: Vanguard, 66-79.

Lutgendorf, P. (2006) 'Is There an Indian Way of Filmmaking?' in *International Journal of Hindu Studies*, Vol. 10, No. 3 (Dec.), pp. 227-256.

Mandelker, Amy (1988). "The Mushroom and the Egg: Lewis Carroll's Alice as an Otherwordly Introduction to Semiotics." *Canadian-American Slavic Studies* 22: 101-14.

Nünning, A. (ed.). (1997). "But why will you say that I am mad? On the Theory, History, and Signals of Unreliable Narration in British Fiction". *Arbeiten zu Anglistik und Amerikanistik*. 22: 83-105.

Onega, S. and García Landa, J.A. (eds.). 1996. *Narratology*. New York: Longman.

Pinto, J. (2004) 'Thinking Out of the Box' *Biblio* July/August http://www.biblio-india.org [Accessed on April 11th, 2013].

Priestman, M. (ed.). 2012 (2003). *The Cambridge Companion to Crime Fiction*. New York: Cambridge University Press.

Prince, G. (1971), "On Readers and Listeners in Narrative". Neophilologus. 55: 117-122.

Rackin, Donald (1987). "Love and Death in Carroll's Alice's." Lewis Carroll. Ed. Harold Bloom. New York: Chelsea House,. 111-27.

Ramaswamy, S. (ed) (2003) *Beyond Appearances?: Visual practices and ideologies in Modern India* New Delhi: SAGE.

Rowe, Juliann. Chazelle, Damien (ed). "Through the Looking Glass Study Guide". *GradeSaver*, 21 January 2011 Web. 27 April 2020.

Stanley, T and Benstock, B. (eds.). (1989). *Dictionary of Literary Biography*. 77: British Mystery Writers 1920-1939. United States: Gale Cengage Learning.

Truffaut, F., "About Suspense and Surprise, an interview with Alfred Hitchcock"http://olympia.osd.wednet.edu/media/olympia/activities/drama_club/hitchcockinterview.pdf (Accessed on June 19th, 2014).

Victorian Web. (2002). *The Critical Reception of Through The Looking-Glass*. [online] Available at: <http://www.victorianweb.org/authors/carroll/downey1.html> [Accessed 5 May 2020].

Vyam, D., Vyam, S., Natarajan, S. and Anand, S. (2012). *Bhimayana: Experiences of untouchablity*, New Delhi: Navayana.

Walsh, Susan A. "Darling Mothers, Devilish Queens: The Divided Woman in Victorian Fantasy." *Victorian Newsletter* 72 (1987): 32-36.

Wordpress. (2020). *The Politics of Storytelling – A Review of Bhimayana: Incidents In The Life of Bhimrao Ramji Ambedkar*. [online] Available at: <https://asociologicalblog.wordpress.com/2017/06/05/the-politics-of-storytelling-a-review-of-bhimayana-incidents-in-the-life-of-bhimrao-ramji-ambedkar/#_ednref1> [Accessed 5 May 2020].

Notes

Notes

Notes